Previous books by To
ryofatdog@yahoo.con

MW00944598

Caloosahatchee

"A wonderfully realistic novel about life on the Florida frontier. *Caloosahatchee*, kept me on the edge of my seat with the stories, twists and turns. It's a real eye opener to a part of our states history the schoolbooks overlook."

- Dr. Marshal Carlton, *Florida Cracker Museum*

"Finally, a writer respective of Florida's culture and heritage."

- Jay Osceola, *Seminole Tribe Of Florida*

Shootoff!

Written with Dr. Robert Norman
"A great book. I could not put it down. This should be required reading for all sub-junior and junior ATA and SCTP shooters."
Bob Feliconio, *N.R.A. Certified Shooting Instructor*

"*Shootoff!* is destined to be a classic in the sports and shooting field. It grips the reader like a tight choke and does not let go until the last bit of smoke pours out of Jesse's gun."

Tom Nowak, *World Wheelchair Shooting Champion*

DEBALO

by

Toby Benoit

AuthorHouse™
1663 Liberty Drive, Suite 200
Bloomington, IN 47403
www.authorhouse.com
Phone: 1-800-839-8640

First published by AuthorHouse 7/9/2007

ISBN: 978-1-4343-1315-7 (sc)

Printed in the United States of America
Bloomington, Indiana

This book is printed on acid-free paper.

PREFACE

We are all of us, it has been said, the children of immigrants and foreigners; even the American Indian, although he arrived here a little earlier. The reasons for coming to America and the method of arrival were as varied as the people themselves. For some, however, immigration was not a choice, but a forced act. Behind them were ancestors, families, and former lives. Those forced immigrants came here into a life of hardship and service and those who survived were characterized by strength, the capacity to endure, and not uncommonly, a rebellious nature.

History is not only made by kings and parliaments, presidents, wars, and generals; it is the story of people, of their honor, faith, hope, and suffering. In writing this story of one young African, whose migration to America was not of his own choice, I found myself looking back again and again to origins, to see the life he left. What a man is and what he becomes is in part due to his heritage and the men and women who came to this continent did not emerge from limbo. Behind them were ancestors, families, and former lives.

Some time ago, I decided to tell this story of the Florida frontier, at the time of the Second Seminole War, through the eyes of an escaped slave, a fictional character, but with true and factual experiences. The name I chose was Debalo. My research has shown Debalo is a real name derived from the Massawra peoples of Africa. These people commonly known as Bushmen, came from a land teeming with wildlife and edible plants and made their livng from the land as hunters and gatherers. Skills necessary to not only survive the wilderness of the American South, but to prosper.

When Debalo's journies are ended and the story comes to a close, it is my wish that the reader should have gained a sense for what life was like in the early nineteenth century of the American South.

ONE

Sleep had not visited him this night. Debalo lay awake in the pre-dawn blackness listening to the stirrings of the overseers as they directed the breakfast preparations. It wasn't their noise outside the cabin that kept him awake, but rather the dread of having to awaken to another day of enslavement. Debalo felt that there was nothing physical that the overseers might do to him that he could not endure. Since having been taken from his home and family several months ago, he already had survived countless beatings, whippings and branding.

The worst was waking up in the morning, after a night of well-earned sleep, to find himself still a slave, which is why this night he had chosen to remain awake. If he did not sleep, he could not dream, and those dreams, dreams of home, tortured his heart and mind with unspeakable longing. Sometimes he would dream, as he slept on the dirt floor of the cabin, of his life in the Okavango delta back home in

Africa. In his dreams he'd hunt zinyoni, birds nesting along the banks of the Luangua River, and collect their mquanda, the tiny speckled eggs they'd lay in those nests when he was a boy. Often he'd dream of past hunts in the mukwa, a forest of hardwoods in the Okavango basin and chasing Mbogo the buffalo out of the thick Mswaki, a tightly woven jungle of underbrush so dense a man couldn't stand up in places. His dreams reminded him of his freedom, family and love, all the things that had been nonexistent to him these past several months.

The crackling of the cooking fire outside in the yard reached his ears and he knew it would be only another thirty or so minutes before the cabin door would open. Then the twenty or so other occupants and himself would be directed out into the yard to receive a cup full of boiled corn meal and a cup of chicory-laden coffee. They would then have ten minutes to finish breakfast and go to the chimbuzi or outhouse as the overseers called it. One was located behind each cabin. They weren't very solidly built structures, made of rough hewn planks with a seat situated over a deeply dug hole.

The cabins themselves were made of the same rough lumber and were arranged in a semi circular pattern beneath a canopy of ancient live oaks that loomed ominously over the complex. There were nine cabins all together, squarely built, low ceiling-ed affairs with one door facing frontward into a tramped down yard of hard packed dirt, and two windows on either side wall. The doors and windows were covered in mud-colored burlap screens to keep out the mosquitoes and yet allow air to circulate inside, cooling the rows of occupants.

The soft snores and groans of the others began to be heard about Debalo as the sleepers began to awaken. A whip cracked in the yard and Debalo rose with the others and exited the dark cabin into the cool air of the early morning. Lines of men formed before the cook fire and each in turn received his meal. Before Debalo could receive his own, however, the overseer Debalo recognized as the one the slaves knew as 'Round-belly' came to him and gripped his upper arm in a black, ham sized-fist and pulled Debalo along with him.

"C'mon nigga', I got a job fo' you!", the words he spoke had no meaning to Debalo, but the tone was unmistakably aggressive and commanding.

Round-belly was a huge Negro of more than six feet tall and outweighed the young Debalo by at least a hundred pounds. Any thoughts of resisting were put quickly out of Debalo's mind and he went quietly along toward the enormous building which was used to house the heavy wagons, team horses and other equipment used in the operation of the plantation. The barn had been built up the hill from the cabins on a level plane. It was a two story structure of dark stained cypress planks with huge double doors in the front center and in the gray light of the now rising sun, it seemed a most terrifying sight and made him want to run and hide.

One word of the new language Debalo was learning was "runaway." He understood this word now and had contemplated doing the very thing himself, but what few Africans there were on the plantation that could speak to him in his native tongue of Fanagalo assured him that escape was hopeless. Once a slave left the plantation, he was told, there was nothing but hundreds of miles of swamp and wilderness in any direction and that the overseers would hunt you down by day and night with great hounds. Once caught, you would certainly die. You would be killed, they maintained, only to discourage others that may wish to do the same. In fact only two nights previous Debalo had lay awake with the others and listened to the screams of a slave and the cracks of a bull whip which came from behind the doors of the very barn Round-belly was now leading him to.

It had been Round-belly lashing away that night with the whip and that same whip was now coiled and tied to the man's belt above his left hip, where he kept it handy in case a worker needed to be sped up a bit or taken down a notch if he got "uppity." On his right side was a huge wood handled knife in a leather sheath. It was the knife that Debalo had admired for awhile. Naturally the sight of the overseer disgusted Debalo the man, but Debalo the hunter admired a good knife when he saw it. The blade of the knife was at least two-hands long and it curved up on the end for skinning. A brass crossbar was just above the dark hardwood grips to prevent the hand from slipping forward onto the blade. The blade itself across the back looked to be the full width of the nail on his little finger. More than once he'd seen the large black man sharpening it and he knew the damage a knife like that could do in the hands of a man that knew how to use it.

Once at the great doors of the barn, Round-belly removed the cross bar and swung open one side of the double doors and pushed Debalo inside. The cavernous room was dark and moist and the acrid smell of mildew and horses attacked his nose. Round-belly moved on past Debalo and led the way to a row of horse stalls built against the far wall beneath the overhanging floor of a hayloft. When Debalo had crossed the floor halfway, he sensed a new smell and winced as he recognized the horrid odor. Round-belly barked a few orders in the foreign tongue that Debalo could not understand, but they soon went through the motions of an admixture of sign language and pantomime until his orders became distinctly clear. He was to move and bury what he was about to find in the low ground out behind the barn. Once Round-belly was satisfied that his orders were understood, he reached for a shovel and tossed it to Debalo.

"I'll be back in an hour an I s'pect that dead nigga' to be underground. I'll bring yo' breakfas' fo' ya', then head on to tha' cotton boy." He brushed on past him and left the barn.

He stood for a moment and tried to steady himself before approaching the stall. When he did begin to move closer the smell worsened to the point of making his head hurt. Upon seeing the mess lying in the straw covering the floor of the stall, he nearly vomited. He was thankful that he hadn't yet eaten. He stepped closer to the thing and a swarm of iridescent green flies flew up from it. Debalo had been a hunter for

5

years and was no stranger to death, but had never seen a death so cruel.

The thing lay face down with its hands outstretched above the head with ropes still tied about the wrists. It was naked and the legs were spread wide, each ankle having been secured to a piece of board that still ran between them, keeping them spread. The entire body, swollen round from the late spring humidity, had been crisscrossed with huge cuts and gouges that had bled freely and now was occupied by innumerable white maggots that crawled everywhere, from the head to the ankles. One horror that was not lost on Debalo was that the soles of both feet had been skinned. There was no doubt it was intended that this man should not be able to run away in his next life either.

He reached for the board tied to the ankles swarming with flies. A grotesque belch of gas erupted from the former man. Debalo drug it out the back door of the barn to the area Round-belly had indicated. He began to dig the grave while planning his escape. He was leaving that day! There could be no uncertainty about that, but first, he would perform the task to which he had been elected. It was the decent thing to do for the corpse and also would allow him time to think.

He knew the direction of the great river that he had arrived upon in the belly of the ship. He had been bound with metal chains, tied to a group of three others, none of whom he knew. Once they had been taken from the ship and led from the platform at the river's edge, they were marched through the streets of an enormous town teeming with more people than he could imagine. They traveled two days south along muddy rutted roads until they arrived at the plantation.

No doubt, with that many people to the north, Debalo planned to continue southward and set a course angling him into the rising sun. As a hunter he knew that mornings were always the choicest times for pursuit. By angling into the rising sun, those pursuing him would have the sun in their eyes should they ever get close enough. When running toward the unknown, any advantage, however slight it may be, was to be used.

He dug steadily into the wet ground. Black water began seeping into the hole before he had gotten more than a shovel's head depth, making the digging a sloppy muddy mess. The fetid water made indecent sucking sounds as he removed each shovel full of mud that smelled strongly of the gasses that arose from the swamps he'd traveled back home. Normally such odors were as unwelcome as a swarm of tse-tse flies, but not this morning. Not compared to the bloated mess resting a few precious yards downwind in the slight morning breeze. The morning air he studied and found, to his satisfaction, tended to rise in the warming of the morning. If he should begin his run within the hour, any animals that may be employed to track him down would not have the benefit of drifting his scent on the wind, but would need to remain stuck to the trail itself or repeatedly lose it.

Once the hole had grown to a depth he found to be satisfactory, albeit a bit shallow, he untied the ropes that secured the board to the corpse's ankles. He slid the thing into the fetid water and partially filled the newly dug grave. It was a horrible way to be disposed of, Debalo thought, but it was the best he could do. He was in the process of replacing the slimy black mud into the hole and had the body covered fairly well when Round-belly showed up at the rear door of the barn with a cup of coffee and a cup of corn meal mush. He motioned for Debalo to come and eat the breakfast and spoke many words, mostly to himself.

Debalo laid the shovel on the ground beside the grave and walked over and received his meal. He had not expected to eat this morning and was particularly surprised that such a hard man as Round-belly would remember to offer him the meal, such as it was. He accepted it quietly in the polite, two-handed manner of his people, the Massarwa, and squatted on his heels to eat. After his morning chore, Debalo certainly felt little or no hunger, but was pleased to get food, knowing well that there may not be time later for finding food. As he was quickly finishing the rations, Round-belly stepped past him and walked toward the grave as if inspecting the job to be sure it met his approval. Debalo's eyes were on the food remaining in one cup and not on the overseer when he heard the sound of running water.

He looked to the grave to see the big negro overseer standing spread-legged, urinating into the muddy hole. Debalo watched open mouthed and still as the big man re-buttoned his fly and returned to the still squatting Debalo. He said a word or two through a pair of sneering lips while nodding his head in the direction of the grave and Debalo readied himself for what he knew he must do.

Standing slowly, he held forth the cups he had been given and as Round-belly accepted them into his hands, Debalo reached for the great knife in a casual, non-threatening manner and as the big overseer looked on in a disbelieving stare, he lifted the thing from its resting place in the large leather sheath and slipped it with surprising little effort between the lower ribs of Round-belly's deep chest. Surprise covered the big overseer's face and he began to react by grabbing for the blade as Debalo removed it from the man's rib cage. As he pulled the knife outward, he gave it a half twist to open the wound for the greatest flow of blood, which was already shooting forth in great spurts, covering them both in the hot thick fluid. Round-belly's fingers tightened on the blade as Debalo pulled it free and two from the right hand hit the ground between the overseers' own booted feet.

Roundbelly looked down at the free flowing blood and back into the yellow, malarial eyes of the small slave and a sad look of acceptance came over Round-belly's large black face.

He held his wounded hands to his chest as if to staunch the flow of blood, but never spoke a word. After several second, which to Debalo seemed eternal, Round-belly sank heavily to the ground and slowly rolled over with fluttering eyes and stilled. Blood no longer shot from the wound in great streams, but slowly flowed out and mingled into the ever-widening pool.

Debalo, covered in the red gore, reached down and unfastened the belt that held the knife's sheath and after pulling it free of the dead man, wrapped it twice about his own waist, replaced the knife back into the sheath and walked into the mixture of trees and undergrowth beginning past the newly dug grave and disappeared into the shadows of the wetlands.

He moved with purpose and speed once he gained the cover of the woods but he was not reckless. A sprained ankle or worse at this stage of his run and he might as well use the great knife on his own self and save the other overseers the trouble. Not far into the forest Debalo found a well used game trail leading in the proper direction and in areas of decent visibility he ran for all he was worth, but in heavier cover slowed himself for safeties sake. He knew that he needed to wash himself of the blood, but distance now was the thing. Later he could find water to bathe, but only after his lead had been established.

He traveled on until the sun was well overhead and he estimated that he probably had come nearly ten miles from the plantation. The ground he had covered was a mixture of swamp and hardwood. Most of the blood had been washed away in the swamp crossing and of course from the sweat that he had flowing freely from him. He stopped for a minute to consider and to listen for sounds along his trail. Flowing water now was the thing he most wished to find. If he could now wash himself clean and let the water carry off his scent, he knew ways to cover his scent trail and he could put them into play, so long as he could do it without wasting too much time.

Having not detected any sound of followers, Debalo continued on into the mid-afternoon before reaching a narrow, yet swiftly flowing stream where he began his first trick to fool any hounds that may be trailing him. The banks of the creek were lined thickly with an odd assortment of low growing brush, spotted with the occasional cypress and pine. Debalo followed closely upriver until finding an opening down a smoothly worn mudslide. After careful scrutiny of the waters and the tracks along the bank, he satisfied himself that there were no Ngwenya present, for he really hated crocodiles and waded in to mid-stream. He bathed himself thoroughly with handfuls of mud grabbed from the streambed. In one hand he grabbed a palm-sized chunk of flint and he delighted at the find. He carefully tossed it to the bank above an eddy, where he planned to exit the water and finished his bath.

Wading over to the bank, he reached into the bottom of the pooled water of the eddy and pulled huge handfuls of dark brown mud, full of rotting leaves and small twigs and piled it upon the bank. Carefully he pulled himself from the water and with both hands, pushed as much water from his body as he could, before thoroughly coating his feet, legs and hands with the stinky mud. He covered the muddy spot on the bank with a scattering of leaves and picking up the flint, he began a course that carried him back over his back-trail and followed it away from the watercourse for about a half-mile where he stood listening for sounds of pursuit.

If a hound was indeed being used to find his scent, it would travel to the edge of the stream and there would hopefully find the end of the trail, now that he had changed his smell and doubled back on his old smell. He back tracked a bit farther yet until coming beneath the low hanging limb of an ancient oak he'd passed beneath an hour or so previously. The limb hung a foot or so over his head as he stood beneath it and he reached up and pulled himself up and onto the limb. With the agility of a cat, borne from a life in the wilderness, Debalo traveled to a place where a large limb crossed over to an adjoining tree and entered that tree and climbed to a point where it adjoined yet another. By traveling in this way, he covered a full hundred yards before having to come back to the ground. The ground had opened up and he set a fast pace and left the area well behind, he was careful not to pass to close to where he imagined the stream to have originated, knowing that searchers would scour the banks for his scent. He was pleased with the trick and was sure that it would take one very experienced hound to sort out that trail and one patient and determined hunter to allow it the time to do so.

Dusk was gathering quickly and Debalo began to search out a place to spend the night. He had crossed many small swampy areas and skirted a few of undetermined size that appeared to hold fairly deep water. But it was the deep water he now wanted most to find. Or, more correctly, an island in the midst of an area of deep water was what he really wanted hoping that the sound of splashing water would alert him of danger approaching. The mosquitoes that had been present throughout the day began to become quite bothersome each time he slowed his pace too much. Debalo knew he was in for a night of misery if he didn't plan for them as well.

Hoping that he soon would find water he angle toward any downhill slope until he came to a slow moving bayou. He walked along its course in the upstream direction and spotted the perfect hide for his evenings rest. Slightly uphill from the bayou's edge a huge oak had fallen during a not so long ago storm, leaving the root base raised up higher than a mans head, making a solid wall overlooking a gaping hole from whence the roots had been lifted.

As darkness gathered and the swarms of mosquitoes began their terrible work, Debalo used the heavy bladed knife to cut a huge pile of limbs and leaves that he used to nearly fill the hole. Atop of that, he heaped as much loose dirt as he could to hold the pile down and after a drink from the bayou, he crawled carefully beneath the gathering of dirt covered leaves and branches, which afforded him protection from the millions of winged pests and warmth from the cool night air. He tried to remain alert and listen for the sounds of pursuit amongst the lively sounds of the night, but the hard traveling of the day and the lack of a previous night's sleep combined to overcome his best efforts and he soon was deeply asleep; being serenaded by the humming of the winged mosquitoes, the croaking of innumerable frogs, toads and gators.

Above it all was the lonesome calling of the owls amongst the treetops and carried along on the cool night breeze, the just barely audible bawl of a hound, searching earnestly for a trail.

TWO

The events of the day had taken quite a toll on him. Soon after having secreted himself beneath his impromptu bedding, Debalo's body took advantage of the rest it was offered and he began to dream.

"Vuka, Debalo, Tiye! It is time to awaken!"

Debalo tried to drag himself away from his nights sleep as his mother busied herself about the hut, rolling up and stowing away the sleeping mats while at the same time preparing the mornings meal. Through his half closed eyes he could see the thin light of the rising sun bringing daytime again, to the African bushveldt.

"Yini lo skati? Is it not too early yet?" Debalo asked his mother with a thick tongue and foggy head.

"It is not and you had better get a move on or I shall not feed you. If you are too lazy to rise, then you are too lazy to eat I think."

The little women handed him a dipper full of soup once he was on his feet and herded him outside and out of her way. The soup was a sweet mixture of boiled meat broth and honey with an egg dropped in. It was his favorite morning meal and he took his time sipping it, so as to fully enjoy every bit of it, slurping just loudly enough to demonstrate his pleasure. His mother was a very talented woman about the cooking fire.

Outside the hut, in the growing light, Debalo watched the activity of the awakening village. Many old man and youngster were being herded out of the huts, like himself and he went through the morning ritual of nodding, waving and acknowledging various neighbors. His mother emerged from the hut with another dipper full of the sweet brew and traded Debalo for his empty one. She rubbed his lean stomach a few times and flashed him a toothless grin before darting back inside to her morning chores.

"It looks like she's trying to fatten you up, eh Debalo?" An old man called out with humor. Much the same as the old fellow did every morning.

Debalo called out then, much the same answer as he gave him every morning, in their long running joke.

"She is Grandfather. She believes that if I should get fat enough, I'll be too lazy to go out on the hunt. That way I'll stay home and she can care for me again as she did when I was a child."

The answer pleased the old man and he smiled his own toothless grin. Debalo liked the old man and made a note to bring him a portion of whatever the days hunt produced. He wasn't really Debalo's grandfather, but he respected him the same. That is how it is, being raised in a Masarwa village. All men older than you are grandfather and all women are mother.

He glanced over the dipper of soup, as he drank, and across the hard-packed earth of the village square to the slender figure of a young woman padding softly through the early light to the nearby lagoon, carrying a cone shaped cage of woven cane. Wiping his mouth on a forearm, he called out to her.

"Is it not too early to trap fish, Futi?"

"Of course not. There aren't as many fish near the shore while the water is still cool, but then, I like the cool water on my legs before the sun heats it." She called back to him in a teasing, almost flirting tone. "Do you want to come and fish with me today Debalo?"

Actually, he did, most definitely he did, but having taken the rights to manhood that past winter, he could no longer think of wasting his time on a woman's chore, even if it meant spending a few precious hours with the lovely young Futi.

"Of course not. I've more important matters to see to this morning. Go along now. I'll see you in time." He told her.

The girl smiled sweetly, then, lifting the cage atop of her shaven head, she turned and disappeared into the bush along the waters front. He watched her go with lustfull eyes. She had not yet been declared as a woman yet, but he and a few others were counting down the days until her next birthday. There would be much fighting for the right to take her as a wife, but they had been friends once and he suspected that she would not turn him down.

Debalo drained the last of the morning's soup from the dipper and stepped to the doorway of the hut and handed it over to his mother.

"Where do you plan to hunt today?" She asked him.

"I think the elders wish to go back to the grasslands. There should be plenty of dik-dik. Those little antelope are bedding up in the grass and I think a drive would be in order."

"Be careful my Debalo. Simba, also hunts the grasses and you know how scared I am of lions."

"I promise, but now I should be on my…"

The scream was low at first, more a cry of surprise than of pain or alarm, then the intensity rose into a piercing shriek of pure animal terror echoing hollowly through the village, up from the lagoon. Again it cut the cool morning air, even higher, a sharp throbbing wail that lifted his hackles and sent shivers racing up and down Debalo's spine like mad.

Reacting, he made a grab for the Asengai style, hunting spear he kept leaning against the wall of the mud and stick hut and ran toward the lagoon. He heard the old man he'd just spoken with, trip and fall behind him, then regain his feet and run on. His heart felt like a stone wedged in his throat as he bulled his way through the light brush along the hundred and fifty yards or so to the low banks of the lagoon, a reedy dry season lake that would join the Munyamadzi river again, only a hundred yards away, during the next rainy season.

Bursting into the open, he could see a flurry of bloody foam fifty yards from shore, a slender, ebony arm flailing the surface at the end of a great sleek form that sliced through the lagoon toward deeper water. Instinctively he raised the spear to throw, but gave pause. The distance was much too great to ensure accuracy and he couldn't take a chance on hitting the girl. Then like a mallet blow, he realized that if he did pierce her instead, the faster death would probably have been a blessing, far better than being dragged helplessly down by that huge crocodile.

Slow ripples rolled across the calm surface, waving the dark, green reeds until they lapped at the edge of the low banks. Once again the lagoon was silent. He stood there, helpless, shocked into muteness, thinking of poor Futi. He could almost feel the bite of the massive teeth around her midriff, the rough scaliness of the giant head beneath her hands as she tried desperately to break loose before her lungs burst and she drowned.

Others came running up from behind. One look at the floating fish trap and the girl's sandals on the beach told them all that had happened. A younger girl waded out into the water up to her knees and retrieved the fish trap, then placing the sandals inside it began a trot back toward the village, from where any minute Debalo expected to hear the wailing cry of the girls mother. Slowly he turned back toward the village, a bit unsteady after witnessing such a tragic death when the old grandfather joined him.

"You are alright my son?" He asked low and slow, almost a whisper in the younger man's ear.

"I should have thrown the spear." Debalo spoke, not looking into the elders face.

"If it would have made you feel better, perhaps so, but there was nothing to do for it. Ngwenya was waiting. It has always been so. Always he will wait."

"Now he must die." Debalo declared simply. "He hasn't left the lagoon and a dozen men on guard along the banks should be enough to get a spear into him when he should surface for air or if he should try to cross the sandbar between here and the river. Go tell the others to meet me here right away. Today we hunt Ngwenya!"

By noon there were seventeen hunters taken up positions around the low banks of the lagoon. There were other crocodile in the area, to be certain, and although Debalo hadn't got the clearest of looks at the one he now hunted, the very size of the creature would be enough to positively identify it as the attacker. From the size of the animals head and the wake he was throwing, he guesed it to be nearly fifteen foot lengths in size and there weren't many of that size anywhere.

He had positioned himself along the sandy embankment separating the lagoon from the river course. All day the sun beat down indifferently upon him as he watched the water until his temples throbbed for some sign of the big croc, but not a ripple betrayed his presence. Crocodiles can hold their breath by showing the tiniest amount of nostril at the surface. As the last of the light was disappearing,

Debalo and the others drifted back to camp pushing aching cramped joints into movement.

He ate early that night, not saying very much and after a few drinks of cool water went off to bed. It was still dark when he awakened and shrugged out of his blankets into the chill of the morning air. It was well before dawn and he left his mother sleep as he quietly left the hut and made his way to the low banks of the lagoon. Arriving at the sand bar in the growing half light of dawn, he could see all too clearly that it was too late.

Across the sand bar, near the spot he'd guarded just hours before, a terribly wide belly-mark flanked by enormous tracks showed where the killer croc had crossed from the lagoon and entered the river during the night. Debalo had figured on at least a chance at killing the croc in the confines of the lagoon. Now, things would be much harder.

Squatting at the rivers edge, he touched his hand to the track of the monster and tried to age the marks by the seepage of moisture in the sand. Not more than an hour he told himself. He'd missed his chance to avenge Futi, by only an hour. Looking back over his shoulder he could see that the others were already drifting back toward the village. He stood at the water's edge, hating the croc, and spit into the dark current, slowly passing by the low sandy bank.

As Debalo turned to leave, he was sent sprawling to the sand by the unseen force of a sudden attack, which showered him with an explosion of river water. He hit hard on the packed sand of the rivers bank, which knocked the wind completely from his chest and sent his spear sailing. His mind could barely comprehend the speed at which it had occurred and seemingly seconds passed before he registered the crushing, searing pain in his legs, now held securely in the jaws of the giant croc.

He screamed for help and reached about himself for an anchor hold. Grabbing, clawing and digging at anything he could find to hold onto in order to stop himself from being dragged backward into the river's depths. Ever so slowly the huge croc backed up, dragging Debalo along, screaming and flailing about. He felt himself entering the water, being pulled in up to his chest when his right hand closed on a solid root and he clung desperately to keep the hold. Reaching across with his left, he made good the grasp and held on for his very life against the pull of the killer.

More than once he felt his hands begin to slip and each time he would find the strength to tighten the grip. The blinding pain in his legs was nearly more than he could stand. He felt the muscles ripping and tearing and the grinding of the broken bones as the croc fought to free him from his grip and he could hear a deep growl coming up from the giant. As he struggled to prevent what he knew was certain death in the jaws of the hated croc, the growling began to grow in depth and volume and began to take on a more ominous tone. It began to sound like laughter. The deep rolling laugh pounded through his head as an even greater fear welled up within him.

Looking down for the first time at the giant croc, Debalo renewed his screaming, for there, waist deep in the water, Round-belly stood looking down on the little tribesman. Debalo watched as blood poured over the ham-sized hands of the enormous black overseer, as they gripped his legs, slightly above the knee, their fingers penetrating the flesh, digging and tearing. The large malarial eyes locked onto Debalo's and he saw the pleasure in them as the overseer pulled him free of his hold and drug him down, down, down...

THREE

He awakened beneath the stack of dirt and branches he'd concealed himself with and laid quietly. His heart was banging loudly in his ears and his breathing came in short gasps. It was all a dream, he knew, but fear had settled so heavily upon him that several minutes passed before he calmed himself enough to take stock of his situation.

He listened for a time to the forest about him, but there was nothing outside of the normal nighttime sounds of insects, the wet swirls of catfish and turtles on the water, the lazy burps and groans of a thousand insomniac frogs. As far away as he was from home, the night's song was the same and in some small way was a comfort. The cricket's however had not yet begun the morning songs so he knew it was still very early.

Slowly lifting a corner of the limb pile, he drew in a deep breath of the morning air. It was moist and clean. The dew had fallen already and peeking out he could see that the moon was doing a fair job of lighting the woods about him. His muscles ached from the previous days running, and his body yearned to return to sleep for a short while, but fear of repeating the nightmare held off the temptation and ever so quietly he slid from beneath the pile and stood erect, stretching out the kinks and knotted muscles.

Visibility in the moonlight was better than he'd hoped for and after answering nature's call, began a fast walk toward higher ground. He was looking for a more open, level plain to put as much distance between himself and any possibility of pursuit. Once reaching a ridge top studded with giant pines, Debalo remembered a trick to disguise his scent, he'd used once while hunting a particular watering hole.

The water hole had been located up against a low cliff, nestled among the stone walls on three sides and was approachable only by using the same trails as the animals he wished to hunt. He was successful often enough, but always on younger animals, for he noticed that the older, wiser animals would detect his odor where it crossed their path and would go to water elsewhere.

Having given thought to the problem of leaving his scent on the trail, he decided to shave the bark from a tall cedar and let the sticky resin pour down the trunk. After enough had begun to gather on the newly scarred tree, Debalo thoroughly coated his feet with the sticky mess. He hopped into a fresh pile of leaves he'd picked and let them stick all over his feet. The results were not unlike a pair of green boots. That evening when the elder animals checked the trail for his scent, they recognized only the strong cedar smell of the resin and the reassuring scent of the leaves he'd chosen. That evening, he'd struck a beautiful Kudu antelope with his spear. It had been a fine older bull with high-reaching spiraling horns.

Choosing a very wide diameter pine, he drew the large knife from the sheath at his waist and set about to recreate the trick. He first cut a ring about the tree waist high and then again at knee level. He then walked around the tree cutting strips of bark away from between the two rings until only white bark shown in the pre-dawn moonlight. Before he'd completed the removal of the bark, resin had begun seeping into the newly bared area of the old tree's trunk. Daylight was still a couple of hours away but he worked quickly, not letting himself get careless with his escape. He still had no idea if he was being followed or to what extent a runaway would be sought, but a man had died and he felt sure that that would never be allowed to pass without an effort to bring him back to account for it.

The spring had not advanced enough for Debalo to locate a good supply of green, pungent leaves to glue to his feet with the pine resin, so he instead set about clearing away the litter of the floor of the pine forest to the barest dirt and after applying a thorough coating of the sticky matter. He stepped off into the fresh cleared dirt. After the coating thickened about his feet, he hitched up the rags he wore for pants and adjusted the belt and knife before striking out again with a new scent on his trail.

The crickets were singing loudly now and pink light was gaining in the east. Debalo quickened his pace, traveling through ancient hammock of beach and oak where the canopy blocked the sun and the undergrowth was sparse. He drew up after awhile, having come upon a road cutting at an angle through the hardwood forest toward a low ridge he'd been skirting. As roads go, it wasn't much more than a deeply rutted lane, but it offered a clear path of travel Debalo opted to follow it at a fast trot and use it to quickly and easily eat up the miles.

Hours passed and the sun rose quickly as Debalo maintained his ground-eating trot along that wilderness trail. The sun, now nearly overhead, had long ago burned off the morning dew and drew thick beads of sweat all over him as he ran. He'd removed the well-worn shirt he'd been given on the plantation and had it tucked securely in the belt behind him. His anthracite skin fairly shined in the light of the morning sun as the daylight passed from shadow to light. He'd no idea how far his run had taken him, but he was proud of his progress. His legs were beginning to ache and his breath came short and in gasps, but he knew he could go on.

Approaching the crest of a ridge before him, Debalo stopped short. The sound of a man's voice reached his ear and fear gripped his heart. His mind spun in near panic. Instinct took over and he quickly moved into the brush lining the trail. A pair of horse-mounted men rode by speaking in casual tones. The two men were dressed alike with fine gray suits and tall black hats. They rode along on horses that showed all outward signs of being well bred and carefully cared for. After what Debalo felt was several minutes, but in reality was much quicker, the two continued past his hiding spot, on their way with an occasional departing laugh to be heard.

Debalo lay in the brush, catching his breath, marveling at his luck in not having been discovered. It was time to slow down again. He'd not take the risk of traveling on the open road again. Realizing how careless he'd been, Debalo vowed himself to maintain better discipline. He kept himself hidden in the brush along the roadway and followed the course past the ridge and soon came upon a swift flowing creek. The road led onto a roughly built bridge of hewn timbers and at the base of the bridge he chose to leave the road course and follow the water upstream along its high banks, lined with low brush and assorted hardwoods. Just under a half-mile from the bridge, he came to a place where the river's bank lowered to the level of the water and Debalo took advantage of it to bathe and drink heavily. Hunger was gnawing away at him and he searched the banks of the river for lunch.

He lay down upon a wide flat rock along the edge of a nearby eddy, pooling against the trunk of a long ago fallen tree. After several grabs he had secured a half dozen minnows, which he consumed whole and raw. The taste of the small fish was of no importance to him. He simply needed whatever energy he could obtain from them. Moving on he spied a cut-bank near a bend in the creek where the current had worked its way beneath the roots of an ancient hickory tree. If these waters were anything like the creeks he'd grown up with in Africa, he'd find catfish beneath those roots waiting for whatever offering the current would bring them.

Wading across the waist high waters of the dark running creek, the cold bringing chill bumps all over his body, he came slowly up to the cut-bank with its wild entanglement of roots. By bending his knees and resting his cheek on the edge of the bank, Debalo freed himself to search the hidden crevices beneath the bank for the soft-slick feel of the catfish. He'd fished before in that manner and knew that to be successful; he'd have to locate the fish's mouth and tempt it into biting onto his hand. At that point, he then would be able to grab a hold of the fish's jaws and haul it out without too much difficulty. Whether by skill or by the luck of the needy, his assumption had panned out, for in short time he'd pulled out from the dark tangles a fat bluish catfish the length of his own forearm.

Wading back across the creek, he pulled himself out of the water and proceeded to the cover of a small grove of willows growing amid an outcropping of flat stones, many as high as his shoulders and many times wider. He's spotted a small game trail leading behind one particularly wide wedge of stone and followed it into a tiny clearing amidst the cover of the willows. Here, he felt secure enough to spend an hour or so to partake of his meal and rest.

Laying the fish out on a flat-topped stone he found at hand, he taken the big knife and slit open the belly and removed the fish's entrails. It twisted and squirmed beneath his sure grip, but once gutted, it lie still atop the stone, the gaping mouth opening and closing quietly in denial of its own death. Of the organs, Debalo selected the liver, heart and gizzard to begin his meal and discarded the rest. After downing the vitamin rich organ meat, he began to remove the smooth outer skin from the fish and remove the meat in long pink strips. The flavor was not unpleasant, but he definitely would have preferred it to be cooked, but the risk of smoke being seen or smelled was far too great. All in all, the fish produced about two pounds of meat. Half of it Debalo ate right off, but the other half he carefully wrapped in his rag of a shirt and tucked away behind his belt. He stretched out his feet and legs and although he felt the ache and tension in them from the hard traveling, he also felt strength and endurance, which lifted his spirits and gave him confidence in his flight.

Slipping from the cover of the willows, Debalo made his way back down to the creek and lowered himself for a drink. He took in long steady gulps to wash down the fish and wiped his mouth off with his hand turned to continue along the path he'd previously selected. A voice from low ridge just above him halted his movement and froze his heart.

"Hey der nigga', who's it ya workin' fo dat ain' got no use for ya dis time o dah day?"

Debalo looked up and spotted the man calling to him. He was around his own age and build, but not quite as dark of skin. He was dressed in much better clothes than the slaves he'd known on the plantation. His overalls were well worn and faded to the color of the mid morning sky, but no patches yet adorned the knees. He had a loose fitting, white linen shirt, tucked in behind the bib of the overalls, the sleeves rolled up to his elbows. Like himself, the man wore no shoes, but did sport a finely woven hat of palmetto leaves. In his right hand, he carried a long slender pole and a small can hanging from a handle.

The first instinct Debalo recognized was the instinct telling him to flee, but the look of the man, who was grinning a broad white grin and coming closer intrigued him and he stayed his fears and returned the smile.

In only a few long strides, the man had drawn quite near and with a gay look about him, spoke again.

"I says boy, how ya come to be down heya, dis time o dah day?"

Debalo hadn't any idea how to react to the foreign language, but in polite Masarwa fashion, held both hands to his mouth for a second and dropped them outward, toward the new arrival.

The man looked Debalo over with a quick eye and noticeably raised his eyebrows at the sight of the big knife hanging at his side.

"Whassa matta boy? You done speak de language yet huh?" His smile lost none of its genuine warmth.

Debalo spoke to him in his own tongue asking where he was and in which direction he should travel, but his words were as unfamiliar to the stranger as the strangers were to him.

"Lemme see sompthin' boy." The stranger spoke slowly while reaching out for Debalo's left hand. Debalo resisted at first, pulling back despite himself, but calmed and allowed the other man to take his hand and turn it palm up, inspecting the scars made there by the overseer's branding iron, a constant reminder of his first day on the plantation.

"Damn yo' hide son, dats Dabria brand. I knowed about dat bunch up de river. I knowed dat dey don' let dey slaves run off ta dah fishin' hole all dis way out, fo' nuttin. Dabria bunch is killa's I hear. I hear tell about dat big nigga dey got fo dey overseer, one what carries a big knife, is da meanes crittur in all Louisiana."

Debalo relaxed in the man's presence and listened to him jabber on with curiosity.

"If dats de knife, I hope ya killed de nigga dead cause ya don't want no Dabria nigga's gittin aholt of yah I swear it. Now look heyah boy," he said, turning Debalo to face upstream along the creek and pointed hard.

"Keep runnin' boy. Keep runnin an' don' look back. Folla dat creek to da river boy an' head sout ta Baritaria. Ya make it deah boy, ya might stan' a chance." He gave Debalo a light shove to set him off.

He started out and smiled a farewell. Behind him he could hear the stranger calling to him.

"You go on now. Me, I'm fo' headin back ta da house. I aint gonna tell massa' nothing bout dis' tho, but I ain't gonna be out heyah alone neitha, case dem Dabria folk come by dis hyar way looking' fer you. Go on ahead boy, git gone!"

FOUR

After meeting the fisherman along the banks of the creek, Debalo had stayed to his course and followed the watercourse for a couple of days. Not yet had he received a hint of sign that he was being followed, but yet he'd no desire to slow down yet. One significant change he had adopted after running into the fisherman, was to crawl into a snug bit of cover throughout the most of the day and carry on the gist of his travels at night, by the light of the moon. He'd seen no more people traveling along the creek, but twice he had smelled smoke and once had heard the far off barking of a hound. The hounds echoing bawl had given him pause, but once he'd taken stock of the situation realized that the noise came from a safe direction and was most likely night hunters out to fill their families larder.

Debalo was beginning to enjoy the freedom of his journey. The ground, along the creek was mostly even and not too thickly covered in brush. Sunlight was no longer a bother and he found he could cover much more ground with less fatigue. Food had been plentiful so far, he having eaten a variety of fish, frog and even an opossum he managed to club with the staff he'd cut and shaped for himself.

He'd even allowed him self the luxury of a cook fire the last couple of nights. By using the back of the big knifes blade striking against the flint he struck a spark into a carefully wrapped nest of tinder which he softly blew on and caressed until a tiny flame took hold. He had built his fires in out of the way nooks that provided shelter from the light and squatting over a cook-fire in the brush, preparing and eating food he had gathered himself, went a long way to help him feel like a man again. Enslavement had not fully broken his pride as a man, but certainly there was a lot of healing needed that time would surely see to. But, now he was living free again and in just a few more days, he thought to himself, he would leave the creek and as long as there were no towns or roads nearby. Linger in an area to find out all there was to know about it. Once he'd learned all there was to know of a place, then he could go into another part of the country and start again. That was the way of life for the bushman for as far as the oldest elder could remember and to Debalo, it was a good way to live.

Often he thought of home and the people he'd left behind upon being seized by the slavers. It struck him odd though that he could not seem to remember the faces of any of his old friends directly. He could recall a name and all of the person's characteristics, but not until he would replay in his mind, a certain event that they had partaken of, could he see their faces clearly. A hunting trip taken, skinning and caring for downed game. Laughing too loudly after filling up with stolen tshwala, beer or many other great stories of some of the most unusual predicaments the hunters could encounter.

One such encounter happened on the dry grassland of the Zambese. It happened one cool mid-winter afternoon. The sun had passed brightly overhead and the leader of the days hunt, an Arab whom Debalo and his friends Simone and Samu, were acting as guides for, had called for a water break and a rest in the shade beneath a huge brachystegia tree near an ocean of tall brown grass. They had been out for hours, hoping to catch the sign from an evasive herd of antelope Debalo knew to be in the area. The Arabs were in a generous mood and were handing out scraps of black shag tobacco wrapped in brown waxed paper which when smoked smelled not unlike burning hair and tasted only slightly better, but it did produce a wonderful, if not temporary buzz the tribesmen enjoyed.

They all heard it at the same time, the sound like a distant tornado, swishing and chugging along. A shiver of fright traveled up and down Debalo's spine as it dawned on him what that sound could only be; Mahoho! Rhino, and coming that way, very fast!

Everyone sprang to their feet and stood listening, straining to locate the noise exactly, the thudding of thick, short feet now audible with occasional squeals muffled by the grass. The Arabs had set about climbing the tree and Simone and Samu split off in separate directions. Debalo made a high jump for a hand-hold on a prominent branch growing from the back-side of the tree and missed, hitting the ground again and watched as the grass exploded with a cow rhino, then a big bull, then yet another bull.

The first bull had a nasty gore wound on his flank and the second one began to overtake him, slashing away at him with his thick front horn. Debalo held his breath as the cow thundered by the tree, oblivious to the frightened little black man pressing close against its rough bark, followed by the foaming, snorting bulls and disappeared back into the tall grass. Debalo raised a hand to his chest, where his heart was trying to beat through and stepped back from the tree when there was a particularly savage snort and a shout of fear from Samu, in the direction the rhinos had just gone.

One of the Arabs jumped down from his perch, clutching his long rifle and together he and Debalo went off into the cover hoping to offer poor Samu any help. As they got closer, Debalo could make out the form of a bull rhino dashing about in little circles around the base of an Umphafa, the tree the Arabs called the buffalo-thorn tree and in the very top of the tree was perched Samu.

From twenty yards away the rhino stopped his running about and stared right at Debalo and his companion, then holding to the old rhino theory of kill it first, then investigate it, the bull lowered his head and began his rush. Debalo had just began his turn to make a jump for a nearby tree when the Arab fired the flint down on the charge in his rifle and the thing went off with the most magnificent explosion of sound and smoke. To be safe, Debalo stepped up into the tree anyway and through the clearing smoke, could see that the rhino was sitting on his haunches, swinging his huge head back and forth in stunned confusion.

It appeared that the ball from the Arabs musket had taken him squarely at the base of the horn and had knocked him completely senseless. In a few seconds, however he was back on his feet and slowly made off into the bush and was gone for good. When the party got back together they realized that Samu still hadn't come down from the tree and slowly Debalo, Simone and the Arabs broke into howling roaring laughs. In his haste to get away from the rhino, which had spotted him and doubled back, poor Samu, in his haste to get away, had chosen a very poor refuge.

The buffalo-thorn tree is a mass of the cruelest thorns imaginable. In his haste to get away, Samu had not even noticed them on his way up; but now it was a different story. Bleeding like a butchered warthog, he simply couldn't find a way back through the barbed branches. Despite the fact that the poor man was obviously in a great deal of pain it took several minutes for the party to compose themselves. The look on the poor wounded Samu's face was most ridiculously humble as he pleaded with the group for help of any kind. Simone finally tossed up to him a panga, which he used to trim a pathway, free of thorns, back down the trunk.

FIVE

Time passed quickly for Debalo and at the rising of the third full moon since he'd made good his escape, he lay resting upon a bed of moss and pine boughs which had been erected in the high fork of a century old live oak. The tree was located in the midst of an enormous hardwood hammock growing upon a low ridge with sparse undergrowth. It was bordered on two sides by deep flowing creeks, teaming with fish, which emptied a mile or so to the east into a huge mud-colored river. Game was plentiful and easily hunted or trapped and Debalo delighted in learning to identify each new species by their sign and habits.

During his time dwelling in this forest, Debalo had taken the time to build a few sturdy lances for hunting and shaped a couple of throwing sticks for rabbits and other small game. He'd fashioned a fire pit, with shelter to keep the flames concealed, and gathered a good stockpile of wood nearby. He hadn't need for much in the way of supplies, but he kept himself living comfortable. Each day he spent exploring the area while hunting, fishing or gathering the plentiful berries and mast.

On the third day after settling into the heart of the hardwood forest, Debalo hunted his first deer in the new lands. He set up on a section of one of the flowing creeks where game often crossed. It was a shallow spot with a firm bottom and plentiful fresh sign on both banks. On the near side of the creek to him and a few short steps from the crossing, a giant oak had blown over and the root base had lifted skyward, creating a perfect blind for an ambush.

Early in the pre-dawn hours, Debalo had risen and bathed himself in the creek a hundred or so yards downwind from the ambush site, then rolled about on the ground in a bed made of freshly picked and fragrant leaves. Once satisfied that his scent would be properly masked, he concealed himself behind the root base with a couple of sharp lances newly made for the hunt. He had taken the precaution of removing all grass, sticks and leaves from the ground around him, less a noise give him away when he moved to make his throw.

He'd been hidden in the blind for nearly an hour when he heard the first unmistakable sound of a deer's feet rising and falling into the creek's water. He remained still, on bended knee, muscles tensed for the coming strike, but the strike he had expected wasn't to come. As soon as the deer had crossed the creek, it made a quick turn parallel to the creek's course, carrying it directly away from the hunter.

He stilled his racing heart, sped by the adrenaline coursing through his veins from the anticipation of the kill, and resolved to remain in position for a while longer. The wait wasn't long before he once again heard the familiar sound. Upon exiting the water, the deer continued on the trail leading around the blind. From a distance of ten feet or less, Debalo let fly with all his strength. He drove his lance half of its length into the chest of the startled deer.

At the moment Debalo struck, the deer gave a terrific kick with its hind legs and sped away, mortally wounded. Debalo stood and leaned against the roots of the ancient tree as he listened for the telltale crash and thrashing of the animal in its death throes. Hearing none, he remained in place for an hour or so before taking up the blood sign left by the retreating deer. The trail was quite easy to follow. Debalo's lance had penetrated through to the deer's rib cage and exited the far side, skewering both heart and lungs along the way, leaving blood sign on both sides of the trail.

After a quarter mile or so of creeping and slipping quietly along the blood-trail, Debalo spotted the deer. It was a young male with twin horns, each horn thin in diameter and as tall as Debalo's hand was long. He lifted the dead weight of the animal upon his shoulders and started for the area he'd begun to use for his main campsite. Once there he proceeded to process the animal.

He cut the meat into long thin strips. Portions he ate right off; he started on the organ meat at first because it would spoil the fastest. He opened the gal sack on the liver and used it as a seasoning to further flavor the raw meat as it was consumed.

Very enjoyable were the intestines, lightly scorched over a bed of coals and eatenlike sausages, original contents and all. The rest of the meat hung on a tall rack of willow branches he had assembled for the task of drying it for biltong or jerky.

The hides was stretched out and staked to the ground with slender wooden stakes he'd sharpened for the purpose. Bones and horn were set aside for tool making and some of the other entrails, which could be used were as well saved. What waste there was from the carcass was carried to the creek for disposal.

Time passed quickly for him in the forest and he was quite content to live from the rich store available to him in this lush wilderness. He was alone. Being alone was not unknown to him, but yet at times he absolutely longed for companionship. For a while, he caught himself slipping into moods, which gave him a brooding self-pity and at those times he would try to busy himself with some chore or another until it passed. He knew that survival in this new land depended entirely upon his determination to live free.

Debalo looked often at his scarred hand, which held the brand of slavery. He lay in the light of the rising moon and listened to the sing-song chorus of the night creatures and smelled the sweet scent of burning pine from his fire. In the night air and rocking with the gentle sway of his tree top bed, he looked again at his hand. He traced the outline of the puckered scars, remembering the evil that had created it, wishing he were in Africa.

Debalo awakened slowly and knew from the moon's position that he hadn't been asleep long. The night was strangely quiet, and had taken on a rhythm he felt more than heard. He lay quietly for a while sensing and feeling the pulse of the humid night, wondering at the feeling, like an old memory coming back to haunt him. Suddenly as recognition flowed over him, he was on his feet, being carried along by the primal rhythms, answering the calling of the night. He traveled a full twenty minutes through the half-dark of the full moon night until he could see the eerie glow of a bonfire with shadows hurling about it.

The volume of the drumming had increased with each step until the sound flowed and ebbed through his mind and body. He began to circle the scene before him, staying in the shadows and keeping himself concealed, yet growing closer with each cautious step. At twenty or so yards away, he halted his advance and knelt behind a maple's trunk and observed.

Nearly thirty men and women gathered about the fire in a large circle. On the far end of the circle, sitting cross-legged upon the ground were three drummers. Each drum was of a different shape and size and the pounding rhythms the three created were like the beat of a man's heart after a long run. In the center of the gathering and dancing wildly to the drumming was a woman. She was tall and slender and moved beautifully to the fast beat of the drums. Her hair had been cut short and in it she wore a wreath of leaves and nothing else upon her body.

Debalo could not tear his eyes away from the nude woman's twisting and turning. Sweat was beaded up and running in rivulets down her dark brown skin and her full breast swung back and forth in time to the beat. Debalo was naturally quite captivated by the dancer's movements. It was a familiar dance he'd witnessed many times back in his home village in Africa, but never performed in the nude by such a lovely dancer.

Much too soon the drumming came to a stop and the whirling dancer dropped to the ground on her knees in apparent exhaustion. At the conclusion of her wild performance a roar went up from the circle of spectators and a young girl brought forth a robe for the dancer to cover with. Once robed the woman held out her hand to quiet the onlookers and in perfect Fanagalo, Debalo's native tongue, thanked them for their love, then asked that they all join in a dance to honor the gods of voodoo.

Kneeling behind the trunk of the maple, Debalo felt more than heard the renewed pounding of the drums as the entire congregation began to dance. They circled the fire in a shuffling series of steps, bending and straightening at the waist raising and lowering their arms in no particular choreography, but in the synchronized rhythm of the primal beat of the African drummers. The rhythms echoed and bounded along deep inside of him, the smell of wood smoke and sweat filled his nostrils and overtook his senses creating a wild and primitive euphoria. Debalo stood and was just stepping from the cover of the tree, hoping to join the melee when a hand reached his shoulder from behind. He instinctively stiffened in alarm at the surprise of the touch, but immediately relaxed from a mixture of the soft and gentle feel of the hand on his shoulder and the comforting calm of the familiarity of the scene.

Turning slowly he discovered that the hand on his shoulder belonged to girl of twelve or so years, but no older. In the foreign tongue he'd heard spoken so much in this new land, she spoke to him in a sweet way that he took for a greeting and reached for his hand. He offered a warm smile and then covered his mouth with his free hand, returned the greeting in fanagalo and followed the youngster into the firelight. Soon he was shuffling and bending in perfect time to match the other dancers and gave himself over to the whirling and pounding of the primitive cadence. Time held no meaning and passed without Debalo's notice. At last, however, the drumming came to a halt and so did the dance. Debalo stood among the dancers, covered in a luminous coating of sweat, which caught the light of the fire and shined brilliantly upon him. The youngster, whom had led him into the fray stood near and he shot her a quick smile despite his heavy breathing.

Others now approached the new arrival, with no small amount of joy and gayety as Debalo found himself received into the gathering with undisguised enthusiasm. Seemingly out of nowhere, food and drink appeared and he endulged eagerly. Many of the dancers spoke fanagalo or kiswahili, which delighted him completely. Since leaving the plantation, he'd spent so much time alone that between mouthfuls of strange and wonderful tasting foods, he found himself chattering on and on to whomsoever would allow him an attentive ear. As the dancing continued anew, Debalo was taken aside by several of the men of the group and he soon learned that many of their stories were very similar to his own. He was not the only former slave on the run from the plantation masters and overseers. At least he was no longer alone.

They remained in the campsite for a week, resting and visiting by day, giving Debalo the opportunity to get to know the members of the gathering. Nighttime, however, was for revelry. The rising of the full moon each night was the signal to again renew the drumming, dancing and feasting. Each night the dancers were entertained first by the woman Debalo had seen on his first arrival to the group repeating her solo performance paying tribute to the gods of voodoo, each time ending up stark naked as before. That was one performance Debalo especially enjoyed and looked forward to.

Her name was Marie and she came to this place each month from the north, upriver a ways from a large and growing city called New Orleans. The name of the place was foreign to his ears, but she arranged the meeting for dual purposes. First and most advertised, was the celebration of the voodoo religion, well known and practiced throughout the region. Second, was the least advertised, in fact quite secretive, purpose of gathering together runaway slaves, called in by the sound of the African drummers.

It was on the second day of the gathering that Debalo was introduced to Marie. She spoke to him about aiding runaways such as himself and asked him what it was he most wanted. He was quiet for a while, not knowing how to respond. She waited patiently as he searched for an answer before offering him some considerations.

"My friend," she started softly "I know you've been hiding out in the forests, but how long will you wish to remain hiding? Wouldn't you like to be among your own people without fear of being returned to slavery or killed outright? I have heard that you also killed a man in your escape from a plantation. They will never stop hunting you. If you want to return to Africa, tell me, I can help you. My new friend, what is it you want to do with your life?"

"I wish to return to my village, of course, but it is so far away. I was brought here in a large ship, I have no ship to return me. I am now to travel in this land." He replied.

"I can make it happen, Debalo."

"How is that?"

"I have a special arrangement with a ships captain named Lafitte. He is a special friend that comes to visit me often. He needs men to work his docks and sail his boats, you will agree to sail with him and he will take you to Africa. It is a system that works out well for us both."

"You say you know this man well?"

"Of course Debalo, he's been one of my lovers for a very long time." She noticed Debalo's look of surprise at her bold confession. "Don't look as if I shock you. He pays me well for my services. Anyway, if you desire, I can direct you to him. Also, I would make a recommendation to you about that knife you carry."

"What about it?" He asked.

"I would sell or trade it. In the least, I would carry it hidden. I've noticed more than one man eyeing that knife and I believe that if you keep it on display, one night it may be taken from you. You may even be killed outright for it. I have seen it done for far less."

Many came and went, most on foot, some by river on makeshift rafts or canoe, all seeking the same thing; refuge from pursuit, food and clothing. Each one harboring the same dream in their heart's which was simply return to Africa. That's where Marie and her gathering were most helpful, Debalo came to understand, for they knew the way to make that dream come true. That dream started in a small island town down river, known as Barataria.

SIX

He lay quietly now, listening to the fast paced slosh-splash, slosh-splash, of the steamboat moving steadily against the current of the great mud-colored river. It had been dark for several hours now, but Debalo took no chances of being spotted by the boatmen. In the bow of the long, double-tiered vessel a pair of torches had been positioned in front of large dish-shaped reflectors, which cast the yellow light of the burning staffs onto the surface of the river. It would take one glimpse of his self or his two companions that lay to either side of him to set off an alarm. The boat would be landed and great rust-colored hounds set ashore to hunt them down.

Marie had made it very clear to him and the others when they departed to travel only at night and to take refuge in the wilderness during the daytime. Slave hunters had kept a steady patrol up and down the waterways searching for runaways to capture for whatever price they could bring on the market in

New Orleans or St. Louis. Providing one didn't mind carrying their human cargo so far up-river, the prices were always better in St. Louis.

Each of the other two men like himself carried a folded letter of introduction which they were told would be their assurance of safe conduct once they had reached the pirate city of Barataria, located on a tributary of the river, much farther to the south. Upon reaching the outskirts of the town, they would be stopped by sentries kept on duty at all times. For the sentries they were to produce the documents she had provided and ask to be introduced to Capitaine Jean Lafitte. He would then direct them further.

The paddleboat finally succeeded in disappearing around the river's bend and slowly the three travelers began anew their trek along the river's edge. The moon was not much help; low-hanging clouds that brought the scent of rain to Debalo swallowed what light it would have offered. He led the trio along slowly in the dark, using his staff to balance himself as he slowly tested each footfall before committing his weight to it. The pace of their advance was very slow indeed, but he found no reason to risk injury by being foolish.

They waded many creeks and small rivers that emptied into the flow of the great river. Debalo approached each crossing with great apprehension and studied each one thoroughly before committing himself to the water. With his staff he checked the depth ahead of him and sought out the hidden snags and possible obstacles he would try to avoid. But deep water and submerged brush wasn't the reason for

Debalo's fear; it was the gators, as his two companions called them that thrived in these waterways. He had seen many along the river and although they were generally much smaller than the ngwenya, or crocodiles, of his homeland, they appeared to be no less dangerous.

He remembered also, a bit of knowledge passed down to him from an elder Bantu warrior about stream or river crossing in ngwenya's territory.

"Remember, it is always the third man crossing that is at the most risk of attack," he had told him one late night as they sat sipping a sort of wine fermented from the plum-like murula near the dying coals of a late evening cooking fire.

"The first man in the water only wakes up ngwenya. The second man invites ngwenya to investigate. The third man, you see, he is taken by ngwenya. Of course that is not always the way of it, but if you live long enough, you will see that I am right more than I am wrong."

Debalo had been a very young man then, only recently had he been accepted as a warrior and a man. But he never forgot the older man's advice.

"I hate ngwenya!" He remembered telling the elder who only smiled at his youthful outburst.

"How can you hate him? He does nothing more than is his nature. Is it his nature you hate, or is it that he is a reminder that you are only meat after all and that one day your turn will come?"

Debalo did not know how to respond to the man's questions, but the elder didn't press him for an answer.

He merely smiled a bit to himself and returned to his wine, leaving the young man deep in his thoughts.

The two men traveling with Debalo were not as accustomed to life in the wilderness as he was and were more than willing to follow his lead. They had met at the gathering place and were also drawn to the sound of the tribal drums. The older of the two, and a few seasons older than Debalo as well, was named Bwana. Back in Africa the name meant that he was a great hunter, but having observed the man in the wilds, Debalo knew the name was only a coincidence.

Bwana was a tall, black man with a stout build. He was shirtless beneath a half rotten pair of overalls and his muscles fairly rippled with his movements. On his feet he wore rags, wrapped tightly, for shoes. He was a handsome man in Debalo's opinion, but he was also the clumsiest fellow he'd ever led through a forest. Several times a night Bwana's rag-clad feet would catch on some unseen vine or bit of brush and send him sprawling head first to the ground. After having been caught a few times by the big man's attempt to break his fall, Debalo was sure to keep a safe distance ahead of him as he led.

He spoke both fanagalo and the local language as well and was a translator for Debalo and their other companion Blue, who spoke only the local English language. Blue was a young fellow of only about fourteen summers. His height and build were similar to that of Debalo, but there was a lightness in his color and features that made him look almost as the white men did. He was the best outfitted of the three travelers. His shirt was almost new and he had a pair of canvas pants that had not yet seen a patch. Blue's shoes were held together with strips of rawhide, but offered him protection from the briars.

During the daylight hours Debalo would choose a suitable spot to hide up and the three would lie together and whisper amongst themselves, trusting the sound of the breeze and the singing birds to drown out their sound to any ears that may come about. It was during these times, concealed in whatever tangled shelter Debalo could find, that he learned the character and history of his two new friends.

Bwana had been born in the small fishing village near the river Nile and was very young when the Arabs arrived and gathered the villagers together by gun, knife and sword. He remembered little of the event except clinging to his mother on a long walk to a barge, which took them down river to the docks. It was there that they remained in a large stone room for a couple of days before a ship arrived and ferried them to the new land.

Listening to the man recount his experience, Debalo thought how fortunate Bwana had been to live the experience as a youngster. Children have vague memories of suffering whereas he still ached daily with the memories of his being brutalized. After reaching the new land, Bwana recalled the shock of seeing a white man. He had never seen a man whose skin was a pale as the belly of a fish and was quite fascinated until one stepped over to him. Taking him by an arm, the white man pulled him from his mother. Having her young son separated from her by the white man, she began a terrible wailing and began to fight the chains that had been placed about her legs. He watched helplessly as a large white man beat and kicked the grieving woman until she quieted down to a mere whimper.

Throughout the telling of the story, Debalo would get bits of the tale and then wait a bit while Bwana re-told the story to Blue, who hung on every word. The rest of his life as a slave, he summarized as having been one of work and quiet living in the black quarters of a Louisiana plantation. He was a field hand and as long as he and the other slaves saw to their work and never bucked an order from the "Massah", they were fairly content. Content, that is, until the old "Massah" died and a new one took charge of the plantation and the slaves.

The new "Massah" was an intolerable drunkard of a man who was quick with the whip and was fond of raping the young women he kept as servants in the big house. The man was apparently not as well versed in the business of the plantation as the former owner and in only a year, money had run out and he had been forced to begin selling off the slaves to pay off his many mounting debts. Bwana was sold to a trader who marched him and a group of others, in chains, to a logging camp in the delta. Once there they began the hard labor of logging out the cypress swamps.

It was one morning while getting the slaves assembled into their labors that the overseer of the crew was stricken by a cottonmouth and died of a fever that night. The body of the overseer was not buried right away because if any other white men were to show up, a couple of the older black men wanted it clear that the overseer had not been slain by his own charges. After the third day in the moist heat of the Louisiana bayou country, his ripeness overcame their caution and he was placed in a shallow, muddy grave. The spot was marked by a large slab of cypress sticking upright into the moist earth and the man's hat resting atop of it.

The slaves stayed where they were for a couple of days, but being without food, shelter or direction, they began to drift away. Bwana was one of the last to leave, not really knowing what else to do. He hadn't really run away, but yet, he had no papers declaring his freedom. He felt himself quite fortunate when he came to the drumming and stumbled onto the gathering in the woods. He had never given thought to returning to Africa, but he did want to keep his newly found freedom and there was no chance of that here in this land.

Debalo understood the man's yearning to keep his freedom. He had not fought hard enough when the Arabs tricked his village into a position to be captured as slaves. Many warriors fought to the death, he himself had fought but little, realizing the probable outcome of further resistance to the slavers, he relented. There were few days that passed during his enslavement in which he hadn't wished that he had died in Africa as a fighter, rather than succumb to the humiliation and cruelty of enslavement.

Blue's story was altogether different. He had been born into slavery in a place he called "Arkysaw". He was the son of a large black woman who served as the cook for a large white family that was quite wealthy. It was told to him more than once that most likely, one of the Ole Massuh's three grown sons was his Daddy, but he was never to speak it.

The ole Massuh kept a stable of fine horses on the plantation and a kennel slap full of fox hounds and bird dogs to which he was given the duties of looking after once he was of age. He was placed under the supervision of an older black man named Jim, who taught him all about caring for the animals and eventually all about their training.

Blue told as how he had been good with the horses and loved the big animals, but it was the hunting dogs and their training that most interested him. He'd never known love from any living person, even from his own Mammy, like he was shown by them dogs, especially a little short-haired spaniel he called Nip. Blue spoke so often of Nip that Debalo grew weary.

Blue had grown up on the plantation and never knew any other way than being a servant. It had only been a month or so before answering the call of the drummers, that Blue had been forced to run away. The story he told was very different from their own, but both Debalo and Bwana understood his situation.

The Ole Massuh's youngest boy Nate had always been a bit on the mean side, but Blue just generally avoided him whenever he could. Then one morning, the day Blue left, the young man came to the kennel and ordered Blue to pick out a couple of dogs for a quail hunt. Blue had wanted to make an impression on the young Massuh, so he leashed up his two favorites; naturally one was Nip.

They had gotten a late morning start and it had been unusually hot that day. Blue had noticed that the birds tended not to move about during the late morning hours and the sun's heat dissipated the scent quickly, which made for a difficult hunt. They hunted through the heat of the mid-day and on into the early evening, putting up no more than two or three birds which Nate promptly missed with his side-by-side fowling gun.

Nate began to cuss the dogs for their lack of finding more birds and the longer they hunted without his getting a shot the more he cussed. The young Massuh had been sipping from a flask he carried in his hip pocket and by the time it had emptied, he had developed quite an anger at the two dogs for their lack of success.

Finally and much to Blue's relief, the angry young Massuh called it quits for the day and ordered the two dogs be leashed. They had began the long walk back from the fields and only gotten about a dozen or so yards when the young Massuh stepped smack into the middle of a small covey bedded down in the cover of the knee high grass. The dozen or so quail exploded from beneath the man's feet with a whir of wings.

After recovering from his start, Nate raised the old fowler and cut loose with the right barrel, which missed completely. After an impressive display of cussing and stomping, the hot-blooded young man turned to Blue and in a raging shout said, "What in hell are we feeding them pot lickers? The only covey we raised all day and I had to raise them myself!"

Without waiting for the slave to answer his question, the young Massuh raised the barrel of the fowler and let go with the left barrel, directly into Nip.

Blue was stunned at the sudden and violent death. He sank to his knees to cradle what was left of the poor little spaniel's head in his lap. He stroked the shiny soft coat of the much-loved little dog and pulled the other close and held him tight. Tears flowed freely and he looked up for an answer to the question he could barely choke out.

"Why'd you kill at dog? T'weren't his fault!" Blue cried out in a sob, but he received no answer. Through his tears, he watched the man leave, marching through the field toward home.

Blue had dug the grave with his own hands and buried Nip beneath a beech tree nearby, saying a Christian prayer over the grave in the way he had been taught. It was nearly dark when he arrived back to the kennel and put away his other dog. Although he had been forbidden to come to the big house, he wanted nothing more than to see his Mammy. He hoped she would say something to help his broken heart.

Arriving at the door leading into the kitchen area of the big house where he expected to find his mother preparing the evening meal for the white folks, he heard a deep grunting sound repeated over and over, much like the sound the old boar hog made when the boy took the slop bucket out to the stye. Looking in through the glass pane of the door leading into the kitchen, he saw his mammy bent over the table where she would cut up the supper meat. She had a hold of the far edge of the table with both hands, her face turned away with the cheek resting on the wooden surface. Her dress hem had been thrown over her back exposing her round black bottom, and the young Massuh was behind her rutting into her like a dog.

He turned away, shocked at what he saw. The hurt from the murder of his dog flooded over him compounded by the shock and terror of what was being done to his mother. Before he could gather his thinking he swung wide open the door and stepped inside.

The young massuh looked over at him, but never stopped his rutting. He just smiled dumbly and kept with the hard thrusts. Blue reached for an iron skillet lying atop of the wood fire stove and before his Mammy could yell no or the young massuh could pull out of her, Blue felt the impact of the skillet with the white man's head. He both felt and heard the skull give way with a sound not unlike that of having dropped a too ripe melon on a hard floor.

Blue's mother spun around quickly and fell to the floor to cradle the white man's head in her lap, just as Blue had cradled his beloved dog only hours prior. She looked away from the white man's broken head with blood trickling from both ears and opened her mouth a couple of times to speak, but couldn't find her voice. Blue hadn't been thinking when he whacked the young massuh in the head with the skillet, he'd just reacted, but now the realization at what he'd done set in.

The room filled with the stink of the white man's bowels as he released in death. He stepped outside the kitchen door and vomited, his mind spinning and feeling sick and weak. His mammy called to him then, finding her voice finally and hailed him back in.

"Why'd ya do such a thang boy? What in the heck got in yo' head?" she asked with a quaking voice and her eyes full of tears.

"He was ruttin' on you! He ain't had no right for that," Blue quietly spoke, another wave of nausea creeping over him again.

"Ruttin' me? Boy, that's my lot in 'dis life. Him an' his brothers been comin' to me for years. It ain't for me to say no neither, they is the Massuh's of this here place. Now you done it sure enough! They gonna hang you boy! You'd best clear out and fast. The only chance you got of livin' past this evening is to get gone and don't never look back. Ruttin' on me?" She shook her head and wiped some of the tears streaming down her face. "Where you think you come from Blue? Mos' likely you coulda' just kilt your own Pa. Now get before someone come along, go on an' get!" She lowered her eyes back to the white man in her lap and her shoulders began to jerk and shake as great sobs began to tear through her.

Blue very quickly grabbed a flour sack his Mammy had lying on a shelf with her dish towels and quickly shoved in a full dozen biscuits she'd recently made for the white folks' supper, a hunk of smoked pork and a small pearing knife on the kitchen counter. Without a look back, Blue began to run for the dark timbered land bordering the nearest field, with memories of his Mother's worried face fading behind him.

After leaving the plantation he'd made his way toward a quickly flowing creek that was said to run all the way to the Mississippi. He made his way along the bank in the gathering darkness and soon after the sun had set and the moon was cresting the eastern horizon, he heard the cry of hound from behind him. He expected that Ole Massuh and the two older sons would be riding hard after him on the very horses he'd cared for and with the same dogs that he'd trained himself. He knew that with the hounds being so used to his scent they weren't very likely to loose his trail. The only thing Blue could think to do was take to the water and let the current speed him along and gain some distance between him and the Massuhs.

He placed his clothes in the flour sack and quickly ate a biscuit, then tying the sack about his neck with the rope he'd used for a belt, he slipped into the water and grabbed onto an old cypress log and pulled it into the rushing waters with him. By holding onto that half rotten and sour smelling log, he rode through the night and most of the next day, until reaching a spot where the creek took a sweeping turn and exposed a small beach of dark sand. He pulled himself out of the water, exhausted and shaking with cold. He dressed again in the wet clothes and ate a piece of the pork, the biscuits having turned to mush.

From there he followed the creek bed to the Mississippi and followed it south, moving at night and skirting around towns and plantations. He'd been out of food for some time and was half-starved when he had heard the drummers in the distance and chose to come in and investigate. He had never before wanted to go to Africa, but if it meant the difference between living free and possibly being caught and hung, then to his mind, Africa didn't sound like such a bad place to try to get to.

SEVEN

All of the animals Debalo came across in his travels were so very different than what he was accustomed to seeing back in Africa. Here he had encountered quite a few small animals whose names Blue and Bwana were quickly teaching him. He had been successful at killing a handful of opossum and coon and was glad to share the meat with his companions who were terribly unskilled at feeding themselves. They had proven to be fair hands at fishing, but neither cared to dine on the raw meat and hadn't much experience at building, maintaining and using a fire to cook with.

Debalo rather enjoyed his role as tutor to the less experienced pair, but he equally enjoyed learning the names of the new animals and figuring out their habits. Deer were not that much of challenge to learn to hunt because they behaved very much like the hoofed animals he grew up around. However the bear absolutely fascinated him.

On their fourth night's travel they came upon the first bear. Debalo had been leading as was usual and as he stepped clear from a thick growth of young trees, he found that he had walked right up on the first real predator he had seen in the new land besides the gators. It was a fairly dark time of the night since the moon had not yet reached it's highest point, but Debalo's eyes had grown very accustomed to the night traveling and he could plainly see much detail of the animal.

When he had first spotted it, the bear was only twenty or so yards away and on all fours, no doubt searching for food. It had been only slightly higher than his waist and looked to weigh a couple of hundred pounds. It was maybe the same size of a young simba, but unlike the lion, it was as black as mbogo, the cape buffalo. The claws were every bit as impressive as a chui, the leopard that was so feared in the night, but they did not appear to retract. It had both the appearance of determined strength and timid demeanor. It took only a second or two before it became aware of Debalo and with a raspy grunt, raised itself upright on its hind feet like a man. Blue and Bwana exited the thick cover behind their leader and both men audibly inhaled at the sight of the standing bear.

At the sound, the bear swung about and in a clumsy lumbering gait, proceeded to put distance between himself and the three men. For some reason, Debalo's two charges were nothing less than relieved that the bear had chose to flee, but as for himself, he had been delighted to see the animal and would have enjoyed watching it awhile to see how it behaved. The rest of the night Bwana and Blue kept very close by and recounted tale after tale of bear attacks they had heard of. It amused Debalo quite a bit that although the two men had heard all about the animal's blood lust, they themselves had never been a witness to it. Nevertheless, the sight of the bear had put a scare in them for certain. Smiling to himself, he wondered how these two would react to an encounter with a charging rhino.

The next morning, they had taken refuge inside a fairly dense stand of maples growing tightly together a hundred or so yards inland from the river's edge. Much to Debalo's delight a mother bear led a pair of young fuzzy cubs along behind her, just past their daytime hideout on their way toward the river. Thankfully the other two men had fallen directly asleep after lying down so that they would not be scared by the nearness of the bear family as they shuffled by. The two cubs were quite comical, as all babies are, and they found much amusement in batting each other about the head with their tiny paws.

The mother was somewhat larger than the first bear he had seen and looked quite formidable. He knew only too well the unpredictable nature of a female of any species, which believes her cubs to be in danger. The wind was coming from the bears' direction to the three men in the thicket, so he expected that she would not become aware that she and her cubs had any company.

A small hint of their scent came to his nose and Debalo was surprised that it wasn't the same as the stench of most flesh eaters; theirs was a stale sweetness on the breeze. The predators he'd known in Africa smelled heavily of rotting flesh from the gore deposited on and about their heads at a kill and the scraps of decaying flesh caught beneath their claws. In fact his father had once slipped up on and killed a young male lion with a spear by following the smell of it's flatulence as it lay sleeping in the shade of a musassa tree. It had been sleeping off a very large meal of warthog and its breakfast had given it a most awful case of apparent indigestion.

Having caught a whiff of the rotting and digesting meat, Debalo's father investigated. He wore the short mane of the lion around his own head and neck in the manner of the Wakumba and Masai tribes for many years. The rest of the skin had been presented as a gift to an old man who had recently taken a young wife and terribly wanted to impregnate her. Sleeping on the skin of a lion was well known as a source of virility and the old man fiercely desired a son. He had had a couple of sons by two of his other wives, but both had died young. One of them died from the bite of a mamba after only seeing four seasons pass. The second child had been carried away in the darkness by a large male leopard, chui, after stepping outside the hut to relieve himself one night. He had only seen six seasons pass.

Bwana and Blue listened closely to the stories he shared with them and afterward they both would have many questions. Blue was always the most anxious to hear more and one morning as they lie in thick cover, through the ever eager interpretations of

Bwana, Debalo told them the story of his first hunt for simba, the lion.

It had taken place in his eleventh summer. The small herds of cattle belonging to the Bantu village that he'd grown up near had been taking heavy losses to a pride of lions, whom had taken up residency in the area. All of the elders felt that the lions were a dire threat to the villagers and ordered the bomas, a protective fence of thorn bushes, to be reinforced around the camp's perimeter. Also, they asked for security sake, that no member of the tribe be permitted to wander about during the night when the lions were at their most active.

The lions had not taken any offensive moves toward the villages, but everybody lived in fear because it is well known that lions consider men as no more than a potential meal. One morning it was discovered that a lioness had made her way through a breach on the boma and during the night had carried off an elderly woman.

A runner was sent immediately to the Masai camp. They were only too eager to arrive for the hunt and before the sun set, two dozen warriors had gathered in the Masarwa village where Debalo lived and prepared themselves for the hunt which would take place with the rising of the morning sun. They sang, danced and made quite a show of sharpening their spears, the blades of which were nearly as long as a young man's arm and kept razor sharp.

As Debalo told the story of the hunt, he remembered how impressed he was with the Masai.

They were very tall, taller than Debalo's Bantu father, and wore a long red blanket wrapped loosely about their shoulders. Their hair had been neatly braided in thin rows down the back of their necks and held in place by handfuls of red clay caked onto them. Most men wore a lion's mane, claws, or some other token of the trrible beasts they killed. They carried with them, besides their spears, tall buffalo hide shields, which they had painted brightly. The older men of the tribe had terribly horrific looking scars about their bodies from their experiences in combat with Simba.

Many of the village men would be permitted to hunt with the Masai as long as it was understood that a Masai warrior must be in on the killing of the lion. Hearing that his own father would be participating, Debalo begged to be allowed to go, but the next morning, many of the Masai warriors objected. He was too young, they said, and only a man could join them on the hunt. Until he was properly circumcised, he would only be permitted to act as a spotter for the hunters.

He readily had agreed to this and as the hunters made their way to the area where they would start, Debalo was directed to a huge baobob tree growing off from a rocky, brush clogged ravine where the lions were expected to be lying up during the day. He had made it to the tree without any difficulty and climbed high into the branches. Once there he was afforded a clear view of the hunt unfolding.

The warriors had split into three columns of men. The first two columns of men were placed on either bank of the ravine with one end touching in the middle so as to form the shape of a "V". The third column was placed across the other end of the ravine in a position that as the first two columns advanced, it would meet with the stationary third column forming a triangular fence of men which then would begin to shrink until any lion caught within the advancing columns would be forced to expose himself to at least one or more of the hunters.

Once the hunters had taken their positions a great shout was sent up and the columns began to merge. Debalo's part in all of this was to keep an eye out for any lions that would try to slip past the hunters early while the men were still spread out. He sat on his perch in the tree waiting, watching and stroking the length of his favorite hunting spear. It was a solid black shaft of ebony wood with a filed iron point his father had traded for and given to him.

As the columns reached one another an enormously loud roar split the morning air and Debalo watched as a huge black maned male rushed headlong into the line of hunters blocking the end of the ravine closest to him. The shouting and roaring was terrific as one after another spear was thrown from point blank range into the beast. At one point he saw the lion rise up on its hind legs and come down upon two warriors who tried to block the terrible claws and fangs with their buffalo hide shields.

After the lion had fallen from its wounds, their wildly celebrating companions helped the two men it had fallen upon from the ground. Even from the distance Debalo could tell that both men had been hurt badly. All of the hunters were on the scene now and a wild dance was beginning around the carcass of the dead lion. Debalo wished to join the hunters around the trophy, but was not sure if the warriors would welcome him or not so he stayed in the tree watching.

After some time, the dancing and shouting had begun to die down. Debalo decided it was time to exit the tree and return to the village. Looking down beneath his perch Debalo received the greatest shock of his young life. A young female lion was crouching beneath the tree, testing the wind and listening to the activities over in the ravine. She sat unmoving except for the tip of her tail, which was twitching back and forth from time to time.

He had climbed to a height of about fifteen feet when he had entered the tree and knew that he couldn't miss his target directly beneath him. At that angle, he would not be able to throw very hard without first rising up from his sitting position. He knew that any movement on his part to rise would only alert the lion and send her off. Moving slowly, he positioned the spear into place and with all of his strength he sent the spear downward.

It struck the memsimba near the back of the rib cage and broke her spine. As soon as the spear embedded itself in her back, she leapt forward on her front quarters and began to turn and spin and bite at the spear's shaft. After a couple of minutes, the lioness quieted and began to pull herself off into the long grass. A handful of warriors were racing toward Debalo's tree after hearing the commotion and he directed them to where the big cat had turned to make her stand upon hearing the warriors approach.

From his seat in the tree, he watched as one after another, spears were hurtled into the body of the lioness. Once it was over, the men began shouting and dancing all over again. After coming down from the tree, Debalo had raced over to where the lioness lie and was grabbed up by the mob of hunters and jostled around roughly during the impromptu celebration. His own father dipped two fingers into the blood of the dead lioness and blazed a red streak across Debalo's forehead, then announced that on the next full moon he was to be circumcised. He now was to be a man of his village for he had done a man's deed that day.

Blue asked him about the circumcision, but Debalo didn't care to tell that story.

EIGHT

It was on the sixth night of travel along the river course when they began to hear the noise of a city in the distance. From this point on, the banks of the river showed signs of frequent passage and eventually had been beaten down into a regular trail. Debalo cautioned his companions against approaching a town or village at night and they secreted themselves well off the beaten path along the river and tried to get some sleep. At dawn, Debalo decided, they would creep about and investigate the small settlement as much as they could to be sure this place was indeed Barataria.

He had selected a place to hide his companions where he felt sure they would be safe from the eyes of any persons that might wander about. He chose a large cypress tree from which he could take a good look around and decide on his next actions. While perched in the top of the ancient tree Debalo saw movement near where he had secreted away Blue and Bwana. He watched hopelessly as the two were marched out of the cover in front of a very large dark skinned man carrying a long barreled pistol. They were led stumbling along on a smooth worn path that led toward a long row of cloth-covered tents.

The fronts of the structures appeared to be made from wood and supported wooden doors, but the two other sides visible to Debalo were made of a dirty brown cloth held in place by a series of ropes, stretched taught and staked in place. The roof was made of the same material and was pitched upward, no doubt by a pair of poles on the inside, to shed the rain. There were several of these in a row along a muddy well used roadway settled about fifty or so yards from a tributary of the river, which flowed less than two hundred yards away.

Farther down the roadway from the tent buildings stood a crudely built barn of unpainted wood and a small corral that held a small herd of oddly colored ponies. On the tributary itself, to the direct front of the tent buildings was a long and spacious dock of roughly hewn planks, its surface area cluttered with wooden crates, bales of materials, wooden casks and kegs. Men were crowding around the dock and in the street as they unlimbered from the night's rest and readied themselves to their daily tasks.

Debalo's two companions were directed to the dock where many of the men, both white and black, began to gather around them. There was a long exchange of words between them and the men present. They were too far away for Debalo to catch any of what was said, but he did see the looks of terror leave the faces of his friends and heard his name when it was shouted out by Blue to let him know it was safe to come in.

Debalo came into the clearing, which housed the assortment of men and structure, cautiously. Blue and Bwana were smiling toward him as he advanced slowly and as he approached the small crowd of men, Bwana called to him in his native tongue.

"Debalo, it is all right. This is not the place, Barataria, but these men work for the man Lafitte. They tell me Barataria is down river and can be reached only by boat."

Bwana was about to say more when a small, dark man interrupted. "I am called Moses." He greeted Debalo in a broken dialect of Fanagalo and Kiswahili. "I am in the employ of the brothers Lafitte. If you are in possession of the same letter as your friends, we can get you to the three Islands of Barataria."

"I have the letter," Debalo answered him.

"That is all fine then. You will stay here with us until the boat comes in. Yes?" Moses asked Debalo.

"Yes I will stay," Debalo answered. "What shall I do, now that I am here?"

"I will put you to work," Moses told him simply.

The assembly of curious workers broke up and returned to their tasks as Moses led the three men toward the stables. Once there he directed their chores for the day.

"You'll find that your life here will be much different than that which you had known as a slave. If you wish to eat, you work. If you do not wish to work, you do not eat. It is very simple. Also, no one is permitted to sleep inside that does not work. Nobody is a slave here and your labors are rewarded."

As the man talked to them and explained things, Bwana kept up a running translation for Blue, who could not understand the African dialect.

"Hold it, boy!" Moses said to Bwana irritably. Then he turned to Blue and asked him in English. "Boy, you don't understand what I've been saying?"

Blue shook his wooly head. "Naw suh. I couldn't understand, so Bwana was telling me everything."

"Yeah, well. You head back over there to where that white boy and that nigga' is catchin' up them hosses. They'll tell you what to do," Moses directed Blue, who turned away and started off as directed.

"Now, you two. Any questions?" Moses asked.

"I have a good many questions." Debalo answered honestly while Bwana nodded his head in agreement.

"Let's have them then. I'll 'splain things as best as I can." Moses stepped over to an empty crate that was sitting outside the barn's door. Taking a seat, he looked up to the two former slaves and waited for them to begin.

Debalo thought for a moment before he asked, "Why do you help us if you are aware that we are running away?"

Moses chuckled a bit, before responding. "I help you because of that letter you and your friends carry. It says that you are not on the run, but that you are property of the brothers Lafitte of Barataria."

"I am no man's property any longer," Debalo let burst in quick rising anger.

"Calm yourself. I know that, but in order for you to remain with us, we must be able to show ownership. Otherwise, those hunting the woods and waters for runaways will take you. You are no longer runaways. For practical reasons you belong to the brothers Lafitte."

Debalo stood as patiently as he could and listened.

"Now, to really answer your question, it is because we need men to load and unload cargo on the ships. Labor is expensive, therefore Jean began recruiting runaways as a work force, in return for passage aboard ship. Once you are taken aboard for the trip to Haiti or Africa, you will be expected to work as a member of the ship's crew. "You see, by helping you, you are expected to repay us by helping us in return. You see, it is a good thing for everyone. Do you both understand now?"

Both of them nodded solemnly and Debalo posed another question.

"You keep mentioning brothers. I was told there was one man to whom I should make myself known. That man is named Jean Lafitte."

"Yes, Jean is the man to whom you will be taken. He and his brother are famous seamen. They are much wanted for all manner of piracy upon the sea, but there has been no force able to interrupt their business. They move merchandise about the Gulf and on toward Haiti and can outrun any vessel on the water. Do not worry though, they are smugglers, but you will be safe enough aboard their ships if you are granted passage."

"You mention piracy. What manner of man is this Laffite?" Debalo queried further with growing apprehension for he knew well many stories of piracy off the coast of Africa.

"Simply that. A pirate, but a gentleman. You will see, he is a good man to work for. It is an easy life. At least we are free, or as free as a black man can be in this country."

"If he is a pirate, how do I know I can trust him?" Debalo wanted to know.

"You don't," Moses answered. "You can trust him or not. He offers help if you want it. I trust him and have worked for him, but then, you don't know me either, so why trust me?" He finished with a laugh.

NINE

Debalo spent a week in the camp near the river and was pleased to leave it when the opportunity arose. Moses had been helpful at first, but once he saw that Debalo knew the routine of the camp, Moses chose to remain by himself as did most of the other men in the camp. A few chose to pair up and go about their day together, but very seldom was there any gatherings of more than two or three at a time.

Bwana had become Debalo's constant companion and they went about their time in camp together. There was little to do in the way of real work and the pair completed their assigned tasks quickly and spent the rest of their time getting to know each other better. Bwana always asked to hear more and more stories of Africa and Debalo didn't mind sharing them. Debalo also had become weary of the language barrier amongst himself and the rest of the people he encountered and asked Bwana if he would teach him some words of the local language, English.

By listening and watching others during his time on the plantation, he had learned a few words, but was eager to learn more. Bwana proved to be a good and patient teacher and by the weeks end Debalo was capable of conversing in short and direct sentences. Learning the new words was proving to be much easier than Debalo had feared.

On the final morning in the river camp, Debalo and Bwana were sitting in the shade of the barn when Blue came running over to join them. They had not seen much of Blue while in the camp. He had attached himself to a mulatto from his home state and hadn't much to do with his former traveling partners.

"Good morning friend," Debalo greeted him when he was within earshot.

Blue drew up wide-eyed in surprise. "Did you just say good morning to me?"

Debalo smiled and nodded, pleased with the young man's reaction.

Bwana spoke up. "We ain't had nuthin' else to do around here, so he asked me to teach him some words. What you doing this mawnin' Blue?"

"I's comin' to tell ya'll that they's a boat comin' in off the river right now. Moses said to get you two 'cause that's the boat goin' take us on the rest of the way."

"Boat? Go Barataria?" Debalo asked in his new language.

"Yes," Blue confirmed, "we are goin' on the boat."

"Well, I don't know about you two, but I'm ready to get out of here," Bwana told Blue and then repeated in fanagalo so that Debalo understand.

The three had brought nothing with them except what they had on their persons, so they had no need to waste any time packing, but rather walked directly to the dock. They joined a small group of others, both Negro and white alike, watching a heavily loaded craft laboring against the current as it made its way to the landing. It was thirty or so feet long and carried many kegs and crates and a crew of six men working three pair of oars.

It took almost no time for the boat's cargo to be unloaded upon the dock and begin its way back down the backwater bayou to the churning river carrying Debalo and his two traveling companions as well as a couple of other black men and one very dirty white man. Debalo did not know if the other three seeking passage aboard the boat were traveling under similar circumstances as himself, but he suspected so. Nearing the main river, Debalo could see the tall mast of a ship traveling upriver. Its pair of triangular sails was full and the ship appeared to be making fair time as it sailed against the oncoming current.

Debalo was very apprehensive about entering the river during daylight hours due to the amount of traffic it received, but he felt he had no choice and hoped these men of the boat knew what they were doing. The ride upon the river took the better part of the afternoon. As the channel widened, it began to look like more of a bay than a rolling river, its deep blue waters extending out for miles. At the far end of the bay, the three islands of Barataria came into sight. The wind was blowing in from downriver and carried the smell of the salt-water. The land had changed and there were fewer hardwood trees visible on the banks and more palms amongst brushy reedy looking land, which lay about them in the distance. Debalo dipped his hand over the side of the boat and took a sip of the dark water and found that despite the river's flow, the water had not remained fresh, but tasted of salt.

The middle island of the three had a natural harbor, which had been developed to full advantage and a large dock had been constructed with roughly hewn, highly weathered planks. There were a half dozen or so buildings scattered along the wharf, but they did not look like residences to Debalo, but rather storage huts. Palm trees towered tall about the island and pelicans strutted about and flapped their wings on the long stretches of sandy beach. In the distance, the roof of an enormous brick house could be seen through the scattering of live oak and palm trees.

They were met on the dock by a pair of hard looking men who greeted them silently, but were quick to offer a hand as they stepped from the boat onto the dock. Debalo greeted each in his newly learned English and received a nod from each in turn.

One of the men, a tall broad-shouldered and middle-aged man took special interest in the knife Debalo wore about his waist.

"Where'd you get that knife at boy?" the man asked.

Debalo was unsure of the words, but the man had pointed to his knife, so Debalo put his hand over it and spoke in English. "Mine."

"I can see it's yours, boy. You wearin' it, aint you? It'll keep on bein' yours too until someone takes it from you, but I've already got one," he told him. The man turned slightly and patted the sheath on his side which bore a knife very similar to the one Debalo wore.

Debalo understood most of what the man was telling him and nodded his head smiling.

"My brother, Rezin Bowie, had a few of these made up a while back in Arkansas. He gave me mine. That knife-maker liked them so much, he's been selling copies of them ever since."

Debalo became lost with all the words and Bwana quickly interpreted for him after which Debalo nodded more then told him, "Very good knife. I am hunter. Very good knife."

"A hunter eh?" the broad man asked. Then as the man talked, Bwana interpreted for Debalo. "Me and Rezin had been slaughtering wild cattle to sell the meat and hides to folks on the river. Powder and shot's too expensive to waste on a cow so we'd rope them then get 'em to chase us around a tree until the rope got short. Once they had themselves tied short to the tree, we'd step in and cut they throat."

The other man on the dock spoke up then, "Tell them honest now Jim, there's more'n cows died by that blade. I seen two men myself sawed nearly in two from it."

Bwana kept translating.

"It's true," Jim told them. "But I never cut a man that didn't need cuttin'," he said with a wink.

After hearing Bwana's translation, Debalo returned the man's wink and patting the handle of the big knife replied, "Me too."

Once the craft was moored in place, Debalo and the others followed the man called Jim up a wide and well worn path leading inland toward a fairly sprawling city built inland from the large, plantation style home, with many large buildings not visible from the approach upriver.

At least one of the buildings, Debalo could tell, was a stable and barn. An open- fronted blacksmith's shop was standing nearby behind which he could see a narrow built chimbuzi, easily identified by the little crescent moon cut into its sides, like the ones he'd used on the plantation. Houses were placed here and there about the shell streets. Smoke was rising from the stacks of many of the houses, many of which were painted white and had little flower gardens in front. The air was filled with the scent of the smoke, but also carried a hint of chamomile along with the salt-tinged air blowing in off of the bay.

The Island was a hive of activity and Debalo felt terribly exposed and wanted to slip off into the woods, but he stayed with the little group as they walked through the city toward the big brick house. He looked over at Blue and Bwana, both of whom wore smiles and looked to be completely at ease.

As they passed through the streets, Debalo took great interest in the people working on the island. Black and white worked side by side. None of them wore clothing as raggedy as those he was wearing. They looked well fed and content. To a man they appeared to be joyful, not like those at the camp on the bayou. Very often, as he would catch the eye of a worker, he would be greeted with a curt nod and sometimes even a smile. Often men would stop and call out to Jim, the man leading them, with a wave. By the time they had reached the heavy iron, gate in front of the great house, Debalo was beginning to grow more at ease with the environment and found that he even liked the place.

As they approached the gate, a tall straight-backed man of obvious black and white origins came forward to meet them. He was dressed in the finest looking set of clothes, Debalo had ever seen. The coat was very shiny and red while the shirt and pantaloons were very white. The tall broad shouldered man that had led them to the gate from the dock called out to him as they neared.

"Pierre, I've got some more nigga's from Marie's bunch. I'm turnin' them over to you until Jean gets back. I'm going out to catch the next sloop heading to New Orleans. I'll be at the blacksmith shop in the quarters if anybody needs me."

"Wi monsieur Bowie, I will tell him."

With a nod toward Debalo and a quick wave to the group, the man Jim left them there and returned back toward the landing.

"I greet you and bid you welcome." Pierre said to the men and opened the gate for them to enter into the yard, which was landscaped beautifully. He led them to a very wide porch, which extended across the front of the house. "I am Pierre De' Phillipe Arraquette. I welcome you to Barateria. You are now standing on Grande Terre, to the east of us lies Grande Isle, and to our west lies Cheniere Caminada. You are at the house of the Coarsair, Jean Lafitte. I must now explain a few things to you.

"Controlling these islands, we control the river trade to the Gulf of Mexico. You see our ships are commissioned to patrol these waters and upon the seas for Spanish vessels. We capture them, keep whatever we wish and sink the rest. It is very profitable and everyone shares in the wealth, but it must be earned. We have need of laborers, both in the warehouse and upon the ships going to sea. You are promised employment, yes?"

Each man nodded.

"Good. Any man who does not wish to work will not be welcome to remain. While you are here there will be no fighting or stealing. Any person found doing so will be severely dealt with. There are women on this island. Any man caught molesting any man's wife will be put to death. Is that understood?"

Each man nodded their understanding.

"Which of you men wish to go aboard a ship to serve that ship's captain?" he asked them.

Debalo did not understand the question, but Bwana answered for him.

"Myself and this man Debalo," Bwana told Pierre. The others remained silent.

"Good," Pierre told them. "You two step over to the side and I'll be with you in a moment."

Debalo asked what was happening and Bwana explained for him. They both looked to Blue to speak up, but he had decided to stay on the island. So, they stood together and waited as the finely dressed Pierre directed the others toward one of the warehouses with their instructions.

Afterward, Pierre led the two over toward a long row of rectangular houses facing the beach. Once there, a small black woman was ordered to provide them with bunks, food, and clothing. They were told to stay there until the next outgoing ship arrived. They could move about the beach and the row-houses, but were ordered to stay away from the docks and the warehouses.

Farther along the beach a battery of cannons had been placed facing out toward the open water. An assortment of several men, were lounging in the shade of the palms nearby it and Debalo wondered about its purpose. He had seen the big guns aboard the ship that brought him to the new land and had even seen them fired once. Their sound was like that of a lightning strike and they belched flame and smoke terribly. He had been around guns more than once in his life and knew what they were capable of, but these giant guns must have unimaginable power.

Life on the island was easy. Debalo and Bwana stayed at the house on the beach or nearby. The old woman cooked regularly and they ate well. There were others staying at the house as well and everyone got along pleasantly. Debalo continued taking English lessons from Bwana and was able to keep up during most of the evening's conversations.

There was a lot of traffic on the bay where the Mississippi River emptied into the azure Gulf of Mexico. It was a scene of constant incoming and outgoing schooners, sloops, corsairs, and brigantines homebound with or seaward for the merchandise they sought. In the silver dawn and the purple twilight, Debalo could always see silhouettes of full masts squared or triangular against the tropical horizon.

On the fourth day, a triple-masted schooner came alongside of the island and anchored about fifty yards off shore. Debalo and Bwana were sent for and it was upon this ship they were to be taken aboard as apprentice sailors. Both men were full of the spirit of adventure and were eager to get aboard. The time on the island was grand but for Debalo, he hoped that soon he'd again be walking amongst the tall grasses of home.

TEN

Shortly after Debalo and Bwana had been taken aboard the ship, they were set to work alongside of the experienced sailors. They were directed to the forward deck of the vessel, clear from the sailing men as the lines were thrown off and the anchor weighed. Soon the ship was under way working its way into the emerald waters of the open bay as the islands of Barataria began to sink into the distance.

The bustling activity began to slow down once the ship was sailing and one of the sailors on the ship called to him. "I'm told to teach you two about this boat. You boys understand that?" he asked with undisguised annoyance.

Debalo and Bwana both nodded slowly. Debalo had indeed understood the man's meaning, but immediately he felt a dislike for the man. His body was unwashed and his manner was offensive. He had darkly tanned, leathery skin, but beneath the tan, he was clearly a white man. His face was unshaved and his long sun-dyed hair was pulled into a tail behind him, held in place by a dirty strip of cloth. The man was terribly thin and had features that reminded Debalo of an old, sick lion. When he spoke, there was noticeable contempt in his voice and his eyes were cold. Even without the smile, Debalo could see clearly that there were no teeth present. Of all the men he could see working about them, there were none that appeared as unkempt as this man.

"This boat you're riding is a schooner," the dirty man began. "She normally carries forty men, four of which are officers, but it takes only five or six sailors to handle her. Because there's always a threat of attack by the gawdamned Spanish, Jean likes us outfitted heavy. That way if we lose a man, there'll always be one to take his place. I'll be learning you my post and once you've got it down, you'll go learn another. Every man to crew this ship knows every job on board her. You got that?"

Again they both nodded and although there were many words Debalo didn't understand, he recognized enough for now and hoped to get the rest from Bwana later.

As he talked, the dirty sailor walked over toward the railing of the deck and leaned against it. They followed silently as they listened to all he said.

"I doubt either of you boys has ever sailed before so there's a lot for you to learn. This ship sails by three masts with sails. In the front is the foresail, the middle is the mainsail, and in the back is the mizzen-sail. The front of the ship is its stem and the back is its stern. We are standing now on the foredeck. The deck in the rear where you see the Captain and his officers, that is the poop deck, below the poop deck there you'll find the Captain's quarters and the galley. Below the foredeck here are the general officers' quarters. You two will find a spot to sleep anywhere you can. Go below, stay on deck, it doesn't matter, so long as you're not in the way of whoever's on duty."

"Either of you boys got a question?" he asked them irritably.

"I do," Bwana spoke first. "I was wonderin' what we goin' to do?"

"You gonna do what you get told to do," the man snapped and turned to Debalo, "What about you boy? You got any questions?"

Debalo nodded and asked, "What your name?"

"My name is Daniel. What difference does it make?"

Debalo didn't understand the question and answered, "My name Debalo," he told the man while pointing to himself.

"I don't give a rat shit who you are boy. You do as I say and we'll get along fine, but if you don't, I'll kick your ass into the Gulf boy. Do you understand me?"

Debalo looked to Bwana with a questioning look and Bwana very quickly related all that the man had just said. Bwana looked back to the man Daniel and nodded. Then in Fanagalo added, "Maybe, Daniel."

The man talked for a very long time before actually giving them a task to perform. He led them down a narrow set of steps into the belly of the ship, which was compartmentalized into three rooms by removable walls with doorways. The forward of the three rooms was for the ship's cargo. The middle was set for the crew's housing although in the tropical climate, most of the crew chose to remain on deck. The rear of the ship was the storage room for the galley and the ship's armament. The smell below deck was of a terrible mixture of mold, feces, and ammonia that caused their eyes to water and burn.

The lower deck of this ship was not nearly as big as the one Debalo had been forced to ride in when he was brought to this new land by the slavers. This one was narrow and there was little room to move about. In the sides of the ship every twenty feet or so, windows were propped open that were the sole source of light in the dark belly of the ship. Beneath each window was a small cannon mounted on a wooden carriage, which could be rolled up to the port to be fired. Below each of the windows and forward of the gun carriages was a pile of cannon balls, in a pyramid mound of four, three, and one.

The forward room was empty of cargo, but the dozens of rows of metal chains and shackles left no doubt in the minds of either men what cargo the vessel was sailing toward. The floor of the room was filthy with the remnants of human waste and some was even caked up onto the walls. A wide spade was leaning against the wall and evidence showed that it had been used to shovel out the waste after the previous cargo had been delivered.

"Over here. Time to get you two working," Daniel spat out while pointing toward a stack of buckets and a row of mops.

"Each of you take up a mop and bucket. There's a keg of ammonia here and I want you to break open this keg and mop this room clean with this ammonia. Use a piece of rope to lower one of the buckets for water to rinse your mops with and get this place cleaned up. That smell gets too much for you, hang your head out of the window for a while. When you finish up, come back up onto the foredeck. You should be finished by the time the cooks are ready to serve us a meal. I promised him afterwards he could have one or both of you to clean up the crockery." Then he turned and headed back towards the steps leading back up onto the deck, leaving Debalo and Bwana to their task.

As they worked Bwana retold everything he could remember of what Daniel had told him. They agreed that neither of them cared for the man and neither cared much for the job they were doing. "Debalo, you don't think we done made us a mistake huh?"

"No. The last time I was on a ship, I was wearing the chains and lying in the filth. Now, I am again on a ship, but things are different this time, are they not?"

"Yes," Bwana agreed.

"If this is what we must do to earn our voyage home, then so it will be," Debalo resolved and his companion agreed again.

As they began to work, Debalo remembered his time aboard the ship that had carried him as a slave. It seemed so long ago now. So much had happened since he'd been taken on board that vessel. It was a bigger ship than this one and the men whom commanded the captives had chained them together at the right ankles, three to a chain. Once the chains were in place, they were made to lie down in rows. Every square foot of the ship's floor was covered with a body. He had not counted the number of captives who didn't survive the trip but was quite aware of the fact that there was much more space available in the floor of the ship when the trip was over. He himself had assisted in the disposal of dead bodies by tossing them unceremoniously through the window port.

For the first several days of the trip, it seemed that everyone was sick. He himself was spared the infirmity, but he spent days lying in the vomit of the others. The sound of crying, moaning, cursing, and retching made sleep nearly impossible, but eventually sleep would come. When it did, however, it was not restful, but filled with dreams of terror and blood. When the cries, shouts, and groans became too loud, the door would be swung open with a shockingly loud thud as members of the ship's crew would quiet the outcries with clubs and whips.

He shuddered at the memory of it and felt a cold, hollow feeling creeping into his stomach. Looking over at Bwana, he saw that the man had ceased to work and was looking very sickly as he stood leaning on the handle of his mop.

"You had better get some air Bwana. Daniel said to hang your head out of the window," Debalo told his partner. He wondered if Bwana was going to become violently ill as the others had before.

Bwana lurched forward a few steps then sprinted to the nearest opening just in time to release his stomach contents into the passing water below. Debalo came to his friend's side and patted him on the back.

"This will pass, my friend. I've seen this sickness before. I think you will survive," he told him with a comforting smile.

"I may. But, I can't be certain," he turned away suddenly as another wave of nausea came over him.

ELEVEN

When the cleaning job had been completed, Debalo and Bwana went above to the foredeck and presented themselves to Daniel.

"Boy," he spoke to Bwana with an amused look. "You look like you're a little sick. Don't sailing agree with you?"

"I feel like I been kicked in ma belly," Bwana answered him.

"Well, you two come with me. You're sailing on this ship, you need to meet the captain and his officers and learn something of what he expects of you while aboard his ship. Rations will be available soon, so let's get going." He brushed past them in his gruff way and walked quickly toward the stern where three men were in a heated discussion, huddled over a large sheet of paper.

"Daniel here, Sir. I brought over the new niggers Jean hired for you."

The three men stopped talking and gave each of the two men a good looking over. The middle of the three, also the shortest and fattest of the trio, spoke up with a deep throaty voice.

"You're excused, Daniel."

"Aye, Sir," Daniel answered and turning away he offered the pair one more hateful look.

"Don't mind Daniel, you two. He's really quite harmless once you've gotten used to him. Now you two have not sailed before, is that correct?"

Bwana spoke first, "No sir, I never."

Debalo began to reply, but held his tongue, not sure how to answer. He subconsciously closed his left hand into a fist, hiding the scar he felt might show that indeed he had sailed. That experience was not what the captain had meant, he was sure, but still this language was new to him.

"You'll learn quick enough, I'm sure. You both look healthy. Well, the cook will fix that," he laughed at his little joke and turned back to his two officers who returned his grin.

"Do you both understand English?" the captain asked directly.

Bwana nodded and Debalo said, "I know English some. I learn it from Bwana." Debalo pointed to his friend.

"Well," the captain told him, "What you don't understand, stop and ask your friend here to explain." Debalo gave him a slight smile and a nod.

"This ship is the schooner Renard Rouge and I am her captain. Captain Henry Hebert. I have sailed this vessel throughout every inch of the Carribean and the

Gulf of Mexico. We sail beneath the flag of the United States, but we have been granted letters of marque allowing us to act on behalf of the French government and confiscate any ship and its cargo flying the flag of Spain. They are at war and we are to act as privateers on their behalf.

"Any value of the cargo will be divided proportional amongst the crew. Any ships seized are returned to Barataria and outfitted for our own service. To remain a part of my crew you must swear to conduct yourselves in an appropriate manner.

"You will be expected to obey orders without question. You will be expected to do a fair share of the work on board the ship. And now," the captain's eyes hardened to glass as he spoke. "Any man amongst my crew found stealing will be tied to the main mast and lashed. Any man instigating or partaking in any fighting on this ship will get the same punishment. Any man guilty of murdering a fellow Baratarian will be hanged. On the same token, however, any man injured in active service will be compensated in gold, the amount to be determined by the extent of his injury.

"Do either of you object?"

Debalo and Bwana both stood silent.

"Good, then swear obedience," the captain commanded.

"I swear," Bwana spoke first, then Debalo followed his lead and repeated the words Bwana had said.

The captain looked pleased and told them both, "Now you are Sailors aboard the Renard Rouge. Go forward until mess call, then Daniel will instruct you further. I have work to do, charting a course to Campeche, and unless you want to sail aground during the night, I had best get back to it. Welcome aboard and you are dismissed." At that the captain returned to the other two men's attentions and huddled again over the papers.

After they had eaten, the sailors all gathered on the foredeck enjoying the cool breeze coming off of the Gulf. To the right of the ship, Debalo could see the green line of land slipping past them and to the left was nothing but an endless sea of rolling waves all the way to the horizon. There had been plenty of talk during the meal and Debalo was relieved to find the others to be a joyous bunch, not like the dirty man Daniel. There were quite a few barbs, good-naturedly hurled toward Bwana and his ailment.

"Seasickness, that's about as sick as a man can get without dying," a few of the older sailors repeated with a chuckle.

"I'm sho' gonna try not to die, but I ain't makin' no promises," Bwana groaned.

"The captain, he good man?" Debalo asked of another black sailor sitting on a coil of rope nearby.

"Aye, Cap'n Hebert's a good man and fair. He knows the waters and where to find Spanish shipping," he answered to a chorus of consenting, "Ayes".

"Is it far to Haiti?" Debalo queried the man.

"A ways I expect. It's through the Tortugas on the other side of La Florida."

"When, until we get to Haiti?" Debalo wanted to know.

A few men chuckled and some even smiled at Debalo's question, although he himself did not know what was so amusing about it. Cursing silently to himself about his difficulty understanding the new language.

"Boy," the black sailor began and Debalo interrupted him.

"I am Debalo," he told him with offense.

"Aye, I'll remember. Debalo. This ship ain't headin' fer Haiti. We sail to Campeche."

"What is Camp-e-che?" Debalo asked the question with alarm. Bwana raised his head with a gloomy look to hear the man's answer.

"It's an island, where Lafitte set us up another island base. It's Texas territory. Some's callin' it Galveston, but I've always known it to be Campeche." It's a safe harbor and from there we'll most likely run across the gulf into the shipping lanes to gather some swag for this empty hull we're ridin'."

Debalo didn't know what to say and he looked to Bwana, whose head had been lowered again. He was so sick that at the moment he couldn't even care. The other sailors lay about the deck, smoking and relaxing as they awaited orders from their captain.

"I go to Haiti!" Debalo said irritably, but the man only looked amused.

"I guess you could swim it, but it's a long way. You'd best accept that you're sailing to Campeche. Captain ain't about to turn the ship around 'cause you want to go somewhere else. Hell boy, don't look so bothered. We sailed to Haiti many times and like as not we'll sail there again.

"If it's Haiti you want, then Haiti you'll have to wait for," the black sailor told him casually. "Here comes Daniel. You two new boys are gonna go to work. Probably cleaning the galley for the cook."

Daniel ascended the steps to the foredeck with a hateful glare in his eyes, "I thought I'd find you niggers loafing already. You've had your rations. Now get your black ass's to the galley."

Debalo returned the hateful look as he and Bwana regained their feet and started off toward the galley.

"It's a wonder somebody doesn't kill that filthy goat," Debalo overheard the black sailor commenting about Daniel as he reached the stairs.

"I'm surprised that hasn't already been done," Debalo thought to himself.

"Get going," the dirty little man directed with a smirk and drew back and gave Debalo a shove toward the steps. He staggered a step or two but didn't fall. He spun quickly to face the filthy Daniel and drew himself upright and rigid.

All of the sailors stopped what they were doing and watched closely, most eager to watch a good fight.

Daniel glared at the black man and repeated his order. "Get your ass to the galley, nigger!"

Debalo raised his hand slowly and extended it palm up. "I no want fight. You no touch," he told him while pointing his finger toward himself.

"You ain't in no position to be tellin' me nothin'. I've orders to get you to the galley, now move your ass or pull that cutlass," Daniel roared.

Debalo slowly lowered his right hand to rest on the handle of the big knife and watched as Daniel's eyes grew narrow and his lips pursed tightly. The captain's orders fresh in his mind, however, Debalo turned back towards the steps and began following Bwana, who hadn't even bothered to turn around at the exchange. "Strange," Debalo thought to himself. "I thought he would have stood beside me." He quickened his pace to catch up with Bwana and to put some distance between himself and Daniel.

"Captain's orders, you two learn every job on the ship. Now, you learn to clean the crockery," Daniel told them at the doorway to the galley. Before going through the doorway, Debalo glanced upward to where the Captain was standing. He had watched the exchange without comment and was now looking at Debalo. He nodded and the Captain returned the nod as Debalo entered the room.

A soft wind was rising and popping the sails of the Renard Rouge as it sailed steadily westward toward Campeche with its crew of privateers and a very worried Debalo.

Shortly after Debalo and Bwana had been taken aboard the ship, they were set to work alongside of the experienced sailors. They were directed to the forward deck of the vessel, clear from the sailing men as the lines were thrown off and the anchor weighed. Soon the ship was under way working its way into the emerald waters of the open bay as the islands of Barataria began to sink into the distance.

TWELVE

Debalo walked aft toward the stern of the ship to stand beside Bwana, whom having overcome his seasickness was now standing tall in the gulf breeze, broad shouldered and content. Debalo didn't speak as he stood beside the man, simply watching the wake of the ship passing as it spread out behind them into the vast loneliness of the emerald gulf. They had been traveling nearly a week and Bwana was quickly growing tired of his life aboard the Renard Rouge. There was something terribly unsettling to him about being confined to the small spaces of the ship. He had gotten along well with the crew and found the work to be not difficult. Still, however, he longed for home stronger than ever.

Bwana had come to love sailing and he described it to Debalo as freedom. "Dis is what I always wanted. A man ain't free that can't go where he wants to go. Bein' in dis boat is the free-ist, you can get."

He didn't share Bwana's opinion of freedom. For Debalo, the boat was a cage without bars. You weren't free on the ship, in his mind. He felt trapped. After the first day, Debalo watched the coastline fade away to a thin dark line then disappear behind the horizon. The uneasiness he had felt before grew. Throughout the daytime, the coastline would reappear, then slip past and behind them until it no longer was in sight. Nighttime was a deep black hole that swallowed them up. Debalo could not find rest in it. He would lie for hours feeling the wind rushing by and the lifting and falling of the ship as it passed over the swelling water. He did sleep, but it was not a restful sleep. Debalo still dreamt of the Ngwenya and the big overseer he had killed. For him, the first light of day was always welcome.

"Bwana?" Debalo spoke after a short while and watched the water with his traveling partner.

"Yes?"

"I hear it said that tomorrow we will reach Campeche," Debalo said. "Daniel says we are not to leave the ship once it is docked."

"Dat's what he told me too, but dat's alright. I don't want to get off no how," Bwana assured him.

"I do," Debalo told him glumly.

"Is Daniel giving you hard time again?"

Debalo switched back to the fanagalo of his home, "It's that too, but I want to feel my feet upon the ground again. I think he doesn't want me to leave, and I will not leave," Debalo assured him. "I hope at least, that Daniel goes ashore if I am to remain here. I'm not aware of what it is that he hates me for, but even as I work I can sometimes feel his eyes on my back. He does nothing to disguise his hate for me."

"You haven't hid your feelings either," Bwana flashed a wide grin at him, "You'll see, it'll get better soon. I don't want to see you throw his sorry ass overboard and get hung for it."

"I will not cause the man harm if I am given a way not to," Debalo tried a smile, but it was weak.

The evening air was cool and the ship was quiet except for the sound of the waves splashing against the prow and the wind singing in the sails. The evening crockery had been cleaned and stowed the way that they had been taught and there was nothing more for them to do until morning. Sailors about the ship were lazing about in the dying light of the evening, some smoking, some talking quietly together, and one or two sat about carving little animals and such from pieces of wood or bone.

Debalo continued to stand with his hands on the railing, looking out onto the water thoughtfully, then said, "Look behind us Bwana; I feel his eyes."

Bwana looked over his shoulder and as Debalo had predicted; Daniel stood at the top of the steps leading up onto the ship's poop deck, directly behind them. On his face was a hateful stare.

"What are you two niggers doing up here? You're supposed to be in the galley!"

"We've finished the work and the cook tol' us to git," Bwana answered.

"I ain't told you that you were through yet!" he spat towards them. "Captain's orders that I see after you two. You report to me when you're done."

Slowly Debalo turned to face the grimy little man. "We finished in galley, Daniel," he said with a flat even tone.

Daniel stepped closer to the pair with a balled fist. "You mockin' me?"

"Naw suh!" Bwana answered, "He ain't mockin' ya a'tall. He's just sayin' we're done; that's all."

Debalo leaned back, casually against the railing of the deck with his hands resting at his sides and staring back at Daniel with undisguised enmity.

"Look here, boy!" Daniel began in a low, hissing voice, "you think you somethin' carryin' that cutlass. Without that, you ain't nothin' but a dumb nigger that belongs back in chains. Why them Lafitte brothers would hire runaways is beyond me. If it was up to me, you'd be back at the sales barn in New Orleans." Then looking down to the big bone handled knife at Debalo's side, "Take care of that blade, boy. You get killed, I might want it for myself." A wicked laugh erupted from his dirty toothless face, and he turned and stalked back to the stairs and down to the lower deck.

"Did you understand all that he was saying?" Bwana asked.

"No, but the way he was saying it, I understand his meaning," Debalo told him.

"I think the man just threatened to kill you and take your knife."

"He wouldn't. The captain would hang him for murder, you heard him say that," Debalo reassured his friend.

"The captain said that he would hang any man aboard his ship for killing a fellow Baratarian. We aren't Baratarians, Debalo. We're slaves."

"No. I am no longer a slave," he looked to the tall man with a serious expression in his malarial eyes. "I am free and I am going home," he told him.

"And you aren't there yet, so try not to anger that man any more than you have. He worries you terribly I know, but do as he says for now and all of this will be behind you. Now, Debalo," Bwana took his friend by the arm and lead him toward a stack of coiled ropes near the starboard railing. "Let's settle down for the evening. I think we both can use a little sleep. Don't you agree?"

"I agree, I need to sleep, but it is hard for me."

After the light had completely faded, Debalo stretched out upon the coil of rope and Bwana lay curled up nearby along the railing. It had not escaped his attention that Daniel was watching closely at the pair as they bedded down and he recalled the man's hidden threat. He lay awake for a few hours in the complete darkness of the night. Clouds had rolled in and blocked any light from the moon and stars.

The dew had settled and moistened the night. The steady breeze kept him cool and comfortable. From somewhere toward the mainsail, someone was whistling a soft tune he'd never before heard, but he enjoyed the lonely tone of the man's notes. He was a talented whistler. The air was sweet and clean as it blew in and Debalo felt himself finally succumbing to sleep.

Before giving in to the temptation of rest, he quietly slid the knife from its sheath and placed the blade between two coils of the rope he was resting upon in such a way that he could not roll onto the sharp blade himself. But, should he need to retrieve it quickly, the handle was placed easily to grasp.

"Debalo, Mamba!"

The cry came from the far side of the village where a small group of elderly women went to work on the hides of the animals the hunters brought in. The hides were staked securely to the ground with the hair side down so that the old women could scrape any fat and tissue away after the animals had been skinned so that they might dry in the hot cool dry air of the African winter. The area where they stretched the hides to the ground was surrounded by a thick, thorn boma, to keep away the night prowlers, attracted to the smell of the blood still clinging to the new leather. The boma had been erected years ago and had been reinforced many times. It now was nearly ten feet thick in most places and nearly as high in some.

The tall grasses of the region had engulfed a large part of it and threaded itself into the tangle of thorny branches, actually strengthening the structure. However, the tangles attracted birds and mice to its protective cover, which happily began to build nests in it. The birds and mice in turn attracted snakes and none were more feared than the mamba.

Debalo had been kneeling at the sharpening log, actually a smooth worn piece of ebony wood upon which Debalo and the other hunters would sprinkle fine sand and grind the edges of their spear points to sharpen them. He leapt up from his work and sprinted in the direction he had been called.

Other men were running as well and most were passing him as he was still having difficulty with his stride. He had experienced the rites of manhood only recently. His hair had been braided tightly in rows and caked into place with a mixture of river mud and buffalo dung for the ceremony. He was then led naked, to the center of the village and made to lie down upon a lion skin. The lipwereri, witch doctor, made passes over his prostrate form mumbling spells and prayers to ward off the evil spirits and to bless Debalo with virility, courage, and strength. Then several men came forward and laid hands upon the young man as the rest of the villagers crowded around to watch. The lipwereri, with a solemn voice asked Debalo a final question before he was made a man.

"Are you to be a man, my son?" he asked.

Debalo nodded his reply and the hands, which were upon him grabbed and held firmly as the lipwereri removed the foreskin from Debalo's penis with a ceremonial knife. The knife had been with the villagers from as far back as the oldest man could remember. The blade had been made of bone, taken from an animal long forgotten and the handle was taken from the horn of a young kudu. Before passing out, Debalo could remember having one thought screaming through his brain, "I wish he had bothered to sharpen the knife!"

Arriving at the gateway through the boma, Debalo shoved past a handul of youths and women staring through the fence at the commotion inside. Entering the yard, he could see that several men were standing about a woman lying on top of a staked hide. Her upper body was convulsing upward and he could tell she was fighting to breathe. His mother was kneeling at the woman's side, offering her companionship as she died. There was nothing else to do. If it was a mamba, which bit the woman, there was nothing to do but wait for her to die. It usually only took several minutes, but Debalo had once seen a man take nearly an hour before he died.

He joined the circle of men watching for any sign of the snake as the old woman died with one last gasp and his mother hurried past him to rejoin the onlookers outside the fence.

As the lipwereri removed the body of the old woman, Debalo continued to stand watch for the snake, ignoring the ticks he could feel beginning to crawl up his legs. The ticks were among the primary reasons that hide scraping was a job for the elderly or infirm. The hateful insects would fall from the skins of the dead animals and re-infest themselves upon the human workers. It was not a job much envied.

One by one the men of the village left the clearing. He watched them as they bent low and passed through the gateway of the protective fence and started their walk back up the pathway through the tall grass toward the village. He continued to stand watch until he was the last to leave. He had been the last to arrive and he knew it was his place as well to remain the longest. Once the others had cleared the fence, he began his own exit from the clearing. At the gateway he paused for one last look behind and there behind him was the mamba!

It uncoiled its dirt colored length from beneath one of the hides staked nearby him. It was as thick as his arm and seemed to grin wickedly while letting out a hiss like that of pissing in the coals of a dying campfire.

He hadn't carried a weapon with him when he ran toward his mother's call. He looked around for something to use to defend himself from the menacing mamba, but there was nothing at hand. He turned to run, but his legs were stilled by fear and his heart was beating so terribly loud in his ears, all else was shut out from his hearing except the terrible hiss and his racing pulse.

He reached back for the fence and grabbed for the thorny bushes to pull himself along. His terror was so complete that he felt as if the sun had gone into hiding and the world gone black as the foul creature came upon him, bringing him his death.

Debalo choked off a scream, which was building in his throat as he opened his eyes from the nightmare and slowed his breathe to calm his racing heart. This dream had been a new one, but just as terrible as the others had been. He lay still on the coils of rope feeling the rocking of the ship as it plowed on through the calm waters, but there was something different.

Debalo came instantly alert, but remained still and quiet. Something was blocking the breeze from reaching him and that something was carrying with it a sour sweaty stench. The clouds were now gone and the nights stars were brilliant and although there was no moon remaining in the sky, Debalo could see enough to distinguish a dark shape looming nearby.

He watched the shape closely for movement and slowly he crept his right hand forward to the handle of the knife. It was cool and firm and its strength gave him confidence. He wasn't afraid, but he was not about to trust the stranger being so near. He watched the dark shape carefully and saw it shift to the right slowly. A slight and gentle touch at his waist confirmed to Debalo that this man was up to no good.

He remained unmoving as the stranger's hand moved across his waist with the lightest touch until reaching the sheath, which had held Debalo's knife. He continued to submit to the touch of the searching fingers until the hand made its way to the buckle of the wide belt he wore and began slowly exerting pressure on the buckles clasp to release it from Debalo's waist.

He'd had about enough of this intrusion as he felt he could stand and made up his mind to put an end to this attempted thievery. In one swift motion, he drew the large blade from between the ropes coils and slashed downward past his belt. Starlight glinted faintly upon the well-sharpened blade as he drew it. There was a moment's resistance as it made its way past his belt and that resistance was echoed by a sharp intake of breath and the sound of an awkward retreat, shuffling across the planks of the deck.

Debalo smiled to himself and replaced the knife back into its sheath. He was confident there would be no more attempts to take it from him that night.

He fell back to sleep and dreamt no more of the giant snake, but rested in dark slumber. He awakened with Bwana shaking him awake and grinning wide.

"It's morning already. It's getting light and we have to get on down to the galley. You must have really slept well, Debalo. You're usually the one waking me up!"

Debalo sat up on the coil of ropes he'd used as a bed and wiped his eyes. Bwana was standing shirtless nearby relieving himself into the gulf water. Debalo looked around for any sign left by his nighttime visitor and quickly spotted a few drops of blood and then he raised his eyes to follow more drops away from him toward the stair well leading down from the poop deck. Two of the ships officers were standing not far from the top of the steps near the big wheel, using an instrument to sight toward the rising sun. He had asked about that instrument and been told that it was a device used for keeping the ship sailing in the right direction. Debalo had no idea how it worked, nor did he care at that early hour of the morning. He had no desire to remain on the ship and whatever magic the white men used to steer it, he was content to remain ignorant of.

He stood and stretched, then felt a gush of bile come up onto his throat as he stooped over to retrieve something from the planks by his feet.

"What you find there, Debalo?" Bwana asked him as he straightened up inspecting the thing in his hand.

"A finger," he told him without enthusiasm.

"A what?" Bwana asked in a startled tone as he fought to replace his member back into the tattered pants he wore.

"A finger," Debalo repeated.

"Is it yours?"

"No," Debalo looked up and started a small smile. "I think however, I'll go see if Daniel wants it back."

"It's Daniels? Debalo what happened?" Bwana was asking with cautious excitement.

"I awoke last night with a man trying to remove the knife and belt from my waist. I stopped him."

"And cut off his finger?"

"He won't forget his mistake now will he?" Debalo offered a weak smile at his grisly joke, but his insides were churning with revulsion.

Just then, Daniel's head crested the top of the stairwell with his customary snarl, "I just came from the galley and the two of you weren't there. What seems to be the problem?"

"We are to go now," Debalo answered him. "I have something for you Daniel," Debalo told him with a glint of humor in his eyes and tossed the finger over to him.

Daniel reached out and caught it in the air and upon recognizing it, yelled out in surprise, "Jesus Christ man! Where, in the Hell, did that come from?" He stood frozen in confusion and stared back at Debalo as the humor left his eyes.

"It is not yours?" Debalo asked quietly and confusedly.

"What do you mean 'is it mine'?" Daniel spat out toward him. "Explain this you black bastard. Where did this come from?"

"I was asleep. Someone came to rob me. I thought it was you," Debalo told him with a dumbfounded look.

"Well, obviously it wasn't me, you ignorant nigger." Turning, Daniel stalked over to the two officers standing at the wheel and paying attention to the exchange taking place between Daniel and the new crewman.

Both looked toward Debalo in shock and the first one turned and rang a bell three clangs. At the bells ringing the decks of the ship became a hive of activity as all hands assembled before the poop and the captain exited his quarters and mounted the deck.

"What is it Mr. Gall?" the captain asked the officer holding the finger up for the captains inspection.

"It's Daniel and the new man, Captain Hebert. Perhaps we'd better ask them."

"Daniel, I would like an explanation please," the captain stood erect and glaring.

"Debalo is the one to explain Captain. I'm mighty confused myself, Sir," Daniel began. "I was just making the steps, Captain, when this man, Debalo, tosses this finger to me and asks do I want it back?

"It's not mine Captain," Daniel explained.

"Yes, I can see that," the captain snapped at him, then turned toward Debalo. "Well, must I wait for you to explain?"

Debalo was scared for a moment and looked about for Bwana to help interpret what he did not understand, but Bwana had moved well off to one side and would not look up to meet his eyes.

"Come now! Please explain this," the Captain demanded again.

"While I sleep," Debalo paused, unsure of his use of the new language. "Hand on Debalo," he told the captain while pointing to his waist and thigh. "Feel for steal of me," Debalo hesitated again, wishing Bwana had not left him.

"Somebody tried to rob you?" the captain asked him and Debalo nodded affirm.

"What was it they tried to steal? Have you any money about you?"

Debalo shook his head and answered, "No, no money. This," Debalo indicated the big knife at his waist and patted the handle for effect.

The captain smiled with a raised brow, "Yes well, I admit. I've eyed that myself a time or two." Then in a seemingly better humor told him, "This will be easy to clear up, now won't it?" Turning to the assemble crew he shouted, "Which man amongst you lost his finger during the night?"

A low rumble of voices as the crew looked about to each other and a shout went up near the mainsail.

"'Ere e is Capn'! Eer's the bloke now!" With that, a scuffle commenced and a light colored man of at least some African blood was wrestled forward to stand before the Captain.

"Show me your hands," the captain ordered in a cold and threatening voice.

The man resisted mightily, but eventually his right hand was produced for the captain's inspection. And as was accused, the first finger was missing below the second knuckle and the remaining three fingers had been laid open with a terrible gash, leaving the thumb, the only survivor of the night. The hand was blood covered, as was the front of the man's trousers. He wore no shirt, but strips of it had been tied about the hand as a crude dressing for his wounds.

"Explain yourself!" the captain hissed.

"No explanation suh. I just never seen such a knife. I wanted it suh," he answered with shamefully bowed head.

"Very well, I must then propose penalty for your thievery. It would appear that you've paid a price already and since the theft was averted, I sentence you to fifteen lashes across the back." Speaking to the two sailors holding the man's arms, "secure him to the mizzen."

"Mr. Gall, as first officer, would you please carry out the sentence."

"Aye sir," the officer answered and the Captain spoke out in a booming voice. "There is to be no thievery amongst this crew. Let it be known that this man has committed his first offence. Shall he repeat it, his sentence will be death." That said, he turned and strode back to the stairwell and returned towards his private quarters.

The crowd of sailors returned to their morning duties and Debalo walked to the stairwell in order to report to the galley. At the rear mast of the ship, the almost thief was being tied and the first officer was straightening out a fierce looking whip. The man was sagging against his restraints and whimpering. Debalo felt sorry for the man, but there was nothing he could do for him. Bwana was nowhere to be seen by now and Daniel met him at the stairs.

"What's this, you accuse me of trying to steal from you?" he asked gravely.

"I thought it so," Debalo told him. "You said you want knife if I die."

"That doesn't mean I'd steal it from you. I like that knife fine and if you die, I want it, but no man calls me a thief. I might not like you black bastards, but I am not as black hearted, a pirate as some of these sea dogs" he told Debalo in the least aggressive tone he'd heard the man use. "Accuse me as a thief again and I'll gut you like a fish boy. And I'll use my own knife," he finished and for emphasis, he reached beneath the wide belt he wore at his waist and pulled out a thin and curved bladed knife about eight inches long with a very impressive edge showing on it.

"Now, get to work boy!" Daniel regained his usual snarling voice.

"Debalo!" Debalo told him unmoving.

Daniel smiled his gummy wicked smile, "Get to work, Debalo." He said and coughed out what could have been mistaken for a laugh as Debalo walked to the galley door and entered.

THIRTEEN

On the morning of the fifth day since leaving Barataria, the Lenard Rouge was skimming along through a bright and sparkling sea with the sun just over the horizon when Daniel came on deck. Bwana was just waking and Debalo stood at the starboard railing with the wind caressing him, catching the spray of the saltwater on his face and tasting the salt.

"Had you two any plans to make your way to the galley?" he growled. "Sun's breached the horizon and the moon sets there, falling fast and you black bastards aren't moving yet."

Debalo turned and started for the galley when Daniel stopped him. Bwana went on ahead unobstructed to assist the cook.

"Debalo, Campeche is just astearn and the Sabine River lies right over there," he pointed a crooked finger toward a thin line of green indicating the coast. Debalo searched the horizon, but saw nothing to tell him of a river.

"The thing is this. When we dock, I'll be going ashore with the cook to gather supplies for the galley. We'll be taking on cargo, so most of this miserable crew will be manning the boats and loading the stores. You will help with that, but while I'm ashore, I want you in that galley. Nobody enters there! You got that?"

Debalo nodded.

"They's rum in there and sugar. I'll not have it looted. If it comes to that, you're responsible and I'll see to it that the captain has your sorry black ass thrown overboard. We'll be seeing the island in another hour or two. Best get to work and mind what I said."

Throughout all of this Debalo was silent, only nodding. Truly, he hadn't understood everything that Daniel had said, but he understood enough to know that he was to remain in the galley while the others left the ship.

He moved past the dirty little man and toward the stairwell that led to the lower deck when a cry arose from the crow's nest of the mainsail. "Sail Ho!"

The cry was repeated a couple of times as the decks came alive with a flurry of activity. The officer on deck rang the ship's bell a number of times and the captain and other officers ran past Debalo at the stairwell to study the horizon. All of the sailors were lined up along the railings of the starboard side trying to catch a glimpse of the ship that was spotted on the horizon and awaited orders from the captain.

"It's a twin master," Daniel said. "Probably a brig and she's got all of her canvas showing. If she keeps

118

coming it won't be long afore we know if she's one of us. You get to the galley," he told Debalo as he started a crooked grin. "If she's Spanish, we'll be needing the men fed and ready. We might get to take on a bit of swag before we make for port."

Debalo shifted his attention from Daniel to the tall ship in the distance. He'd been uneasy since stepping aboard this ship and now he was terribly disturbed. He didn't understand all that Daniel had told him, but he understood enough to know that this ship's arrival could be a terrible omen.

In the galley, Bwana was already at work readying the crockery for the sailors' morning meal. The cook was busy at the fire pit stirring vigorously in an ancient iron kettle, sweat rolling down his red, beefy face.

In Fanagalo Bwana asked him, "what is taking you so long this morning? Daniel will be after you."

"I just left Daniel. There is another ship in the distance and everyone is looking to it," Debalo explained.

Bwana's eyes widened and he stopped what he was doing, "is it chasing us?"

"It is behind us, but off to one side. I do not think it is chasing us, but I do think that there will be trouble."

"Why is that?" Bwana wanted to know.

"Because Daniel was too excited. The whole crew lined up to see it and the Captain is now looking it over. It could be that they are bringing slaves to this new land as I came before, but I do not know why that would bring about so much interest." Debalo tried to tell him what he knew without showing how upset he was about it.

"Blast yer hides," the fat old cook called to the pair. "Stop all that jibberish and get to work. We've men to feed yet and we'll not be to it with all this talking."

Debalo nodded once to the man and stepped quickly to his tasks.

Once the men had been fed and the crockery cleaned and put away, Debalo and Bwana went forward and joined the other sailors along the railing to get a better look at the other ship.

It was much closer than when Debalo had first seen it and he could easily make out the square set to the full sails and the wide, low-riding bulk of the vessel as it cut a swath toward them through the green waters of the gulf. Debalo noted that the crew around him appeared to be in very good humor and bantered excitedly. A dark-skinned man with a leathery face bearing a wicked scar across his left cheek and eyebrow called out, "She's Spanish, boys! A low riding galleon waiting to be plucked." He sported a grin that terrified rather than humored Debalo.

"What does that mean?" Bwana asked the man.

"What that means is that we'll be arriving in Campeche with a little money in our pockets for a change," he answered excitedly.

"Debalo! Bwana! Come along now!" Daniel was shouting to them from before the Captain's quarters. "Come with me!"

They both hurried back down the stairs and followed Daniel down into the ship's hold. Once they were with him below the deck, he started to explain.

"It's a Spanish vessel and we've orders to intercept and loot that ship. As it continues to close on our course, the Captain will order us to arms. When we receive that order, you will come here. In the stern there is a large barrel of sand and sawdust and another foreward. When the shooting starts, the boards are going to get wet and slick from seawater, sweat, and blood. Men manning these cannons will be calling for sand. Your jobs are to keep these floors dry and their footing firm.

"You have to be on the spot. These gunners will be firing hot and fast at first and the wood and steel is going to be flying. If eitherof you get struck and can't manage the bleeding, call out for the iron. It'll sear the wound closed to get you back to work. Now, get yourselves topside and make yourselves useful," Daniel finished and started back up the steps leading to the upper deck.

Bwana stared after the grimy little man until he had disappeared above the stairs and Debalo noticed that a bit more white was showing around the eyes of the big man's black face than was usual.

"You are scared, Bwana? What was he saying?" Debalo asked him.

"He said that we got to get this here dirt on the floor when the shooting starts so that the gunners don't slip in the water and the blood. He said they might be blood all over the floor and we could get hit with wood or something and go to bleedin' too!"

Debalo could clearly see that Bwana was terribly upset by all that had been said and he didn't want to alarm his friend more by admitting his own fears.

"I'm sure we are safe enough if we are to stay down here. I do not like this at all, but if we stay here and do as we are told, we will survive and return to Africa. I keep telling myself that this is something I must endure in order to go home and I will get there Bwana. We will get there," Debalo assured him and with his stomach tying in knots still, he started up the steps to the upper deck.

When he arrived again near the railing, he noticed the other ship was drawing away from them and was smaller in appearance. Men were grumbling and cursing as they moved about the vessel and the man with the awful scar across his face looked toward Debalo and the others and shook his head.

"She changed course, boys. The Captain doesn't want to chase her down since we're so close to Campeche. Damn Campeche!" he said looking toward the Captain up by the big wheel. "He has a whore on the island he's looking forward too. He should be giving chase, our hold is empty and we've no reason to be taking ourselves to this port, but that the Captain agreed to carry mail to the island and he wants his whore." The man shook his head again and walked toward the stern of the vessel.

Debalo sensed that there would be no shooting and that comforted him mightily.

A cry arose from the watcher seated atop of the mainsail and a bell rang forward. Campeche had been sighted.

In a couple hours time the Lenard Rouge was at anchor in the sprawling harbor of the island. A pair of wooden longboats had been lowered over the side and the officers of the ship and members of the crew rowed the short distance to the landing. There were three other ships at anchor nearby and the crew that remained aboard the ship called out to the men left aboard the neighboring vessels and all of them were in a celebratory mood. Each man would get ashore for their turn at drinking and recklessness.

Debalo stowed himself away behind the locked doors of the galley as he'd been instructed and did not mind at all being denied the opportunity to go ashore here. The part of the town visible from the Gulf was not dissimilar to that of the Islands of Barataria. It was a sprawling complex of warehouses, cattle pens, and houses amidst the towering palms and pine. Prominently located near the beach was a large red brick mansion that had about it a comfortable, welcoming look. However, that image was marred a bit when one noticed the dark muzzles of canon protruding from the several top floor windows of the structure.

To either side of the landing, in the not too far distance, Debalo had spied an area of raised ground topped with a small battery of the big cannon numbering five guns.

The oppressive heat in the galley drove Debalo to remove his shirt and stay near the open port that faced the gulf. There was a very light breeze blowing across the window, but it carried no relief from the heat. He watched as the distant clouds towered high and dark and moved across the waters towards the city of Campeche. He knew that the clouds carried heavy rains, but wished for rain all the same as a means of relieving the heat.

On the breeze by the window, he could smell the sweet salt of the air and amused himself by identifying the different types of wood being burnt by the scent of its smoke being borne upon the wind. The nearer the clouds came, the cooler the wind at the window, and he began to smell the sweet scent of the rain being borne upon the breeze.

He had been locked in the galley guarding the stores and listening to the activity outside for hours until Daniel's voice boomed to him from the other side of the barred door, "Open that door and get your ass busy loading these supplies. That rain will be on us soon and we've got dry goods to load. Open up!"

Debalo quickly un-barred the doorway and opened the galley for Daniel to pass through, both shoulders loaded with sacks of goods. Behind him came the cook carrying a wooden crate and sweating heavily, his fat jowls flushed deep crimson.

"Debalo, get over to the railing where they're unloading the stores and get to work. We've got to hurry," Daniel told him, breathing heavily.

They gathered all of the supplies into the galley and finished just as the first drops of rain began to splatter down upon the deck of the ship. Men ran here and about, clearing the deck and many going below into the hold to keep dry. Debalo looked about for Bwana, but didn't see him and asked Daniel about him, "is Bwana coming?"

"I sold him to the slavers," Daniel croaked out.

"Sold him a slave?" Debalo asked in an astonished voice. A knot of worry choked him and he did not know what to say.

"Naw, he's coming. Look there, now," Daniel cackled at his dark humor while Debalo looked to see Bwana and four other sailors crawling over the starboard side-rail. Relief flooded over him and slowly built to anger at the vile little man's joke.

He wanted to hit Daniel in his gummy mouth, but instead walked out into the rain and watched as Bwana and the others stepped lively toward the opening leading down into the ship's hold. The rain was cool and felt good to him and he walked to the rail and looked across the waters to the buildings of Campeche. He wondered to himself if he should swim ashore and take his chances on the land or remain here on this ship he was growing to hate.

FOURTEEN

The Renarde Rouge slipped silently into the hollow blackness of the Gulf of Mexico in the still hours of the predawn. Word had been passed amongst the crew that the Captain had issued orders that all hands were to remain silent until the ship had been gotten underway. Debalo moved to the galley door and stood clear of the experienced sailors as they darted in and out of the blackness readying the ship for departure. On land, most of the fires had gone dark as the city slept. The only sound in the night was the barking of a dog carried over the waters.

Debalo moved from the doorway and stood near the stairwell leading up to the rear deck. He watched as the mainsail was unfurled, showing barely a silhouette against the empty, overcast sky. It made a series of hollow, popping sounds as it caught the night wind and filled. Debalo listened to the strained grunts coming from the foredeck where members of the crew were slowly raising the giant anchor that had held them fast to their mooring in the bay. All around was the stamping and padding of bare feet upon the wooden planks of the ship's deck and Debalo wondered that they had not been discovered in their flight.

He didn't understand the reason for the stealthy withdrawal from the pirate port, but he knew instinctively that it must not be good and wanted to say as much to Bwana, who had moved up beside him and stood tall and silent. Debalo, however, decided against conversation and just stood for a while as he waited for the dawn.

The night had grown cool and Debalo was glad that the rains had died off earlier in the night. With no sun to dry them, the crew worked on in the blackness, shivering and miserable. His mood was as dark as the stygian night and he wondered out loud if he would ever see the tall grasses of Africa again.

"Ya worry too much, Debalo," Bwana scolded him under his breath, "Why ain't ya happy to just be here? They feed us good. They ain't nobody hurt us or asked us to do nothin' bad. I think the Cap'n wants a early start, that's all."

Debalo was surprised that Bwana had heard him, and ashamed that he had been caught talking to himself. He sheepishly opened up to the big man. "Bwana, I do not know why I feel the way that I do, but I do not trust that we are safe here," he said.

Bwana patted his shoulder with a hard calloused hand and moved off into the dark. Debalo started to follow his friend into the dark, but remained where he was. Daniel had not sought him out to give him any special orders, so he stayed where he was and listened to the activity around him. The mast creaked and groaned beneath the weight of the wet canvas and the hemp made tiny, high-pitched noises as it stretched under the tension. As always, the sound of the waters being parted by the keel speeding into the invisible waters of the nighttime Gulf kept up a continuous moan.

Debalo heard splashes in the water near the starboard bow and recognized the sound of dolphins arcing in and out of the water, racing the ship. He had seen them on several different occasions and at first was humored by their permanent smiles and the playful way they would dive in and out of the ship's wake. In the cold dark, with the silent crew working about him like specters upon the water, his recollection of the dolphin's grin became more a recollection of a snarling smirk.

Closing his eyes, he could see their dark bodies in his mind hurling upward out of the ships wake as if leading it to some watery abyss. It was as if they mocked him, grinning wickedly at his gloom and despair. He opened his eyes to the night and was glad for the blindness. He didn't want to see the dolphins and he didn't want to see the pirate crew. He wanted to be away. He missed home more than ever.

Daylight did arrive eventually and with the light of the morning sun, Debalo could see no land anywhere, just the lonesome flatness of the emerald Gulf surrounding him. Daniel found him sitting on a pile of hemp coiled near the starboard railing of the foredeck and summoned him to the galley.

"I should expect to find your ass sitting around when there's a fast to break this morning! To the galley with ya' and when yer done of the work there and all be fed. Come below. You've a thing or two to learn this day if ye plan to remain aboard this ship. I'm to teach ye' the drills below deck to assist the gunners. If we get lucky enough to cross paths with a fat brig loaded with swag, you'll be needed to take a part."

Daniel snorted a time or two as he left and Debalo rose and made his way to the galley. The meal was unusually large for a morning, but with the new provisions taken aboard at Campeche, the cook was generous. Late in the morning, as the sun rose high in the gray overcast sky, Debalo made his way to the galley to find Daniel below the decks.

Once down into the dimly lit belly of the ship Debalo found himself amidst a flurry of activity as men worked at the cannon. The customary stench of the ship's hold assaulted his nostrils and was compounded by the sweat of the dozens of men laboring in the cramped quarters and the rancid greases being used to treat the cannons for protection against rust.

"About time I see yer' black ass down here. I've shown you the sand barrels. That's yer job in the opening volleys. To stand near and be ready to sand the floors for the gunners unless the other ships returning fire be accurate. If so, men will die and you have to be able to jump in with a crew and make yerself useful to the gunners."

"You understandin' all of this?" Daniel asked, annoyed at the confused look upon Debalo's face.

He shook his head slowly and Daniel turned and roared for Bwana, "Bwana! This ignorant bastard needs you!"

Bwana ran forward, shirtless and sweat soaked, from where he had been stacking ammunition for the guns. He stopped beside Daniel and faced Debalo in the stern of the ship.

"Tell him what I told you and get it right. Show him to stack the ammo by the gun carriages and have a gunner explain the firing procedure. I've got fuses to roll and don't have time to go over this with him again." Daniel huffed and headed for the ship's stern.

"Yessah, I'll teach him right," Bwana called after him. He turned to Debalo and spoke softly in Fanagalo. "Overlook that man. I will show you what we need to know."

Debalo forced a smile and he followed Bwana to a gun carriage. There was a lot of activity going on in the cramped and dimly lit belly of the ship. Gun carriages were being arranged at the portholes and the guns were being serviced. Bwana led him over to where a crew was working and in Fanagalo began to explain their responsibilities to Debalo, with obvious pride in his newly acquired knowledge. He listened intently and asked a lot of questions. The answers Bwana did not know, he would ask a crewman working nearby. As always, whatever Debalo could not understand, Bwana would quickly translate.

The cannons had been turned facing the open port windows on both sides of the ship. In all there were twenty-four cannons in the belly of the ship mounted on compact wooden carriages with small wooden wheels. They were slightly longer than Debalo's height and had an opening as wide as the width of his hand. Each of the guns had been well oiled and the carriage wheels greased. A crew of three to five shirtless, silent men attended each gun position; some stacked ammo and others rigged the ropes and pulleys that allowed the cannons to be rolled in and out of the port windows for loading and firing.

Each gun carriage had a long pole on either side of the barrel with one end bundled with canvas. These were the ramrods used for loading and swabbing the barrel. To the rear of the carriage was mounted a pair of small wooden containers, in which the various tools of the gunner were stored. Debalo could not guess the purpose of the tools, but did not ask.

As they traveled through the hive of activity, a gunner's mate called to them to assist with the handling and positioning of the ammunition. Bwana quick stepped forward to the mate and Debalo fell in line with others, carrying ammunition forward to arm the forward gun positions. There was a good variety of ammunition being delivered to different gun positions, but the most plentiful were two types of projectiles that were stacked near each gun. One, he learned, was called "solid shot". It was a heavy round ball and most commonly Debalo heard it referred to simply as "shot". The smashing effect of the solid cannon shot was used to tear great holes into the belly of an opposing ship at the waterline to disable it. He was instructed to grease each ball with black, foul smelling grease that was kept in small wooden buckets, to prevent rust from gathering on it. The grease also served as a lubricant so the shot would load easily into the gun's muzzle. The weight of the things made it quite difficult to handle. After a while his arms and hands ached.

He'd been instructed to stack the shot into a ten shot pyramid of five balls on the bottom, four balls placed atop of them and a single ball alone atop of the stack. These stacks were placed to the front and left of the guns' position allowing enough room for the gunner's mate to move about between it and the carriage. To the left and to the front of the carriage, Debalo was instructed to place the second stack of ammunition described to him as "grape shot" or simply "grape".

The grape shot consisted of short stacks of nine small iron balls stacked in three tiers between two wooden plates with an iron pin connecting them. The balls were stacked around the pin and wrapped very tightly in a canvas cover that had been sewn together giving the stack a quilted look. When the grape shot was fired, the canvas would blow apart allowing the nine iron balls to spread out and scatter. These rounds were very effective when used to fire into the cannon ports of an enemy vessel to kill and maim the gunnery crew, or fired upward onto the decks to help clear the decks of sharpshooters.

It was well after the noon hour when the job was completed and the gunners began assembling their crews for gunnery practice. A pair of the captain's junior officers came below to direct the final preparations and the handling of the gunpowder.

Daniel appeared in the hold, calling Debalo and Bwana back up to the galley. They slowly ascended the stairwell, and stood for a moment on the deck, relishing the cool Gulf breeze as it blew over their tired bodies. They washed up quickly in a bucket of seawater in an attempt to get most of the grease and sweat off of them before reporting to assist the cook in preparation of the evening meal.

As they went about their usual duties in the galley, the crews below deck had finally readied for their first practice shots. The sudden and unexpected roar of the guns nearly frightened Debalo to death. Once he'd recovered from his start, he noticed that he was not the only one affected by the cannon fire, for Bwana stood trembling, showing a bit too much white around the pupil of his eyes. The cook shook his head a time or two and laughed a low chuckle to himself, amused at them.

In another minute another volley was fired and soon after another. The entire ship shuddered at the pounding of the big guns and the roar and concussion was so great that his head began to pound and his ears ached from it. As soon as he would hear a new volley begin, Debalo slapped his hands tightly over his ears and waited for it to finish. He looked out the side port window and was terrified at the amount of smoke coming from the sides of the ship, leaving a dark gray and blue trail behind them as the wind carried them steadily over the waters of the Gulf of Mexico.

Debalo was grateful that the cannonading had not lasted very long. After the evening meal had been served and the galley put back in order, Debalo wandered out to the stern of the ship and watched the ship's wake fanning out behind them as the sun sank lower and lower to the green waters. He thought of the tall masted ship they had watched on the horizon as they neared Campeche and wondered if the readying of the cannon and the gun crews practicing was in any way connected. He was aware of the disappointment the crew felt for not having attacked that ship. Try as he might, Debalo just could not understand the predatory nature of these men.

The captain and another officer were standing near the big wheel where a small table had been erected. Spread out across the table was large sheets of paper with drawings that drew quite a bit of attention from them. Debalo watched them for a while and studied their faces, looking for signs of evil or despair, for he was convinced that they all were doomed men. But no matter how hard he stared or how long he brooded, he could not deny that these men seemed content and confident, their talk bright and with no hint of tension or angst.

Debalo wondered if Bwana was right after all, that he was wrong to feel so desperate to be away from the ship and the sea, but inside of him was an emptiness that he had never known. Even when he first was put in chains and beaten and starved and sold as a slave, he had never known this feeling. It was a mixture of terror and loathing, lonesomeness and sorrow and it would not go away. He was about to turn away from the men and look again toward the sunset when the captain straightened and beckoned to him.

"You there. Debalo, isn't it?"

Debalo responded with a nod and stepped over to the captain, "Yes, I am Debalo."

"Will you be a good lad and tell the cook that I will be having my evening tea here on deck tonight? There is a lovely breeze. Will you do that, Debalo?"

Debalo answered slowly because he hadn't understood everything the captain had told him, but he knew enough to understand what it was the captain was asking. "I will, Captain," he said and started to move away.

"I meant to ask you before now, Debalo. Where did you come by that knife?" the Captain asked him. "As I've said before, I am rather fond of it."

Debalo reached down and covered the handle of the big knife with his right hand and answered, "Overseer's knife, his name Roundbelly."

"I don't imagine he was too happy about parting with it. Did you steal it from the overseer when you escaped?" the Captain asked seriously as the other officer watched Debalo closely.

"He did not need it," Debalo told him matter of factly, "he was about to die."

The two officers stared back into the yellowish, almond shaped eyes of the young African and did not need to ask what he meant by that. It had been stated, not as a brag, but as an honest answer to the Captain's question and they couldn't help become amused by it.

"Well then, wear it in good health. Now about that tea, Debalo?" the Captain asked as he turned his attention back toward the papers on the table and the other officer.

Debalo walked briskly to the galley and relayed the Captain's message to the cook. He took a seat atop a flour keg in the corner of the room and sat quietly as the cook went about preparing the captain's tea and thought of home. He knew that he had to focus on returning home, where he understood the land and the people and a way of life that made sense to him. He wanted more than ever to return to the hunt. Debalo closed his eyes in the gathering dark and thought of the evenings he'd spent along the banks of the Munyamadzi River listening to the honking call of the imvubu, the hippos, and the laughter and hooting of fisi, the hyena. Hundreds of birds flew in and out of the mswaki, or underbrush, growing so thickly along the water's course and he knew every sound and song they sang; and he missed them terribly.

One of his favorite places to hunt was along the river's bank at an ancient crossing where congoni, the zebra and impala, the quick little antelope would come often to drink. There was a huge stand of ngamo, fig trees nearby that provided excellent cover for a hunter. The wind was always right in the evenings there and often he would go there just to watch and observe the animals, even when he wasn't hunting.

He thought about the first time he had gone there to hunt. His father had shown him the crossing and sat beside him in the shade of the fig trees while waiting on the animals to arrive for their evening drink. As the sun sank closer to the horizon, bathing the riverbank with an amber glow, a small herd of the congoni arrived. Debalo had always admired their black and white stripes and thought their meat the finest of all. He had not yet killed one of the lovely striped animals himself, but on that day, his father told him that he was going to let him throw first.

He was carrying a new lance his father had fashioned for him out of the black ebony wood. It had a beautiful straight grain to it and it tapered nicely and threw with a terrific balance. Hours of skillful care had gone into the straightening and curing of the wood and the tip had been tapered to a fine point, hardened over a fire. As the congoni drew closer, he found it quite difficult to breath. He had actually begun trembling in anticipation of the kill. His father's hand reached out and rested on his shoulder and had given him a little squeeze to help him calm his nerves.

After what had seemed to the young hunter to be a terribly long wait, an old stallion of the small herd finally made his way cautiously to the water's edge. Debalo began to raise the spear, but his father put a firm pressure on his shoulder and he knew to stay his throw and wait. Once the stallion had drank his fill, he moved back, farther up the bank and a couple of young mares crept slowly down, stopping every few steps to test the air and watch for danger until they came to the water's edge. Once they had lowered their heads to the dark rushing waters of the Munyamudzi, Debalo felt his father's hand withdraw with a gentle tap. It was time to strike.

He raised the ebony spear slowly until the point was inline with the chest of the nearest mare. Without hesitation, Debalo hurled the weapon across the short distance of muddy ground separating them. He saw it sink all the way up to midshaft into the ribcage of the striped mare.

With a shriek of surprise, the stricken mare dove headlong into the river and attempted to swim across. The others disappeared back up the bank and fled away with the rest of the small herd in a boil of dust and thudding hooves. Debalo stood and watched his congoni as it weakened and stopped swimming. He let the dark waters carry it downstream a way before it came to rest against a tangle of brush snagged near the bank. He turned to his father, who had stood up behind him and looked up into the scarred, leathery face with pride. His father had reached out and patted Debalo on the head and with a grin had said, "Jumbo!" good job, before stepping around him and leading the way across the river to recover the kill.

"What is it you're brooding over, Debalo?" the cook asked him.

He had been sitting on the flour keg with his head down staring into his clasped hands as he thought of the hunt with his father.

"Africa," he admitted in a melancholy tone.

"Ahh, yer homesick eh?"

Debalo didn't understand the question, so he shrugged his shoulders and offered a half-hearted smile.

"When we sail to Haiti?" Debalo asked him.

"I don't know," the cook answered him and sat on a small wooden stool nearby, "that be up to the Captain, see? I expect us to cross this Gulf a time or two looking to pick up a bit of Spanish swag. The Captain, he'll find us a ship or two to fill up our hold.

Depending on what we claim is how the Captain knows where to sail to next."

"Why take from other ships?" Debalo asked him.

"That's what we do boy," he told him, a bit surprised at Debalo's question. They sat quietly for a moment and the cook got up and went to check on the water for the Captain's tea.

Debalo went back to his thoughts and leaned back against the galley wall and closed his eyes. He was tired from lack of sleep, as well as the day's labors, but did not want to sleep however. He feared more bad dreams would visit him and he dreaded falling asleep because of them.

FIFTEEN

Debalo was not sure what he hated more about the cannons: the incredible noise that hurt his head and made his ears ring, or the smoke that billowed from the guns and filled his nose, mouth, and chest, and made him struggle painfully to breath. Each day since leaving the port of Campeche, the Captain had ordered gun drills. At the noon hour, the ship's bell was rung four times. Each member of the gun crews raced below decks and took their positions at the gun carriages.

A gunnery officer would call the drills as the crew went through the motions of loading the cannons. Each step was done with great care until each gun was ready to fire and the order was given. They would fire only two volleys each evening and afterwards the gunnery officer would comment on their performance and order each man a ration of rum. After the first day's drill, when Debalo had been called away to the galley, he had sat at his assigned station in the stern of the ship near the sand barrel while Bwana stood ready at the stern of the vessel.

After participating in the drills, each of the men would gather with high spirits as the rum was poured and even Debalo began to look forward to it. It wasn't the rum itself that he looked forward to, but rather that it marked the end of that day's cannonading.

As the gun crews rested and sipped their rum, Debalo reported to the galley to assist with his usual duties. He and Bwana would get together afterwards and talk as Debalo continued to practice his English. He was becoming quite fluent with most basic phrases and Bwana was very proud of his role as teacher. After their lessons he would always ask Debalo to tell him more about Africa and together they would pass the early night until sleep would claim them.

On the eighth night after leaving Campeche, they sat with their backs against the starboard side railing of the foredeck. Dark had closed in around the little ship as it rode steadily upon the deep green waters. The foresail and the mizzen had been stowed and the heavy wooden mast of the full and billowing mainsail creaked and groaned in the quiet dark as it rode the gentle swells. Even with the steady sea breeze, Debalo could still catch the scent of the cannon's smoke and the many fish he'd helped prepare for the evening meal.

Neither had been very talkative since taking their nightly leave of the galley; Bwana was content to lounge and rest while Debalo, as was becoming customary for him, sat quietly brooding their situation. Bwana yawned and stretched his legs out further and asked in a tired voice, "Do you want to talk English tonight?"

"I should," Debalo whispered in a melancholy tone, which brought a low chuckle from his companion.

"Why do you laugh?"

"You, Debalo. I'm laughin' at you. You can't quit worryin'. There ain't no doubt about it. You da worryinest man I know." Bwana said chidingly, "We gonna be fine. You gonna get home and I might to. I like livin' on this ship. I don't know what spooks you so bad, but I wish you'd get past it. You worryin' me over worryin' 'bout you."

"You know I ain't for purpose. I feel trouble, Bwana. It stinks like smoke of a cannon. I smell it," Debalo told him gloomily.

"Even so. We may get into trouble, but it ain't happened yet. As surely as we may get in trouble, we may not, too." He snorted for effect, "You can't change what we're doin' no more than you can change what we done. You learn that we're here and you got to be happy about that."

Debalo had to agree on that point.

"We no more slaves," Debalo conceded.

"Tha's right! I ain't gonna be ever again. Now, let's get started on your talkin.'"

They talked quietly for a while and Bwana asked Debalo to tell him again about the animals in Africa. He was fascinated and a bit afraid of animals that regularly caught and fed upon humans. He had heard stories all of his life about bear and wolves and gators, but the animals that Debalo described for him must really be something to see.

"Simba," Debalo began, reverting to his native language, "is the most feared of the animals. He can take the chest of a man in his jaws and crush him. There is no fear like the fear of simba. In the night you will hear him roar and it is loud like the cannon. You can hear him roaring for miles. It's at that time that he is telling the world that he is there and that there is no escape. If simba wishes to have you, he will have you."

Bwana appeared mesmerized, his mouth open and his eyes riveted on his little companion as Debalo told the story.

"There are many stories, Bwana, of people being taken by simba after he has entered the hut while they sleep and step over and around other sleepers as he selects among them for his meal. It can be read in the spore, the tracks, after simba has left how he will walk silently from one person to another smelling their heads as he decides. That is why the people from the villages of the Warusha and Masai cover their heads with the dung of their watusi, cows. So that they will not smell inviting to simba."

Bwana whistled low and spoke softly, "I would be more scairt of livin' around such as them lions than you are of livin' on this boat. The way you worry, didn't you worry about being eaten?"

"There was nothing to worry about," Debalo told him matter-of-factly, "simba either came or he didn't."

"I'd like to see one of the elephants. The jumbos. Momma told me some about them and I know you hunted them, but I can't figure out something that big. Seems like he'd have to move awful slow."

"No," Debalo told him, shaking his head, "jumbo will run a man down quickly. Once he has selected you to die he will hunt you. It is very difficult to hide from him. He will smell you out. To avoid jumbo, you have to use the wind and keep it blowing from him to you or he will kill you."

"They eat you too?" Bwana questioned his young friend.

"I have heard of it, but I have not seen it. Most of the old men of the village say that that is not so, but I do not know. Most jumbo are too fond of the fruit of the marula, or fig trees. It makes them drunk like a man with too much rum. Like men with too much rum there are some who remain happy, some who turn sad, and there are some who turn mean. So it is with a jumbo. If they become mean, they may tear up a village and run down any who come in their way."

"I don't like 'em!" Bwana spat out contemptuously, "I've never seen them, but I don't want no part of them if they act that way. Which one do you think is the worst?"

Debalo thought for a while. "Neither." Given the nature of the question, he answered in the only way that made sense to him. "They do what they are supposed to do. Do we not kill as well? Like simba, I am a hunter and I kill to eat." He answered honestly and simply.

Bwana was not happy with the answer and pressed his friend a bit.

"So, you think you're like a lion or something?" Bwana asked with an amused ring to his voice.

"No," he answered.

"If you could be an animal, would you want to be a lion?" Bwana pressed the question.

"No," Debalo told him, becoming a little amused by such silly questions.

"Simba is dirty. After hunting them and you get up close you can see that they are often covered with fleas and bugs. It is ingwe that I should wish to be like. The leopard is silent and stealthy. He is much smaller than simba, but hunts with much more skill and patience. He is a clean animal and by far the best hunter I know."

"We better get some sleep if we goin' to," Bwana told him, satisfied at Debalo's answers. "I'm pretty well tired and haven't had…"

Bwana was interrupted by a shout from a crewman near the starboard rail of the ship's stem.

"Ship, Ahoy!"

Debalo and Bwana rose quickly as the ship came to life with the activity of the crew swarming to the starboard side of the ship to see what had raised the cry. As they moved across the deck in the near complete darkness Debalo spied the source of the alarm as the cry was repeated and the ship's bell sounded twice. A light was to be seen, dimly glowing upon the far stretching waters of the dark Gulf of Mexico, which could only be the light of a ship's lantern appearing on the horizon.

It was becoming dark enough that Debalo could not see clearly, the faces of the crewmembers about him, but he knew their excitement. He heard it in their words and the tones of their voices. He felt it ripple through the assembled crewmembers like a small wave washing across the ships deck. In the rear of the vessel, he heard orders being given and members of the ship's sailing crew began carrying them out. The foresail was hoisted and a watch was set up in the platform above the mainsail to keep an eye on the light. The light crept slowly to the stem of the ship as the Renarde Rouge, turned toward the light in pursuit.

"We goin' huntin,' Debalo. Just like the leopard!" Bwana clasped his hand on his friend's shoulder.

"No," Debalo answered, filled with despair. "We are more like simba," he told the big man, then to himself added, "I feel dirty."

He wandered back to the place he had been sitting with Bwana and left the others staring after the light. He was still very close to the assembly and their excited talk wore on his nerves. He got up again and moved to the far rear of the ship and found a coil of hemp to use for a seat and tried to make himself as comfortable as was possible.

The Captain and his officers were assembled near the great wheel of the ship. He could not make out what they were saying and for that he was glad. He really didn't want to know. He still watched them as they stood together in the faint light of the rising moon and wanted to tell them his fears, but knew they would not listen. He was destined to be a part of their plans, however reluctant, and he knew that he must try to rest. He had no idea what to expect if they should catch up to the other ship and tried not to think of it. He was sure that he was in for another bad dream, so he tried to clear his mind of everything and think of nothing. Waking up in a sweat soaked terror had become a nightly occurrence and sometimes more than once in a night. It was wearing him down and he knew it, so with the sounds of the wind in the full sails and the black water rushing past the ship's stern, he tried to clear his mind and slept.

The palest shard of an African moon was just rising over the broken strand of mopane scrub when Debalo placed another log on the fire. The bright blue tongues of flame licked hungrily at the dry wood and he hunched closer, his almond shaped eyes squinting as he scraped with a small knife at the tiny bits of flesh still adhering to the zebra skin. He had worked for many hours now and most of the hide lay across his lap, as clean as parchment. He would finish it in the morning, he decided, knowing that the cool dry air of the savannah would not let the hair begin to slip.

Placing his hands into the small of his back, he stretched his young muscles and took a long sip of water he'd kept in a gourd at his side. The cooking fires of the village had all lapsed into round red pools of dying coals and the little Masawra bushman laid aside his work and stood up for a better stretch. He looked across the village compound and stared toward the round-topped mud covered hut where his mother was sleeping.

Debalo sensed something was wrong and looked searchingly into the dark shadows of the village. One of the red mounds of coals caught a brief wisp of wind and flared up, lighting the pathway between two of the huts. There, Debalo saw the leopard stretched flat against the cool sand. His seven feet of steely muscles rippled hard beneath the rosettes of his glossy, dappled hide, his hind claws digging into the sandy earth to grip for his charge. An electric jolt flew up his spine as he slowly formed the word on his lips, "Ingwe!"

Faster than Debalo could claim his next breath, the leopard made good his charge and flattened the little bushman beneath the weight of his attack. He felt the hooked, razor sharp claws grip deep as he wrenched his body for that bite that would bring quick death. The force of the impact had driven Debalo backward into the halo of light in the center of the compound. Lying there beneath the ravages of the leopard, he could see his mother's face peaking from the doorway of the hut with a look of disapproval. With a shake of her head, she turned away. Grabbing him with long fangs across the middle, the terrible cat lifted poor Debalo into the air and leapt for the darkness.

Quickly, through the terrible blackness of the night, Ingwe dragged his prey. Debalo could feel the cool wind blowing across his bloodied body and the heat of the leopard's breath on his side. He had not cried out, nor tried to resist. Debalo felt himself being carried away, but was either too terrified to fight back, or too tired to care. He began to cry as he traveled in the jaws of the big cat and his sobs grew to wails of anguish and misery and he knew he must fight. He knew he must resist, and gathering whatever strength he could muster, he began to scream and kick and punch until he felt himself dropped. Debalo quieted and lay still. He waited for that bite to the base of his skull that would end it. It didn't come. Instead, there was laughter.

He could not see, but he knew the laugh. He rose to his knees and tried to pin point the location of the laughter, but it swirled around him. It was evil and he was scared. Debalo drew the little knife from his belt that he had been using to scrape the zebra skin only moments before. He slashed out with it, but found only air. Again he stabbed and again he slashed, but there was nothing. The laughter intensified and a pair of yellow eyes began to grow in the darkness, and the laughter turned into a hideous growl. Slowly the eyes came to him out of the dark and revealed that they belonged to the face of a man. It was the face of the overseer he had killed while fleeing the plantation.

"Roundbelly going to get you, boy," the face spoke to him in a deep, ominous growl. "You can't wash away my blood. I smell it on you. It leads me to you wherever you go." The beefy face snarled and exposed long white teeth, like that of a leopard. Still growling wickedly, the face dissolved back into the blackness of the night.

Debalo came awake, shivering with fright. About him men were still moving to and fro, waiting on daylight. After a quick look toward the horizon, Debalo felt certain the morning's glow was still a good ways off. He stood on shaking legs and gripped the ship's railing to steady himself. He turned his back to the rail and decided to go toward the galley and wait for the cook to awaken. Dreadful exhaustion consumed him and his eyes burned for sleep. His head swam with the frightful residue of the dreams.

Dawn did arrive, despite his most dire wishes and with it, the sight of sails high on the horizon. The captain had ordered a large meal for the morning. Debalo completed his prep work in the galley and came forward to the ship's railing to stand amongst the men. His heart sank as he looked upon the ship they were pursuing. It had every inch of sail showing, but was wallowing deeply in the water and Le Renarde Rouge was closing fast.

The mood of the crew was joyous and high-spirited. Even Bwana had gotten caught up in the excitement onboard the ship. Debalo could not understand the celebration for what they all knew was about to take place. It would be frightful enough to be below deck in the stinking hold while cannons fired upon another ship, but Daniel and the others had well guaranteed that the other ship, when pressed, was bound to fire back. He left the gathering and returned to the galley for a cup of the strong coffee the cook had brewed.

A candle had been lit in the galley and when Debalo opened the door he found the cook wide-awake and slicing meat.

"You couldn't sleep either, eh Debalo?" he asked as he glanced quickly toward him.

"No," he replied, embarrassed about his sleeplessness.

"Step in and close the door, or we'll have the crew comin' round for a bite. Help yourself to some coffee and sit if you wish. You've no need to ready the crockery at this hour."

Debalo nodded silently and moved into the room and picked up a cup. He poured the steaming liquid into his cup slowly and wished he had remained on the stern railing. He didn't want to talk with anybody; he had planned to be alone.

The cook went on about his meat cutting and didn't pay Debalo much attention. Debalo sat on a short, fat keg of flour and sipped at the hot, bitter liquid. He never cared much for the flavor of the strong drink, but did appreciate the way it helped a man wake up and feel energized. "I need to drink a lot of this," he thought to himself, still groggy from his lack of sleep.

"What is it that won't let you sleep, Debalo?" the cook asked casually while still paying attention to his task. "I know it's not the ship we're after. You've not slept a night through for sometime. What is it that wakes you?"

Debalo shrugged his shoulders and sipped the hot brew.

"I've seen you sleep. You have bad dreams, Bwana said. Is that it? Bad dreams?"

Debalo was embarrassed to admit that he could not sleep for fear of being afraid.

"Coffee's not the drink for you if you can't sleep. You should be asking for a tankard of rum. That will help you sleep," he told him.

"I don't want to sleep," Debalo uttered, then looking from his cup and up to the cook.

"Bad dreams?" the cook persisted.

Debalo nodded and confessed, "In my dreams I die. I die many ways and in many places, but always there is one man responsible."

The cook looked down upon the young African, "Then kill that man," he told him.

Debalo was silent for a moment, then slowly spoke, "I did."

The cook nodded in understanding, "I see now, lad. It's not the killing that's hard, but livin' with the killing, eh?"

Debalo nodded and looked back to the metal cup in his hands.

"Well, no time to worry about that. Last time I checked, we were gaining on that ship out there and I 'spect ther'll be a bit more men die this day. Killin' to some comes easy. Lord knows there's a vile bunch on this ship to be sure, but you rest easy, lad. Try to put what is behind you, behind you."

"It will be easier to do when I get home," Debalo told him before taking another sip from the metal cup.

The cook came over and filled a cup for himself, then looked at Debalo and winked, "Lad, you're home now. Home is where you are, not where you want to be."

"I don't want to be here," he said, looking up to the cook.

"Aye, lad, but you are here and there's not a thing that can be done about it."

"Maybe not," Debalo thought to himself, "but I will."

SIXTEEN

He had known all morning this was inevitable. He had not dreaded anything more in his life. They had closed the distance to the ship the crew was calling a Spanish Frigate. It was turning in a wide arc to the larboard to position itself for the attack of the Renarde Rouge.

After all members of the crew had partaken of an especially generous meal and the galley put back in order, Debalo followed Bwana and the cook out into the bright, mid-morning sunlight. He was shocked to see how close they were to the ship as it kept up its attempt at flight. They had pursued so closely that Debalo could see the individual members of the Spanish ship's crew lined up along their ship's stern returning the crude gestures of the crew of the Renarde Rouge, whom were gathered still in the stern of their own vessel.

Bwana had joined the others on the foredeck and, caught up in the excitement of the gathered sailors, was shouting his own insults and grinning from ear to ear. Debalo watched the big man as he removed his shirt and flailed it around over his head. More than once, a fellow member of the crew would greet Debalo with a slap on the back or a hand on the shoulder, while delivering some gay banter. He returned the good cheer with a forced smile and politeness, but was in awe of the joyousness being exhibited by all hands.

He took a walk to the rear deck and ascending the short stairwell, noticed the Captain and his officers standing about the great, spoked wheel in as merry a mood as their men. He acknowledged them as he passed and received a nod from the Captain. He sat on the railing at the rear of the ship and watched the men in the riggings of the ship as they crawled about, seeing to the ropes and riggings.

As he watched those men, working up high above the decks, they each set up a shout and began pointing toward the Spanish vessel. The Captain called out, "To arms!" and rang the ship's bell.

Debalo sprang from the railing and joined the other sailors as they ran for the ship's hold to man the cannons. He ran into Daniel and four other men who were coming topside with buckets of powder and shot and bundles of rifles to be distributed amongst the crewmembers remaining on deck.

"I told you we were headed to a fight. You remember what you are to do?" he asked Debalo as he paused in his work.

"I remember," Debalo answered.

"Then see to it. We'll be rich men again by nightfall; them Spaniards have begun to turn into us, to fight it out. There'll be a battle for sure," he croaked out happily and scurried off to finish his job.

Through the open door of the galley, he could see the cook sharpening his big knives he used for butchering and laying them out atop of a large pickle barrel. The table had been cleared and the fire stoked in the cook pit. Several rods of steel had been inserted into it. Those rods, Debalo knew, were for cauterizing wounds to prevent a man from bleeding to death. His stomach sank as he watched the fat jowly man go through his preparations. He hoped he would not have to come to the galley for that.

"Get below, you black bastard! Below!" Daniel bellowed from across the deck and Debalo descended the ladder into the hold. The cannon ports were open and everywhere men were busied with their preparations for battle. Cannon crews were loading and positioning the big guns as others were lighting candle lanterns, which hung from the ceiling.

Bwana was squatting at the sand barrel in the rear of the hold and Debalo made his way to the foreward area and took up his position near the other sand barrel. There was much good-humored banter going on between the individual gun crews. Debalo was reminded of young hunters leaving camp in the morning, jeering with the others about what each would pledge to accomplish, but rather than young hunters boasting of wart-hog or Impala, these were desperate looking sailors egging each other on toward the destruction and capture of other men.

He fought back a wave of nausea and his yellowed eyes filled with tears. They were doing no less than the Arab murderers, who came to his village and enslaved them. A vision of his mother standing in the doorway of their mud and stick hut came to him. She was holding out a gourd of soup to him and he wanted terribly to take it from her and to have her hold him the way she did when he was little, but the vision left him and he felt terribly alone.

A giant splash occurred nearby and a spray of water came though the cannon port to the immediate cheer of the gunners. A second behind the cheering, Debalo heard the distant boom of a cannon and knew what it was that had made the splash. Another splash and a splintering sound from above as more cheering and a pair of distant booms were heard. Another boom sounded and the officer below deck began calling the foreward, starboard gun crews to action.

Debalo watched as the gunners commanded the sighting of the weapons and the order was given. "Fire!" The gunners pulled hard on the lanyards, which triggered the firing mechanism and three big guns jumped and roared to life. Smoke blew back through the ports as the crews hauled on the ropes to pull back the cannons. A swab was quickly inserted down the barrel of each piece and as quickly removed. The gunners called for solid shot, and a pre-measured bag of powder was inserted into the gun's muzzle in front of a wooden disc. The greased ball was inserted and all the ammo seated by the big ramrod that was thrust down the cannon's barrel. The crew hauled back on the ropes again and the three guns moved forward in unison, reloaded and ready to fire.

More cheers followed the firing of the three cannons as smoke poured back into the ship's cannon ports and swelled over the crews in the rear of the ship's belly. It was a very short time until the orders came to open fire and the entire starboard battery opened up and continued firing. Round after round was expended toward the other ship and occasionally Debalo could hear more wood splintering above him on the upper decks. A few times there were tremendous impacts that shuddered the entire vessel. He could hear men crying out from the smoke, their screams of agony mixed with the shouts of the gunners and the roar of the cannon.

"Sand! Sand!" the shout went up and Debalo carried two buckets of sand toward the command. The smoke was thicker than he'd experienced it and it stung his eyes and burned his chest to breathe it in. He could not see well at all in the thick swirling smoke, but could see daylight showing through a couple of new holes that had not previously been in the ship's wall.

"Sand, Damnit!" again the cry and Debalo arrived at a gunner who directed the dirt be thrown at his feet and cried out for Debalo to get more. Water again splashed in through the port holes, soaking the gun crew and Debalo was suddenly knocked off of his feet with a piece of board that flew into him after tearing loose from the impact of a cannon ball.

A searing pain burst forth through his mid-section as he tried to lift himself from the wet planks of the ship's floor. He cried out and reached downward to find a splinter of wood, about two fingers thick, protruding from the skin in his lower left abdomen. He placed his thumb and forefinger to either side of it in order to slow the flood of blood that was running from it and staggered to his feet. His head swam from the explosions of so many cannon and he thought that he would faint.

With a burst of new pain, he bent and retrieved the sand buckets from the floor and turned to go back for more sand when a bearded sailor grabbed him, shouted something incoherent and snatched the wood from his stomach. He yowled with the pain, but he was not heard over the cannons. Debalo did see, to his relief that the wood had not gone very deeply. Another shattering blow to the ship knocked him and the bearded sailor sprawling onto the floor together. Rising, Debalo could see that the other man's arm was torn and bleeding.

He got to his feet and ran to the sand barrel in pain and confusion, filled the two buckets and returned amidst the firing to the place where the gunner had ordered the dirt thrown. The gunner lie dead, his body torn and lifeless, face down in the sand Debalo had spread earlier. Two of the gun's crew grabbed the dead man and rolled him out of the way. Debalo spread the fresh sand quickly in the wide pool of blood and hurried back for more, holding his own blood soaked side.

From the time he first heard the call, Debalo never stopped carrying the sand. The fight lasted for not quite an hour before the officer was calling out, "Cease fire! Cease Fire!"

At his call the guns quieted and a tremendous cheer sounded. The ship's bell was ringing above them and Debalo knew that the Spanish ship had surrendered. Smoke was so thick in the ship's hold that he could only see the men of the first gun crew. They finished reloading their cannon and rolled it back into place, each man standing at the ready in case the order to resume firing came.

Debalo held tightly to his wound and after re-filling his buckets sat down on the nearest one. His sand barrel was emptied by nearly a third and spilled sand was all about him. He struggled to catch his breath from the exertion, but also from the lack of clean air. He correctly guessed that the ship had stopped moving, because there was no wind blowing the smoke clear of the hold. Debalo sat still on his bucket, chest and nostrils burning, eyes stinging and watering, and his side burning with pain. It took a long time for the smoke to clear from the hold, but a light breeze was blowing in from over the water and it did help to blow it off. Debalo was summoned forward to assist in disposing of the dead.

There were only two dead men, and after the officer of the deck had removed any items off of the bodies that were to remain on board, Debalo and another man lifted them to an open gun port and quite unceremoniously dropped them into the emerald waters of the Gulf of Mexico.

One quick look out the window showed the Spanish frigate with its sails lowered and railing filled with sailors. Blue smoke was blowing lazily from its open gun ports and the ship appeared to be leaning heavily on its side. He returned back to his place at the sand barrel and through the assembled gunnery crews, he tried to catch a glimpse of Bwana, but could not make him out. Debalo sat quietly holding his side; the bleeding had stopped and he was sure he would recover with a little time, but the pain was distracting.

"Ay mate, Deeblo," the nearest gunner called to him, pronouncing his name terribly, "yer best to see about that gut now. Not careful, them guts might roll out and we'll be pitchin' you in the deep," the man chuckled and winked.

Debalo didn't answer and just sat there with both hands on his wound.

"Go now, mate," the gunner called again, "If firing starts again, you might be a long time seeing the doctor. Just be sure he don't try to cook you," the man ended with a laugh that caught on with the rest of the crew. He jerked a thumb toward the ladder leading to the upper decks and Debalo slowly stood and made for the galley.

He slowly ascended the ladder, one hand on the rungs and his left hand on the wound in his side. Coming topside, he could see right away that several men had been injured and they waited at the door of the galley for attention. Looking about him he could see the other ship lowering a longboat over its side as his own crewmates stood watch along the starboard rail armed with muskets. There were signs of damage about, but none like he had expected to find. Splintered boards lay here and there and he could see that many ropes in the rigging hung loose and some dragged along the deck. The only real damage he noted was to the mainsail mast, which had received a hit from a cannon ball that removed a large portion of wood. He wondered how it could still be standing.

There were trails of blood all about the deck, leading to the galley where the cook had set up his hospital. As Debalo approached, a hissing sound and a muffled scream reached his ear along with a few loud curses afterwards. Moments later Daniel emerged from the galley holding his left thigh and wordlessly limped past Debalo.

Another sailor stepped in and Debalo watched as a red-hot iron was laid against a gaping cut on the man's forearm. It hissed and smoked and the sailor yelped and pulled away, retreating from the galley. A dead man was lying on the galley floor and the cook was busy moving about over the body of another blood soaked patient that was stretched out on the table. The patient was Bwana.

"Bwana!" Debalo cried out and moved past the others to get inside.

Bwana was unconscious and his eyes had rolled upward into his head. His left arm had been torn away along with part of his rib cage. The bleeding was not terribly bad due to the arteries having been seared shut with the hot iron. Debalo was sick and felt the vomit rising in his throat looking at the torn hulk that was his friend.

"Don't stand there gawkin' boy, give me a hand," the cook told Debalo. "This man's not going to make it.

I can pull the skin over the stump of that shoulder and sew it up with a little catgut, but there's not enough skin to pull over that chest hole."

Looking into Bwana's wound Debalo could see the lungs rising and falling with jerky stops and starts as the big man fought for breath, the pink organs jumping wildly. Amidst the torn flesh and bone, Debalo could see the top of the poor man's heart beating out a staccato rhythm.

"I know he's your friend, but he's dead already. It's best to put him over the side and let him drown. He'll not feel no pain," the cook told him softly.

Another hissing sound as another bleeding sailor's wound was closed with the iron.

"No. Bwana drowned still alive?" Debalo cried out in alarm.

Before the cook could respond, the patient came awake with a gurgling cry and began to struggle with his arm and kicking his legs. Two men rushed in and seized the legs and the cook grabbed onto the arm. Bwana cried out in a pitiful sobbing wail and tried to scream, but his voice was dying and weak. He continued to struggle weakly, writhing in pain, and Debalo grabbed his head and laid a hand on his blood-slicked stomach.

"Bwana," he called to him, "Bwana be still."

He continued to struggle and wailed again in agony.

"Kill him boy!" the cook looked up at Debalo who stared back in shock.

"It's the best thing for him. He's hurt too bad! End it quickly for him boy, now!"

Debalo stood there numbly, knowing the cook was right, but he couldn't do it. Another sailor stepped around them and taking Debalo's knife from its sheath, he slipped it lightly into the wound and neatly punctured the heart. A long stream of blood spurted forth, but the cook threw a rag into the hole and instead the blood boiled out around it and spilled over onto the already blood slickened floor.

It took only a few seconds before Bwana ceased to struggle and quieted, his big eyes rolling upward again in their sockets.

Debalo was horrified, but made no protest. One man grabbed a hold of the head and shoulder and another grabbed his feet. Bwana was carried out the door to the Gulf. Debalo leaned back into a pickle barrel and held his own wound, numbed by what he had just witnessed. He looked at the cook, blood spattered and sweaty, laying a hot iron on another man's leg. His mind was whirling, but not thinking. For the moment he wasn't capable of thought; he just leaned there against the rough wood of the barrel and watched.

"Let's see yer wound, Debalo," he was startled to hear the cook speak to him.

"My wound?" Debalo asked him.

"Aye, yer wound," he told him and took Debalo's hand and pulled it away. The bleeding's stopped, so you won't need the iron lad. Wash it with water from that bucket there and I'll sew it closed in a minute." He told him and walked over to another man Debalo recognized as one of the gunners and looked over his shoulder where he had been holding a piece of cloth to a nasty looking cut.

"Hand me that needle and catgut there Debalo," the cook called to him and he stepped forward to comply. The needle looked like a large fishhook and through the eye of it, the cook already had threaded about a foot and a half of black suture material.

Taking it from Debalo, the cook began pulling the sides of the cut together and sewing them back together. The gunner winced, but remained silent. He caught Debalo's eye once and a bit of a smile formed at the corners of the man's tightly pursed lips.

He waited for his turn to be sewed together, numbly sitting on the short fat barrel of flour, wanting to cry for his friend, but too tired and filled with pain to do so.

After the cook wordlessly sewed together the small ragged hole in Debalo's side, there was no time to rest. The galley had to be cleaned, the water buckets re-filled, and the crockery readied as the cook prepared the evening meal. The fat old cook was looking weary and drained as he went through the preparations of a large soup. Debalo wanted to rest and his movements brought forth the angry red monsters screaming in his side, but it was not in him to complain. He was tortured by the death of his friend, yet happy to have survived the horrid event; he was terribly confused by the conflicting emotions.

He had spent his life around death and knew its many evil faces, but Bwana's loss was more than that of a friend and companion; he had been Debalo's teacher and interpreter. His loss left Debalo more alone than he'd been since leaving the slave plantation and he felt the loss especially hard.

That night Debalo slept in the galley. So exhausted from the fright and horror of the day, his sleep was dreamless. When he awakened to find the sun lighting the galley window he felt a great rush of relief at having escaped the dreams, but soon after, the horror of the previous day flooded in on him and the weight of it crushed him. He felt as if the small room were shrinking in on him. He left out of the door as the cook was beginning to stir from his corner pallet. Debalo moved quickly to the foredeck and stood in the breeze.

The Spanish ship was nowhere to be seen. He had not left the galley after the Spanish surrender, so he could not know that the ship was then on its way to Barataria Bay for refitting, manned by members of the Renarde Rouge sailing crew. All members of the Spanish ship's crew had been given the option to join the crews of Jean Lafitte, be put ashore at the next available port, or to be lifted overboard at the discretion of the Captain. It was the second officer and twenty armed men that boarded the Spanish ship and set sail for the pirate base.

Daniel found him standing there by the railing and limped over as surly and irascible as ever. "Lost yer nigger, eh?" he asked with a low grumble. "I can't say I was glad to hear it."

Debalo looked at the man. His face was a mask of pain and the skin was gray and dull. "He was my friend."

"I know," Daniel said turning away, "it's too bad. In the least we could have gotten three-hundred dollars for him."

Debalo stared after the hateful man and felt the handle of the big knife at his side and thought terrible thoughts.

As the sun began to creep beyond the horizon, Debalo returned to the galley and was surprised to find two olive skinned men with dark black hair and beards. They both looked frightened as Debalo walked in and found them unstacking the crockery for the morning meal. The cook had set them to work and Debalo eyed them suspiciously and greeted them with a nod.

They nodded in return and one spoke a word he could not understand and they returned to their chores. Debalo took the nearly empty water buckets for cleaning the crockery after the meals and left for the starboard railing to drop them into the Gulf with a length of rope and returned them to the deck filled with the salty green water. As he bent to lift them, the red monsters again screamed out in his wounded side and he set them back on the deck and leaned against the rail. As he stood there, he took in the activity about him.

The sailing crew swarmed over the riggings and replaced ropes and pulleys that had been damaged in the previous day's engagement. Several sailors were busy with buckets and scrubbing brushes and cleaned the decks, and others were going about their morning routines of waking and meeting nature's call by hanging their denuded backsides over the side of the ship's railings. He spotted Daniel limping about and shouting out obscenities to a trio of Spanish sailors, crewmates of the two he'd encountered in the galley.

The crew was still in a fine mood and most wore the look of contentment, some even pleasure. There a few others, such as Daniel, whose wounds prevented them from enjoying the victory they had so eagerly pursued, but all in all, spirits seemed to be running high. Even though his own were as low as ever.

The gunner with the wounded shoulder walked past and chucked Debalo on the shoulder. "We'll be eating soon, eh?"

"Soon," Debalo reassured him.

"Cap'n expects we're to be near the coast of Florida. Gulls were on the horizon last night and he's set a course for Tampa Bay. Could be we'll reach it by evening."

"Tam-pa Bay," Debalo formed the word slowly. "In Florida?"

"Aye mate," the gunner assured him. "There's timber to be had there for the new main mast. That one'll never survive a storm, even with the sail stowed. We'll have the repairs to finish there and time ashore I'm wagerin'. Cap'n Hebert, he's in a high spirit."

"Time ashore," Debalo thought to himself. Then forcing a smile for the gunner, "Yes, I would like to be ashore again."

The rest of the day, Debalo thought of nothing else. Once on land, he knew he'd be able to slip off from the ship. He'd not been allowed ashore in the port city of Campeche, but surely, he could ask the cooks permission to leave the boat to fill water barrels or some such task for the galley as Bwana had done.

He felt a stirring of hope and his spirits lifted a little as he thought of his escape from the hated ship and the piratical crew.

SEVENTEEN

The heat of the galley was stifling beneath the noon hour sun. It was a small room and what space food and the fire pit, oven, and preparation tables hadn't already occupied took water stores. In the small bit of work area left in the cramped room Debalo worked silently alongside the fat cook, who smelled as rancid as the meat he was carving for the evening stew. The pain in his side was as angry as ever, but he suffered it without complaint. There was no one to complain to that would understand anyway, now that Bwana was gone.

Debalo was slowly becoming acclimated to the heat of the small room and for that he was sickened. He wanted nothing about the ship to become commonplace. He hadn't wanted to be aboard long enough to adjust to any of it. As he stood shirtless above the tub of dirty seawater, rinsing out the bowls and cups of the morning meal, he held onto the thought that he at least might have the chance to get away soon.

He was most comfortable without talking. It was a terrible burden to go through conversation in English. He was unsure of the words still and although he understood a great deal of the new language, there was always doubt about the words he selected to speak. He wanted to ask the cook about going ashore, but he held back from speaking it.

"Debalo," the cook addressed him, "let one of those Spaniards finish with that. You go rest and let that side heal, eh?"

Debalo nodded and turned to leave, and saw one of the sailors of the Spanish vessel waiting behind him in the doorway to take over his place at the tub. The cook pointed to the Spaniard and spoke sternly to him, "Marinero," then pointing back at the tub of dirty seawater and crockery, "enjuagar."

The sailor stepped quickly past Debalo and attacked the chore with vigor. The cook again dismissed Debalo from the galley and he made his way to the rear deck to a spot amongst the coils of hemp, placed near the starboard side railing. As he began to take a seat amongst the rope, he could see Daniel on the lower deck being half carried to the galley, presumably to see the cook. His wounded leg not once touched the ground.

He suspected that the dirty little man's leg was turning putrid. He had seen it many times before, when a man became injured, the wound could fester and begin to rot. He knew the foul smell well, for it was such a wound that had killed his father when he was young. He hoped for a moment that Daniel as well would die from a green stinking wound, but stopped the thought as soon as he began it.

What type of a man would hope for such a horrible death? Daniel may well be an intolerably miserable man, but even he did not deserve such a fate. He looked down at his own wound and felt around it for signs of the affliction, but found none. Relieved, he settled himself into a comfortable position and thought of asking the cook to go ashore.

He had not been there long when the gunner whom he had watched get his shoulder sewn walked over and joined him uninvited.

"I see you're getting about well enough, eh?" he asked Debalo with a closed smile.

"I am." Debalo answered.

"This arm's giving me grief, but I've been 'urt worse I 'spect. I can't fairly raise the arm 'tall, so the Capn's got me on rest for a few days. I've no complaints." He spoke without really looking at Debalo as if he didn't care whether he was listening or not. "Word's we're set for Tampa. It's a fine spot we're in. They's mosquitoes all about the coast. It's not likely we'll get in and out without notice, I'm thinkin'." He reached out and nudged Debalo on the arm.

"Those mosquitoes are stirrin' the waters somethin' terrible I'm hearin'. Afore we left Barataria, word came in of two of Laffite's ships burned to the water line and the crews hanged. We get boarded with these damn Spanish onboard; one of them's bound to speak up. I say, we pitch 'em overboard and let them swim a bit, that's what I say. Better them than us, eh?"

"Drown them?" Debalo questioned slowly.

"Aye, mate," The gunner replied, "if it comes down to it. No Mosquitoe can show us to be anything other than a trader, but if they's proof of piracy. Well then, the Admiral will see us all set to swinging."

"Because of mosquitoes? I do not understand?" Debalo told him with dreaded confusion.

"Mosquitoes, mate. That's what the navy's calling themselves. They're sworn to clear these waters of pirates once and for all. These have been open waters since anybody's ever sailed her, I say, but now that Florida's a part of the United States, the navy's gotten together a real fleet out wanting to claim the Gulf too."

Debalo didn't understand every word of what he was hearing, but enough was sinking in that they were in very real danger.

"How much longer to Tampa?" Debalo asked, misery crowding in on him.

"Cap'n says tonight we'll be along the coast and we'll enter the bay sometime tomorrow. They've a fort there now. We'll outfit and be off in a day or two I expect. Too bad if we don't stay longer; I could stand to have a woman again. There's places in Spanishtown Creek if'n you got a bit of specie about ya mate. I don't expect it'll do you any good, beein's they don't let no niggers lay with the wenches," cracking a bawdy smile he nudged Debalo again, "too bad fer you then right?" then he croaked out a low laugh.

"We will need water there?" Debalo asked the gunner.

"Aye mate. Never let an opportunity pass when the barrels can be filled. You never know what's to encounter after ye sail again. Run out of water, you'll be obliged to drink yer own piss or die for want."

Debalo cringed at the suggestion, but the assurance that the cook was expected to go for water raised Debalo's spirits. Certainly he would need help and Debalo simply nodded in response.

Another member of the gunnery crews limped over and joined them at the coils of hemp with a cheerful greeting, that Debalo did not understand, but which brought a low chuckle from the other. They spoke for a short while, ignoring the little African beside them before the third man spoke to him directly.

"That knife you've got there boy. Word tells that you've killed a few men with it. That so?" he asked him pointedly.

"Why ask me of that?" Debalo queried back in defense.

"Calm down boy, I'm just askin'. You don't look the type," he told Debalo as the two pirates smirked at his discomfort with the questions.

"Look the type? I don't know," he puzzled at the words, still uncomfortable, but much less defensive.

"He means, mate," the first gunner spoke up, "You don't look like a killer. Man carries a cutlass of that make, he out to know how to use it. You took Will's fingers, but could you keep it if another wanted it bad enough to try to take it from you?"

"No," he cast his eyes aside, growing very weary of the conversation.

"Trade it then," the second gunner spoke up. "I'll give you six dollars gold for it."

"I'll keep," Debalo answered, covering the bone handle with his right hand loosely. "What am I for gold?" he stumbled over the words with frustration.

"Think on it mate. You might want to get yerself a jug in Spanishtown," the gunner grinned and nudged him again with a happy chortle.

"Will I go Spanishtown?" Debalo asked.

"Up to you I guess. Ya get back in that galley, tell Ol' fatboy yer bound to go," He told him with a shrug.

"Will Daniel allow it?" he wanted to know, hope building within him.

"Daniel?" the two gunners exchanged an amused look. "That bastard's got a green leg. You don't have to worry about him much longer."

"I thought it," he said in a low voice, then rising from his seat, he told the other two, "I should I'll go see him," then left the two gunners chatting in high humor behind him.

He found him in the shade of the galley wall near the larboard side railing. What color had been in his dirty face, had drained away leaving his skin the color of raw fish and there was no small amount of perspiration trickling from his brow.

"What are ye gawpin' at?" Daniel squawked at him in a dry weak voice.

"I heard that you are not well," Debalo told him softly.

"I'll be dead in a couple of nights, I expect. Not wantin' to have no nigger rubbin' ma nose in it, so go on with ya!" he barked out with great effort.

When he'd finished his tirade, Debalo could see how tightly the man's jaws were clenched and could guess at the pain he was in.

"I am not happy for this," Debalo told him softly.

Daniel stared back at the stoic face of the little Masarwa and slowly let his temper abate. "Why did you come here then?"

"I don't know. I wanted to see you," he told him.

They remained quiet for a while and Debalo turned over a bucket and took a seat near the stricken man. The day was hot and there was little breeze blowing across the deck. The shade, usually provided by the billowing mainsail was not to be had due to the damaged mast, so he and Daniel sat in the bright afternoon sun. Neither of them really wanted the others company, but Debalo still felt obligated to try to make a peace with the man.

"Do you hurt?" Debalo asked with genuine regret for the man's pain.

"Aye," Daniel growled, squinting at Debalo, "hurt it does."

"Are you hungry? I could get food," he offered.

"No," he winced in pain as he tried to sit up a little higher against the wall. "Tell the cook I could use a bit of rum. You do that, damnit."

Debalo nodded and moved back to the galley and the small kegs of rum stored there. A moment later he was back sitting atop of the over-turned bucket watching Daniel sip from the tin cup. He thought how pathetic the dirty little man looked and how alone he must feel, knowing that he was dying and not having a friend.

"Where Daniel did was born?" Debalo was sure he was asking wrong, but still hoped that Daniel understood him.

"It matters not where a man is born, but rather where a man goes in life."

He thought on that for a moment and was sure that he understood the meaning before asking, "Where have you been?"

Daniel took another sip from the cup and with the sleeve of his shirt, wiped the sweat from his brow. He adjusted his seat against the galley wall and his face screwed in pain. "Been?" he asked with a cracked and weak voice. "What cares the likes of you, where I've been?"

Debalo didn't answer, he just shrugged his shoulders and waited for Daniel to tell him. Whether he did or not, didn't bother Debalo, but he knew that a man should have someone to talk to before he died.

"I've been across the world," Daniel began, hesitant to talk to him. "I know I'm dead in a night or two, but those that know me, if there be any thought of me once I'm gone, can say that; I been across the world." He paused long enough to take another sip of the rum. "You too, I'm guessin', but you were dragged across it chained up proper. Me? I went to see it on my own. I never missed the land beneath my feet. My home has been on the decks of a ship at sea. Huh, what sort of question is it to ask a man where he's been," he began slurring his already affected speech as the rum took a grip on him.

"I told you, you ignorant nigger, it matters where a man goes, not where he's from," he drained the cup and passed it back to Debalo. "Aye, it matters where a man goes. Yesterdays matter for naught, it's tomorrow that counts. My tomorrow will see me dropped over the side of this fine ship for the sharks and crabs to feed upon." He stopped talking and looked into the eyes of Debalo.

"Where are you going?" he asked softly.

Debalo didn't respond at first because he was still trying to understand everything Daniel had told him.

"Damnit all! I asked ye a question you stupid bastard!" Daniel exploded in a drunken stupor, and cried out with the pain that it caused him. He was sweating more profusely and his breathing grew uneven.

"I don't...Africa. I go back to home," Debalo answered.

"Get on with it then," Daniel croaked out. "D'ya hear me? Get on with it!"

"Yes. I hope to soon," Their eyes met and Daniel nodded once, then closed his eyes tightly for a moment.

When he opened them again, he said, "I don't want no more talkin'. You go on and stay away from me. I'll see another sunrise I expect. See me then if you wish, but now, I want to be alone." I will come to you after the sun rises," Debalo told him and took the empty cup and returned it to the galley.

The cook was opening small canvas bags of dried vegetables and pouring them into the big pot he used for stews and soups and sometimes his own laundry. The Spaniard was on the floor with a large brush scrubbing away at the wood and rinsing it with the dirty seawater he'd cleaned the crockery in.

The cook turned as he walked in and said firmly, "No more rum for that bastard. He's dead already, it won't do him any good."

"I did not come for more rum," Debalo told him.

"Good, we have to let it last. No sense in wasting it on the likes of him," the cook snorted out and Debalo was reminded of the man's lack of charity toward the dying.

"If it calms him, does it matter?" Debalo asked, ashamed for asking.

"What he needs I'm thinkin' is to be tossed over. His pain will end sooner that way," the fat man snorted again and turned back to what he was doing.

"Tampa tomorrow?" Debalo questioned the fat man, wanting no more talk of Daniel's doom.

"That's what they say, but we ain't even along the coast yet. Could be tomorrow though." He answered over his shoulder.

"I want to go on land for water," he told the beefy cook.

"More'n likely you've heard about the whores in Spanish town. There'll be none of that. Cap'n wants to get in and out of that port as soon as possible. If there's time, suit yerself, but don't be disappointed if you can't buy a whore. Them boys there is particular of what breed they lets lay on their wimmen." He laughed a chuckle to himself, then turning back to face him again. "You might could find someone to rent you a goat though," and he turned away howling laughter at his own disgusting joke.

Debalo didn't care that the man was foul at his expense. His spirits had been lifted to high by the knowledge that he was to go ashore in Tampa and once ashore, he expected to never see the miserable Renard Rouge again!

EIGHTEEN

By the light of the growing moon, which had risen high in the night sky, the Renard Rouge limped along the Florida coast in a generally northern direction until finding and entering the mouth of the large bay of Tampa. Late into the night Debalo awoke from another bad dream, sweat soaked and trembling. The night was quiet but for the soft murmur of the waves against the ship's hull. He listened to the night as he regained his composure.

There was enough light to see by and as he rose from his place of rest upon the rear deck, he could see the few sailors on duty now, quietly going about their nighttime chores. He thought of Daniel, as he lay dying near the galley wall, and wondered if he was getting any sort of rest in the night.

Debalo stepped to the railing and relieved his full bladder. He looked across the dark surface of the bay and could make out the shadowy outline of land. There were no lights visible from across the water and he wondered if this was the place they had been bound for. He walked forward, the length of the ship, stepping around the prostrate and sleeping bodies of his fellow crewmen.

He stood in the stem of the vessel testing the air of the night. What breeze there was, was blowing out to him from the land and although no fires were to be seen burning, Debalo could detect the smell of wood smoke in the air. It was a faint smell and his senses recognized the musky thickness to the smoke as that of a hardwood such as the oak trees he'd seen growing so prevalently in this new and foreign world.

Slumbering men were scattered about the deck taking advantage of the cool night air, but nearby was a large roll of canvas left unattended. He climbed atop of it and lay back, hoping to sleep again. The stars were shining brilliantly despite the light of the near full moon and not a single cloud was to be seen against the blanket of starlight flickering overhead. He had left his shirt in the galley and the legs of his well-worn breeches he had rolled up and folded above his knees. Always present was the wide black belt upon which hung the thick bladed knife so envied by his fellow crewmembers. He dared not leave it unattended for a minute. They could steal his shirt for all he cared, but not the knife. It represented the sum of his possessions and he did not wish to part with it.

He had given thought to gathering a few supplies to carry with him as he made his escape once on land, but he could think of no way to carry them and knew that such a thing would only draw attention to himself. He closed his eyes and thought of his escape from the plantation. He doubted there would be much of a pursuit, but knew he could not count on that. It was the unknown that was now twisting his insides into tight knots. He knew that he'd find a way to distance himself from the others, but until he was ashore, he could not make any plans.

He closed his eyes and tried not to think and just be content to lie there in the dark, but his mind was too full. As much as he wanted to sleep, he remained wide awake. He let his hand travel down around the wound in his side and explored it. The pain was greatly diminished and he knew he was healing fast. It should not become much of a bother if he should have to make an extended run.

Debalo continued to lie upon the rolls of canvas as the early morning dark began to lighten. The sun was approaching the horizon across the bay and Debalo could now see buildings and boats along the shoreline. There appeared to be the mouth of a river opening into the bay to the right of the buildings. As he watched, a long-oared craft emerged from the shadows and began a slow crawl across the water towards the ship.

He got up and made his way to the galley, as he knew the cook would be stirring already and readying for the morning's meal. He was stiff with fatigue due to his lack of sleep, but that was nothing new to him lately. At least the wound was healing and didn't hurt him as before. He stopped near the doorway of the galley and looked toward the wall where Daniel had lain; he was gone. He hadn't heard any splashes during the night, so there was a good chance someone had taken the pitiful man below decks, but it wasn't likely. It was a cruel and uncommonly indifferent bunch that he was sailing with and he could not wait to put as much distance between himself and them as possible.

He reached for the water buckets and walked over to the starboard side railing where he tied the buckets to a length of rope. He hauled up seawater for washing in the galley. As he knelt to untie the rope from the now full buckets a voice called to him quietly.

"Diablo," he looked up to see a Spaniard walking toward him. The man was young, about his own age, Debalo guessed. He tentatively reached for the buckets and finished untying the knots and lifted them to carry to the galley for him.

Debalo offered the young man a half-smile and said, "water is to galley for cook."

"Si, senor Diablo," the Spaniard spoke to him and turned back toward the galley leading Debalo to the door. As they entered the small, dimly lit room, Debalo could see the cook feeding kindling to a small fire he'd started in the fireplace with one hand while holding a steaming tin cup of coffee in the other.

"Let's be to work, now. There's a hungry crew to be risin' any minute now and we've a big day. You get that barrel of meal open Debalo and Juan, you get the crockery down," the cook barked out his orders and took another sip from the steaming cup.

The Spaniard stood fixed to his place, unsure of the orders due to his mis-understanding of the language. Debalo noticed the man's confusion as he went over to the barrel of meal.

"Vajilla, taza, ahora!" the cook shouted out to the Spaniard, then gave a conspiratorial wink to Debalo, whom despite himself, winked back with a smile.

It wasn't much of a meal provided for the crew, but it was over quickly and soon they were gathering up the crockery.

"Has food been taken for Daniel?" Debalo asked the cook as he filled the washing tub from the buckets of seawater.

The cook stopped what he was doing near the fire pit and turned to ask, "what cares you, about the likes of him?"

"I would not want to be hungry," Debalo answered with a slight shrug.

"No matter," the fat cook went back to his work, speaking over his shoulder, he told Debalo, "he went over the side last night. He's needin' no more food."

Debalo stood in silence for a moment, before resuming his chore wondering despite himself if Daniel had elected to go overboard or if he'd been helped by the merciless cook.

The crew began to come off the ship, six or seven at a time. As he jumped from the large rowboat behind the fat cook, Debalo thrilled at the feeling of the cold bay water and mud beneath his feet. Soon he was walking along the well-worn and muddied pathway up into the settlement around Fort Brooke. He was terrified, yet exhilarated to be on land again and his eyes swept the outskirts of the settlement, as much of it as he could see.

There were palm trees and tall oaks towering above the main buildings of the settlement, of which there were only eight he could see. Small buildings had been erected near the mouth of the river he'd spotted in the morning light while aboard ship.

He spotted a sea wall, erected from upright logs that had been buried at the river's edge to retain the soil.

The little settlement around the fort was much smaller than those he'd seen in Barataria and Campeche, but it did appear to be thriving. A sawmill was in operation far inland from the water's edge and the shrill whine of the saw sent shivers down Debalo's spine. It sounded to him like the scream of a witch and he knew better than to go too close to the loud machinery.

The sawmill's blade was hardly the only sound greeting the ship's crew as they entered the street of Tampa. The rhythmic falling of a blacksmith's hammer, the lowing of cattle in the small pastures cleared nearby, and the laughter and cries of rough men at work met them as they arrived. Debalo studied the people of Tampa as they encountered them and was very surprised at what he found.

Dark black faces were mixed in with the city's residents; the disparity in dress, and that the small building near the water had barren yards before them, confirmed to Debalo the presence of slavery in Tampa. His anxiety rose high and his mind began to reel with fear. What if somebody noticed his scarred right hand, what if...

He stepped closer to the cook and tried his best not to look concerned as they walked into the streets. Nearby one of the small pastures, there stood a dozen or more armed men, with long barreled muskets cradled in the crooks of their arms. These were men the likes of whom Debalo had not before seen. They were coppery skinned with fine features. They wore loin-clothes, long cloth leggings, and leather footwear. Some sported close fitting, turban-like hats similar to those he'd seen worn by Arab traders, but these men were clearly not Arab. A few of the turbans were decorated with long elegant feathers and they wore long, brightly-patterned shirts and scarves about their necks. Earbobs were easily seen on a few of the men standing with the gathering and Debalo suspected correctly that these were the natives of the land. They made up a handsome bunch and Debalo felt himself drawn toward them.

Debalo followed the cook toward a low building erected beneath the shade of a cluster of palm trees. It had the darkly weathered look of having been there a very long time and there was no door hanging in the frame. The cook called into the building and a short, yet thickly built, white haired man came waddling out. He appeared glad to see the cook and the two struck up a fast paced and joyous conversation after a quick shaking of their hands. Debalo didn't care to listen in on what was being said, he was busy looking about him for clues as to which direction he should sprint when he felt the time was right to make his run. He noted the direction of the river as it disappeared behind a screen of brush and he saw the tops of hardwood trees growing thickly in the not too far distance to the North of the river. He guessed that the hardwoods would provide enough shade to keep the undergrowth to a minimum and allow him to make better time.

A wide and well-used trail took off to the east and Debalo was sure that it would run fairly parallel to the river for a distance.

"Debalo, you listenin'?" the cook barked toward him. He turned his attention to the pair and the short man who reminded Debalo of a small buffalo was pointing to a pair of barrels, each standing waist high.

"Take these back to the boat. Just roll them easy, these lids are tight, but don't take a chance," the cook was ordering him.

"Just hold up," the buffalo man was saying to the cook, "that yer nigger?"

"Yeah, I picked him up in New Orleans a ways back," the cook answered, while giving Debalo a stern look.

"Why you let him go around with a pig sticker like that?" he asked the cook, pointing toward Debalo's knife.

"He earned it some time ago, so I let him carry it," the cook replied casually, then addressing Debalo, "get goin' boy, we got plenty to do. Get that grain over to the boats."

Debalo tipped one of the barrels over onto its side and began rolling it to the boat as directed. He understood enough of what was being said to know that the cook was lying to protect him. He was surprised that the fat man would do such a thing and he was grateful. He quickly returned for another barrel and looked quickly to where the Indians had been assembled and saw that they were retreating across the small pasture in the general direction of the hardwoods Debalo had spotted earlier. He was now certain that there must be a trail leading through toward the open forest and that that was the direction he needed to go.

He found the cook sitting on a crate talking and laughing with the buffalo man and neither gave him much notice as he tipped over the second barrel and started it back toward the boat. Upon his return there was three small wooden crates waiting to be carried back to the beached craft and Debalo carried them quickly away.

Several more trips back to the bufallo man's building and the cook declared that they were finally through gathering the supplies and walked with Debalo back to the boat. The cook sensed Debalo's unease and told him, "now is not the time."

"The time?" Debalo asked confused.

"The time to run off," the cook told him. "What, you think I don't know what you're plannin'? I see it in yer face as plain as day. I ain't gonna stop you. You don't belong on that ship, but you got to wait a bit yet if'n you plan on getting' away."

"When?" Debalo asked, too surprised to say more.

"Soon. The Capn's getting' that new mast loaded onto that longboat over there and they'll all be busy about it in about an hour. You go when they're busy and they'll less likely see you when you go. Give me a hand filling these casks with water," he indicated to a dozen or so wooden kegs, "When you go, I'll give you a head start before I start yellin'. I have to cover my own ass with the Captain. I saw you watchin' them Seminoles over by the pasture. That's Pacheco and his boys. He's got a head start on you, but if you can follow them and catch up to him, they'll take care of you.

"He's a scout for Colonel Brooke, but he grew up Seminole and his Mammy's a nigger sow, so I expect you can trust him."

Debalo listened carefully to all that the fat man was telling him and when he finished, Debalo asked him the only question that was running through his mind, "Why help me escaping?"

"Damned if I know...I 'spose it's easier than watchin' you sulk."

"Pa-che-co, he help me," Debalo asked him doubtfully.

"There's quite a few niggers mixed in livin' and fightin' 'longside them Seminoles. I reckon you'll do well to join him. If not, yer as likely to wind up getting' caught by some slaver or shot as a deserter. Florida's a big place Debalo. Go catch up to Pacheco and get Tampa behind you. If you can't find them, head south, across the river. That's Injun territory still, won't be no soldiers patrolling there least ways."

Debalo looked into the sweaty face of the cook and for a moment he had second thoughts of leaving. He had no one since Bwana's death to call on as a friend until then when the cook showed himself to be a friend indeed.

"I thank and remember," Debalo almost choked on his words of appreciation and his stomach began to twist and turn inside of him as he readied for the cooks signal.

Walking back from the well, each carrying a cask, the cook whispered, "Now!" to Debalo, who fell behind the cook, gently set down his keg and walked purposefully back toward the well. After reaching the well, he continued to walk in the direction the Seminoles had left the field and just as he reached the line of brush and trees that marked the field edge, he saw the trail as it led into the forest and at the same time heard the cook's shouts to stop.

He turned once to look back and saw a puff of smoke belch from a long rifle that had been leveled toward him and he heard a bullet sail past him, clicking through the brush nearby. He turned and ran.

The path was narrow, but well used and free from obstacles. He ran on, making good time, but pacing himself. He didn't bother to stop and listen for the sounds of pursuit, he just assumed that he would be pursued and that there was no time to waste. The trail did lead into and through a large hardwood forest, where the canopy was so tightly grown together, the daylight was shielded and the soil of the trail changed from soft sand to hard packed black earth. The air was cooler in the shade of the giant trees and it felt good to him, to stretch out his legs with the long strides.

He had been running for a little over an hour and had long left the hardwood forests near the river and followed the foot trail as it wound it's way through dense stretches of palmetto and pine, skirting around dozens and dozens of swampy sections of cypress, bay, and magnolia trees. There had been many other trails coming into and intersecting with the main path upon which he traveled, but now as he passed through a stretch of high, thickly matted trees with little red berries, he came to a very large intersecting trail, which ran fairly straight north and south. The ground along the trail was packed tightly and showed recent use. He studied the tracks and could tell that many horses had been by and more than one wagon track was plain to see.

He knelt for a moment and inspected the footprints in the sand. There were many that had been made by the hob-nailed boots of white men, such as the ones he'd seen around the plantation, others were more rounded with large squared heals, but atop of those were ten different pair of smooth leather clad footprints. He had counted a dozen Indians in Tampa and counted again, but still could only make out ten.

He stood where he'd been kneeling and looked northward along the trail in the direction the footprints led. He stood, breathing deeply, thinking about the two missing footprints and reasoned that two must have turned off of the trail onto one of the smaller trail forks he'd passed and glanced back over his shoulder. His eyes widened in fright and he jumped around, with his right hand reaching downward to the handle of the big knife, to face the two Seminoles standing behind him.

He was clearly startled by the unexpected appearance of the two Indians, but relaxed quickly as they began laughing. Both of them were leaning on the long barreled rifles they carried and wore very amused expressions on their dark faces. He stood quietly appraising the two as they in turn assessed him.

It was very obvious that they were in no way threatened by him, but he was so very confused as to whether he should feel threatened by them. Each of them carried a long rifle and as well, each had knives stuck in sheaths worn about their waists, and each carried a satchel and flask, which Debalo recognized was needed for reloading the rifles.

One of the Indians said something to Debalo, which he certainly did not understand and Debalo spoke a greeting in kind, "Jambo," he said in his native tongue.

One of the Indians raised his hand out toward Debalo with the fingers turned up, palm outward and spoke a few words in a calm voice. When Debalo didn't respond, he looked over to his companion and they shared an exchange of amused talk before one of them whistled loudly.

From a hundred yards down the wide, well used trail, the other ten Seminoles stepped out of the brush and came trotting back to where Debalo stood. He was both frightened and curious at the same time. He knew he should be embarrassed for missing the sign and walking into a trap, but he was too busy to think on that at the moment. He studied the faces of the men addressing him and he raised his hands and covered his mouth in a gesture of politeness, then bowed slightly. All of them were in a high spirit and were talking strange words amongst themselves.

There were two men amongst them whom were not smiling as carefree as the others and he addressed them first in his native language, which brought no reply, then he tried again in the new language, "Hello."

"You speak English then?" one of the two men whose faces wore expressions of concern asked him with a firm monotone. Debalo noticed the man's cold gray eyes above his high cheekbones and firmly set jaw.

"I do speak some," Debalo offered meekly.

"Tell me then, why are you following us?" the others grew quiet and listened intently for his answer.

"I follow for," he hesitated as he remembered the name, then slowly and carefully pronounced, "Pa-che-co."

The gray eyed Seminole stiffened slightly and told him, "I am Louis Pacheco. What is it you want?"

"I am told go Pacheco for help to..." Debalo let his words trail off as a couple of the Seminoles stepped closer. Their faces having grown quite serious, Debalo began to doubt the wisdom of trailing these men.

"Help to...escape?" Pacheco asked with a raised brow. "What is your name?"

Debalo understood the question perfectly and told them all proudly, "I am Debalo."

Some of them smiled again, but Pacheco remained unaffected and asked Debalo, "Tell me about yourself, Debalo. Tell me why we should help you make good your escape?"

Debalo nodded, but didn't answer right away. He had begun to grow uncomfortable under the scrutinizing stares of the Seminoles and he drew himself up to his full height and set his jaw before explaining.

"Not to escape. To live. I come here from Okavango in Africa. I work as slave, now I am no slave no more! I came to the Lafitte in Barataria and they take me to ship in Gulf and I will not go back. They say they are pirates and they hunt other ships as Simba, the lion hunts the Impala...like the deer?" he paused as he fought for the words, "They brought me to Tampa and I will not go back. My friend told me to come to you and I followed you to here," he finished with a shrug of his shoulders and an honest look into the eyes of Pacheco. He was unsure of their reaction to his words. Not all of them understood English and they watched the faces of the ones that did, but Debalo kept his eyes locked on to those of Pacheco.

"What do you want from me?" Pacheco asked him with a softening glance.

"I will not be slave. No slave, no more! I want to go home. I do not know where to go." He told him with a touch of the sadness that had been plaguing him.

"You will come with us then. We scout for the soldiers at the Fort and follow the trading routes between the tribes and settlements. I am as well, the interpreter for Colonel Brooke. We're traveling fast toward Tsala Apopka for a council with the Baton Rouge. The Army knows them as the Red Sticks," Pacheco paused. "What do you know of Florida?"

Debalo shook his head and shrugged.

"I thought so," Pacheco told him. "Come with us and I'll tell you what you need to know if you plan to stay with us. War is on the horizon and these are troubled times. Do you understand everything I'm saying to you?"

Debalo shook his head slowly, and answered him with an embarrassed, "No."

"No matter. I know someone that can help us overcome that," he reached out for Debalo's hand and shook it firmly, saying, "Welcome to Florida, Debalo."

His solid features broke into a wide grin and the others joined in with their own greeting.

Debalo relaxed as a wave of relief rolled across him. Any doubts he had about following these men he put aside. He would know in time what type of men these were, but for now, he was too happy to be back on solid ground and among free men.

NINETEEN

The Seminoles started up the well-worn trail to the north at a slow run. Two men had sprinted ahead a couple of hundred yards and two others remained behind and followed at about the same distance from the main body of warriors including Debalo. Even though he had run so far and so long already, Debalo had no difficulty matching the pace of the Seminole men as they followed the trail past miles of pine and palmetto flat-woods, large dark stretches of hardwood forest, and wildly tangled growth around the swamps and marshes.

As they ran, there was very little conversation, none of which was directed to Debalo. He spent his time reading the sign of the land about him, taking note of the landmarks in case he ever should pass this way again. As they ran, Debalo would take quick and subtle glances at his escorts, trying to read a little more about the character of the people in whom he had chose to trust an alliance. He noticed that these men were each healthy in appearance and kept themselves clean and groomed properly. That was definitely a difference between them and the white men he had met aboard the pirate ship, although the white men of Barataria had been of a similar quality to these men.

Their clothing, he noticed, was of good quality and certainly not ragged as that worn by the slaves and himself. Debalo had not given much thought to his appearance until now and wondered at the image he must portray to these men. He felt a little ashamed. He was in need of a bath, wounded, his hair matted and unkempt, and he was clothed in rags. As he ran along, he slid a hand up to his face and felt at the few hairs curling upon his chin. He had never had more than a few hairs to sprout upon his face and those he would pluck regularly, but he hadn't bothered in quite a while. He pushed his appearance out of his mind. There was nothing to be done about it then and it was no good to brood upon what he could not help.

As the sun began to lower itself to the western horizon, the two Indians whom had ran out in front slowed and then came to a stop, waiting for the others to gather up to them. Pacheco spoke a few words to them that Debalo did not hear clearly and they began to file through a dense palmetto thicket in single file until they were totally enclosed in the thickly growing bush. There did not appear to him to be a marked trail, but he could see that they were heading toward a small hammock of hardwood trees, where he guessed they would be making their camp for the night.

Arriving into a stretch of open ground bordering the hardwoods, the Indians began to go about the chores necessary to set up a night camp. Debalo jumped right in with the work, gathering wood for a fire and using his knife to cut away the tall grasses in the area to clear a place for a fire. The grass he kept to one side to use as bedding later.

The Indians went around gathering armfuls of dry wood to fuel the fire and cutting limbs from some dark green, low growing brush and arranging it for their own bedding. They talked amongst themselves and often a comment or question was directed at Debalo as they went sociably about their tasks. Pacheco kindled a fire quickly using a piece of flint rock and a ring of steel to create a spark which he caught in a small bundle of tinder he had carried in the wide leather bag hanging from his shoulder. He blew softly into the small nest of tinder until smoke erupted and quickly disappeared as a tiny flame licked skyward, eating hungrily at the dry twigs and grasses he added atop of the burning pile. Soon the flames were high enough to support themselves without constant attention.

Pacheco stepped back from the fire and took a seat close by Debalo and while the others talked quietly among themselves, they began to talk.

"Debalo, when you were brought here as a slave, where did you go?"

"I do not," he began slowly, for he was unsure how to answer, "ship came into a river and we were taken other places," he shrugged, then pointing toward himself began again. "Me, Debalo, walk with some a long time to plantation. We stop and we were kick and whipped to made walk some more. We go to the plantation and worked. It was not hard work, but it was not a man's work."

"If the work was not hard, why did you run away?" Pacheco interrupted him.

"Because I was not a man," Debalo told him, but was not satisfied with his answer. As he looked into the gray eyes of the Indian he tried to explain, "At plantation a slave is not a man. A man can go there," he pointed to the north, "a man can go there," he pointed to the south, "a man can go there and there," he pointed off toward the other two directions. Taking a breath he tried to explain further, "A slave can not go there, but only where told. Slave does what other man wants...can not be a man," he raised his hands palms up with a shrug and looked hopefully into the face of Pacheco for signs that he understood.

Pacheco glanced at the puckered scar adorning the palm of the left hand and nodded his undestanding; Debalo was pleased.

"Do you know where the plantation was?"

"No," Debalo tried to tell him what he did know. "I run and walk many nights. I came to big forest near good water and from there I met those who would help."

"Those who would help?" Pacheco asked him.

With a nod of his head, he began again.

"Runaways, too. They would help and two others and I followed the river to Barataria."

At this Pacheco brightened.

"Barataria," he said quickly. "The mouth of the river. The Mississippi River. You were in Louisiana territory. I've been there with the army to New Orleans. But now you find yourself in Florida. Still a long way from home, eh?"

"A very long way," Debalo agreed.

"I can well imagine that you've no desire to return to the white man's service, but where shall you go and what shall you do?" Pacheco asked him in a friendly way.

"I don't know," Debalo answered honestly and lowered his eyes to the ground as he thought over the question.

After a moment's hesitation Pacheco asked him, "Debalo, what did you do in Africa?"

"I am Massarwa," he answered, looking back up to face Pacheco. "I hunt for my village."

"A man accustomed to a life in the wilderness, eh? You might prove valuable as a runner, a messenger. You stay with us, Debalo, and I'll see to it that you are made to feel at home among our villages. There are other Negroes, like yourself, living free in Florida and among the Seminoles. Most are farmers or craftsmen of a sort, but there are some, like you, that bring in meat and soldier."

Debalo smiled in recognition.

"Debalo, Florida is on the brink of war. Do you understand the term, war?"

Debalo shook his head and bit lightly on his bottom lip as he listened and tried to understand.

"The white men have come to Florida and they take away Indian land as if it were their own and they tell us that we are not welcome in this land. The whites push harder and harder and they take more and more land. Each year their numbers increase and there are still more coming here. The Indians and the Negroes living as free men are forced to abandon their homes and fields to move farther away. The flood of the white man must be stopped or there will be no room for the Indian or the Negro. Do you understand this?"

Debalo nodded, for he understood quite well. It had occurred between many tribes of Africa and he had heard stories, as a child listening to his father and the other older men of the village, of many battles fought over such issues.

"Our fathers, Debalo, fought the white man in the territories up north. My own grandfather joined Tecumseh at the tall timbers. He came to Florida with others after the white man defeated them and drove them from their homes and lands. He was Ghonkaba, a sachem, or holy man, of the Cherokee Nation. He came here to join the Semi-nol-agee, the Wild People, as they were known. Now, I am Seminole and I pledge my service to the people here in Florida. "

Pacheco leaned forward and spoke more fervently.

"The white soldiers came through our town and asked for volunteers to scout and guide the soldiers. I volunteered and have been in the service of the soldiers for six years now," Pacheco saw that Debalo wasn't following him well enough due to the language barrier.

"You work for white soldier?" Debalo questioned.

"Yes," Pacheco answered, "I help the white men so that I can in turn help my people. For instance, we are being sent north along this trail to Fort King, so that I can alert the soldiers that there are a number of Seminoles joining the Red Sticks for war against the settlers. First we will stop by Tsala-apopka, the place to eat the trout, and deliver this message to Osceola and the Red Sticks.

"There are two companies of soldiers marching to Fort King to join them in hunting down Osceola. Once that news has been delivered to him, I go to Fort King and deliver the message," he grinned at his own cleverness.

"What if it is told, that you tell this man, Osceola?" Debalo asked.

"They will hang me," he answered. "Now, Debalo, let us have some tea and rest. The moon will be up around mid-night and we will continue then to Tsala-Apopka."

Pacheco got up and walked over among a few of the others and spoke quickly with them. The man whom had retained his seriousness upon their first meeting was seated nearby with a worried look upon his face. Debalo spoke to him, wanting to know more about the war Pacheco had spoken of.

"I am Debalo," he spoke kindly, "I am to ask for your name?"

"My name is Micanopy," the serious one answered.

Debalo nodded politely and repeated the man's name, "Mica-no-pee."

The man nodded with a slight nod. He did not appear to be in the mood for conversation, so Debalo offered a smile, but said no more to him. Clearly the man was troubled, but about what, Debalo could not guess.

He knew that he should be worried about this turn of events. He did not know these men, but already had entrusted his well being to them on the word of a fat pirate cook, whom he had not cared that much for anyway. It was only hours since he had left the hated Renard Rouge and much had taken place. Yet he was so happy to once again be upon dry land, he could not care at the moment where his travels might lead him.

One of the others of the group stepped over to where he was sitting and offered him a small tin cup of tea. Debalo accepted it in the polite, two-handed manner of his people and bowed slightly.

"Deebaloo," the Indian tried to pronounce his name while smiling in a friendly manner. He was a young man about Debalo's own age. In character he appeared to be Micanopy's opposite. He rattled off a few words to Debalo that he could not understand, then spoke over his shoulder toward the others. A ripple of laughter went up from around the campfire. Through sign, he was able to make Debalo understand that he was glad Debalo had joined them. Then he asked a few questions, which Debalo tried to understand.

The Indian seemed to be asking about his skill as a hunter, but Debalo was unsure, so he remained quiet, but very attentive to the young man's mixture of sign language with his foreign tongue. Finally, his curiosity got the better of him, so he called out to Pacheco for assistance.

"He's asking you if you think that you are man enough to travel with us to Tsala-Apopka. Can you keep up with us at a warrior's pace?"

Debalo looked back into the questioning eyes of his grinning companion and nodded while returning the grin. "I can keep up," he said.

The other Indian said something else to make the others laugh again and Pacheco translated it for Debalo, "He says, he doubts it. You have skinny legs."

Surprise showed across Debalo's face and the group laughed again at his expense. Even sour-faced Micanopy cracked a smile at the teasing.

"Tell him to set the pace when we leave out. I will stay beside him as long as he runs," Debalo told him.

The smiling Indian's smile widened at the reply and he pointed to his breast saying, "I am Renno," in broken English.

Debalo smiled and holding up his cup of tea said, "Thank you, Renno."

"Renno is the brother of one of our Micco's, or tribal leaders. His name is Coacoochee. He will be with Osceola in Tsala-Apopka with Juan Gavallo. Juan, the American's call him John Horse, is the leader of the maroons. They are a militia of free black men who refuse to give up their lands to once again be another man's slave. They're Africans like you."

Debalo shook his head, to show that he did not understand. Pacheco sat beside him again holding his own cup of tea and patted his shoulder, "When we get to Tsala-Apopka, there should be some among Juan's people that we should be able to find you an interpreter. Now, let's get something to eat and rest a little. We will have far to go tonight."

Debalo relaxed a little and sipped his tea. The others were staying quiet as they sipped their tea and ate small cakes of ground corn. Some were offered to Debalo and he ate them quickly. He noticed that his hunger wasn't lost on his new companions and more corn cakes were offered as well as strips of dried meat. He washed it all down with a second cup of tea. When everyone had finished their tea and corn cakes, they all stretched out long upon the ground and rested.

Nighttime had fallen and the temperature of the moist night air had dropped much lower than Debalo had expected. He had tried to sleep while his new companions rested nearby, but too much had taken place during the day and his mind was hard at work, trying to sort out and understand as much as he could about what Pacheco had told him. He was still awake when Micanopy arose and stepped a respectful distance away from the small band of warriors to relieve his bladder. Afterward, he stepped over to the nearest sleeping figure and nudged him with his toe to awaken him.

He walked around the camp, nudging each man in turn until he came to Debalo and could tell that he was already awake.

"You sleep at all, Debalo?" he asked, with a dry, but not unfriendly voice.

"No," Debalo admitted as he came to a sitting position, "I sleep only a little."

"You should have slept," Micanopy told him in a concerned voice. "You must learn that a warrior needs rest."

"I am well without sleep," Debalo, "I have a lot I thinking for."

"I know you do, but we have much hard travel ahead of us and you will want to keep up."

"I will," Debalo assured him, then coming to his feet, "I was raised Massawra, a bushman. My home is on the hunting trail, you will see," he reached a hand out and placed it on Micanopy's shoulder. Debalo could feel the man tense up at his contact and pulling his hand back he told him, "I will sleep when I told."

Micanopy nodded his assent and as soon as each of the warriors had readied himself, they slipped quietly through the palmetto field toward the open trail they had earlier traveled. At the trail's edge, they sat motionless for several minutes, listening. Debalo did not understand all the reasons for the extra caution, but soon two members of the party stepped out and began a slow run up the trail to the north. A few minutes later several more of them stepped clear of the palmetto field and took up the run, while two others remained behind to follow after a short interval in order to protect the rear of the warrior party.

Pacheco ran just ahead of Debalo and he matched his strides in time. To his right he saw that the smiling Renno was running alongside of him, carrying his long rifle over his shoulder with the butt-end of the stock skyward and holding on to it by the barrel. He ran smoothly and with an even stride.

This was something very familiar to Debalo. He had many times set a warrior's pace while going to or coming home from a far away hunting place. The pace of these Indians was what he had grown accustomed to since childhood and Renno's tease about his skinny legs was very similar to the teasing, playful way he and the other hunters would carry on before taking to the trail. He was comfortable with these men, despite the language barriers. He had learned already that time would resolve that issue. As for now, he was pleased to be traveling in their company.

A large tree had fallen across the trail and the runners leapt on to the trunk and off again, back onto the well-used trail. Debalo's feet landed lightly, avoiding making noise in the refuse of the fallen tree as if they had eyes of their own. He began to breath heavily and felt the burning pull of the big muscles in his thighs and long sinews of his lower legs. But he pushed past the pain and discomfort and soon his chest seemed to expand and his breath came more easily as he found his wind and adjusted to the trail.

He ran and was pleased to do it. Running had always been cathartic for him; it was in his blood to cover great distances with a tireless flow of movement. He felt he could run forever and as they ran, the trail began to turn more eastward. As he ran with Renno beside him, he remembered other times when it had been necessary for him to run in such a manner so as to cover great distances quickly. He could smell the fresh, clean air of the plains along the Monyumodzi River back home in Africa. He could feel it as if he'd been there just yesterday rather than having awakened aboard that stinking ship.

They ran for hours, past large hammocks of oak, skirting the swampy ponds of cypress, bay and magnolia, until the eastern sky lightened and showed promise of a new day's birth. The farther north they ran, the more hilly the trail became. The group crested ridge after ridge past the piney flatwoods of palmetto and scrub, until after bounding up one ridge and then casting themselves downward full tilt came to another line of giant oaks bordering a narrow river. Pacheco, still out front from Debalo, began to slow his pace and as they neared a treeline, Debalo could see that the two warriors that had ran ahead were kneeling down on opposite sides of the trail, their rifles at the ready.

One of the kneeling Indians gestured for the others to edge up slowly. Quietly, in pairs, each took up a position on opposite sides of the trail, facing a well-used crossing of a shallow river about twenty-five yards wide and moving slowly. The opposite bank had been disturbed by many foot prints and where water had been splashed up onto the bank, the newly risen sun reflected brightly.

Pacheco motioned to one of the warriors to move forward and he rose to a half crouch and slunk cautiously forward to the river's edge. He studied the far bank and stood erect, peering as far along the trail as he could before slipping back to Pacheco and the rest of the waiting Indians and Debalo.

This Indian spoke some English and he listened as the young man reported on what he had observed.

"Across the river is the camp of white men. They camped with no fire and have not been gone very long. They do not travel with horses."

Pacheco stood and led the others to the bank of the river. He spoke something to the group in a language Debalo didn't understand and stepped into the river and waded silently across. The others didn't move into the water. Debalo, not understanding that Pacheco had told the others to remain where they were, followed suit.

On the far bank were several different sets of tracks made by men wearing rounded toed boots with square heals. Debalo traced the tracks with a finger and studied the ground. Having been born to the job, he took in all he needed to see at a glance.

"No horses," Pacheco noted to himself.

"No horses, but many guns," Debalo told him, pointing to the marks in the dirt where several rifles had been stacked, leaning one against another. He walked off a little ways towards a small opening in the underbrush and came back to Pacheco as the others were wading across the river, "Two of white men sick."

"Show me," Pacheco asked of him and Debalo led him to the opening in the underbrush and pointed to the separate piles of uncovered human waste. Both piles were terribly watery.

"Not well," Debalo said, rubbing his stomach. "White men sick."

"Good," Micanopy spoke as he stepped close up to them. "These tracks were made by militia. They are not far ahead. We can catch them in a couple of hours," he said as a faint smile crossed his lips.

"No," Pacheco spoke with what sounded like regret to Debalo. "We must carry the news to Osceola first. If there is to be another war, there will be plenty of opportunity to kill militia. "

"Let us wait a while and travel until we come to the Withlacoochee. There we will turn toward Tsala-Apopka and meet with the counsel of Osceola and his Red Sticks."

Debalo did not like all of the talk of war and killing. He'd seen enough of that already to last him a lifetime. He also did not want to leave the company of these new companions. These were men he wanted to know better.

"Deebaloo," Renno reached out and put a hand on his shoulder. With a smile, he spoke haltingly in English, "good...run?"

Debalo understood that it was a question he was being asked and placing his hand upon Renno's opposite shoulder and answered with his own smile, "Yes, good run."

TWENTY

They left out of the white men's camp and slowly followed the winding road as it ascended a high ridge. At the top, Debalo waited with a few others as Pacheco and Micanopy crawled to the crest and studied the ground below them for signs of the militia men they knew to be somewhere out in front of them. Debalo studied the trail as he waited and noticed that one of the boot tracks had been dragging and he quickly surmised that the man leaving such a track, must have been injured or terribly fatigued.

He pointed the drag marks out to Renno, who signed that he understood and then jogged forward to pass on the information. Both Micanopy and Pacheco looked his way and offered a curt nod before returning their attention back onto the trail ahead.

Soon, they were descending the long slope of the trail, which led into a deep dark hammock of giant oaks and other hardwood trees. In the shadows of the open forest beneath the canopy of the ancient trees, ferns grew in profusion. Spiderwebs stretched upward from the carpeting of the ferns and attached themselves to the scattered saplings, offspring to the giant trees, whose canopy engulfed the sky above them. The tracks of the white men were still clearly visible in the moist, dark dirt of the forest floor and Pacheco called the others close.

"We are gaining ground on these men ahead of us and it is not wise to risk an encounter without Osceola's council. Florida's on the brink of war and I don't want to be the one to set it off. I say we follow this hammock to where it meets the river and follow the Withlacoochee to the bluffs. What say you?" he asked the others and Micanopy spoke first.

"It will take another four hours by that route. We must hurry to Osceola and tell him of the soldier's deployment. There is no time. Would it not be better to overtake these men, kill them, and hide their bodies?"

"It's not that easy. What if they get lucky and kill some of us?" Pacheco asked shortly. "We've all got jobs to do that cannot be done if we are dead."

The others remained silent and Debalo looked from face to face trying to read the thoughts of the other Indians, but he found no emotion to betray their feelings. Each man remained stoic, even the light-hearted Renno.

"We must go now to the river," Pacheco was saying, "I feel it is the best way. If you wish to remain with me, I will be grateful, but if murder is in your hearts, go then and kill these men, but know this; Osceola is meeting with the Indian agent, Thompson. If the meeting goes well and the treaties are amended, a war may be avoided, but if we follow and kill these men, any peace that could be, certainly will not be."

They stood for a moment letting his words sink in and Debalo, whom had understood enough of what was said to recognize that Pacheco was in favor of peace, knew that he would continue to follow him.

No one objected to Pacheco's reasoning and they started out beneath the canopy of the hardwoods in a direction away from the trail, towards the east. It was cool in the shadows of the hammock and they found a deer trail, which they followed at a fast trot. By necessity, the pace they had enjoyed running along the open trail had to be slowed along the narrow trail. There were many fallen branches littering the ground and the trail wound around and passed beneath some of the larger ones. They changed trails many times and the green ferns passed quickly as they ate up the miles.

Not many hours passed before the small warrior party reached the river and they paused along the shore for a short rest. Debalo took a seat at the base of a smooth barked tree and was quickly joined by Renno who was in the process of digging out a small parfleche of dried meat. He handed a piece to Debalo who accepted with a smiling nod and popped it in his mouth. The meat was dried, yet tender and had a sweet smoky flavor, which he enjoyed.

After only minutes of rest, just enough time for a light snack and for each man to drink deeply from the clear river, they started out along the banks of the river, following whatever trails they could. They were strung out single file as they jogged through the forest, quietly, but with a swiftness born of a life outdoors. In this manner, they continued to follow the Withlacoochee's northwest flow, until coming to an area where the wide river narrowed and was lined with huge stands of cypress and bay.

Water marks on the surrounding trees told Debalo that this was a year that the river was low in its banks and that at times the open forest surrounding them would be covered in water. With the river deep in its banks, it opened the land around them and the party was again able to pick up speed to a run and they again ate up the ground.

The sun had slid half way to the horizon when Pacheco slowed to a stop and signaled for the others to gather around him. He knelt amongst them and the others took to their knees and waited for him to speak.

"It is another mile or two to the west, where we will come to Tsala-Apopka. I do not care what your personal feelings about the different tribes are. We must not fight amongst ourselves. You must not be tempted into a fight, do you all understand?"

Each man nodded and one asked a question in words that Debalo could not follow and Pacheco responded with the same foreign tongue.

"Debalo," Pacheco addressed him.

"Yes," he asked.

"You are not familiar with the politics of this region, but you do know that these are dangerous times. There are maroons and Negroes expected to be present. When we arrive, you may remain with us, or join one or other of the different bands of free men as you wish. You've proven to be an excellent tracker. I hope you'll remain," Pacheco told him and then spoke something to the Indians he didn't understand and they all grunted approval. Renno leaned forward and slapped him on the shoulder good-naturedly.

"I am glad for being with you, I like run," Debalo told him.

A few of the men who had stripped their shirts during the run, brought them forth from the large bag each of them carried at his side and dressed themselves. Each man checked and rechecked his turban, hair, and gear to be sure that everything was in its place. Debalo recognized that they were preparing themselves to arrive amongst their people and wanted to make a good impression.

He donned the torn shirt he'd been given in Barataria and tucked it into the top of the baggy brown breaches he wore. He'd long thought about cutting the legs off of the breaches to just above the knee rather than fold up the tattered ends, so he pulled the big knife from its sheath and trimmed them. He replaced the thick belt carrying his knife around his waist and over the top of the pants. He snugged it up tight and adjusted the big knife until it hung at a comfortable angle holding his shirt tightly tucked into his waistband.

"Deeblo." Renno tapped him on his shoulder. "Knife," he said, pointing to the big bone handles with one hand and holding the palm of the other open, upwards. Debalo nodded and loosened the thong holding the handle in place and slipped the big blade from the sheath. Renno's eyes widened as he gently accepted the knife from Debalo.

He clearly was impressed and he made a couple of slashing and stabbing motions through the air with it. He smiled and handed it back to Debalo, who replaced it back into it's sheath. "Bonita, it…" He struggled for a moment with the words until Micanopy broke in.

"He's trying to tell you how much he admires that knife."

"So, tell him thank you," Debalo said.

"He understood you," Micanopy replied almost bored with the talk.

Debalo looked back to Renno who was nodding his head, then reached out and patted the handle of the knife. Renno lifted the long rifle that he carried and handed it over to Debalo to inspect.

He had some small experience with firearms and knew how the weapon worked, but had never fired one. This particular gun, when sat on the ground, had a length that brought the barrel to just under the point of Debalo's chin. The hole in the barrel was large enough to fit his thumb into easily, so he knew that the bullet fired from that gun would be large and deadly. The wooden stock came all the way to the end of the barrel and a wooden rod had been inserted into the wood, which Debalo recognized as the ramrod used to clean and load the gun. Renno had carved pictures of little bears all along the rifle's stock and all over it had a well worn look that told Debalo the gun was very old, yet it was in very clean condition, so Renno obviously had cared for it well.

He handed the weapon back to Renno and nodding his head told him, "Good rifle."

Renno repeated his words holding the rifle upwards, "Good rifle," then adding, "kill soldiers."

Debalo smiled to him, but wasn't smiling inside. He'd seen enough of death. He had seen it come in many forms, but when men killed other men, he thought that such a death was the worst kind of all. Men being killed and eaten by simba, the lion or by ngwenya, the crocodile, those deaths made sense. Those animals must eat, but there is no reason for men to kill other men that he could understand and as the little group headed away from the river toward Tsala-Apopka, he began to worry.

They left the open forest of the dry cypress swamps and climbed a low ridge into a country of pine and tall grasses. Palmettos grew here in isolated patches, but the land was fairly open and visibility was good. They spooked a small herd of deer and as they ran off, Debalo followed their bouncing white tails with his eyes and thought how much they reminded him of Impala, the medium sized antelope he grew up hunting.

He took note of their tracks as he passed over them and at a glance could tell they all were female. Since leaving the plantation, he had learned quite a lot about identifying the sign left by the animals in this new world. The sign he hoped to find most, however, was the sign of the bear's passing. He thought often of the bears he had seen before coming to Barataria and he did want to see them again.

Other than alligators, they appeared to be the only large predator in this new land, but they didn't carry that foul carrion smell about them, as did the predators back in Africa. He remembered the clean, almost sweet smell of the bears and studied the trails for their sign. He was so caught up in reading the ground that he nearly stumbled into one of the Seminoles as they slowed to a walk.

"We're almost there," Micanopy spoke from behind him and Debalo looked ahead to see the lead warriors stop to face a pair of armed black men, dressed in the same manner as the Indians.

Renno sped ahead of Debalo, nudging him as he ran and Debalo picked up speed to match the young warriors stride as they approached the sentries. The two leading warriors continued on past the black men as Pacheco and the rest of the group arrived.

The men were clearly glad to see Pacheco and his men arrive and after a quick exchange of pleasantries, Micanopy led the way beyond them and onto a wide and well-worn trail that led up a shallow ridge. Debalo looked back as he stepped out onto the road beside Renno and saw that Pacheco had lingered at each of the black men, grasping their hands in affection before trailing after the rest of them.

The road led beyond the ridge and through a wide plain toward the west where the sun was sliding slowly toward the horizon. Looking up towards the sun, Debalo spotted the first line of smoke rising out of the pine forest ahead of them. In no time they were entering a large encampment of both Indian and Black men. Many shelters had been thrown up around the area and in the center was a large open compound where several large thatched buildings had been erected. They had been made out of large sturdy timbers and covered with the leaves taken from the palms and palmetto that grew readily all about.

The largest of the thatched, open sided structures had several rows of half hewn logs situated around a large fire pit and Debalo recognized this as the council house. Several men were standing around it and Pacheco headed toward them with Micanopy in tow. A group of Pacheco's warriors gathered with them and others, both Indian and Black, came from different directions of the camp until the gathering had swelled to thirty or more. Renno took Debalo by the arm and gently led him away from the gathering and off toward a group of older black men.

Renno called out to the pair who turned and greeted him with warm smiles and hand shakes and introduced his new friend. These were tall men and powerfully built, wearing the same dress as the Indians, including the turbans adorned with flowing feathers of bright pink. Also, it wasn't lost on Debalo that both of these men carried rifles and the pouches of supplies to load them, as did the majority of the men he could see about him.

Debalo was a little shy to meet them at first, unsure if he would be welcome among them, but their enthusiastic greeting soon laid his reservations to rest. Both of these men were very interested in his escape from the plantation and in his plans for the future. They walked him over to a couple of hewn logs that were being used as seats in the back row of the central council house. He sat facing the both of them and answered their questions as best he could while taking looks over his shoulder toward Pacheco who was still standing amongst a throng of listeners.

"Now I am come with Pacheco. I go with Pacheco," Debalo told his audience as he ended his story of his travels after leaving the plantation.

"Pacheco is a good man." The larger of the two black men agreed with Debalo, "Osceola's counting on him to act as an interpreter and council to the white soldiers."

Debalo shrugged as he asked, "what is inter-pre-tor?"

"He knows all of the languages. He can talk for anybody," the man explained to him. Debalo thought of Bwana and the manner in which he relayed the words between himself and the young man they traveled with after leaving the gathering on the banks of the big river.

"Pacheco no can talk for anybody," Debalo corrected him, "He no talk my language Fanagalo. I am learn to English for talk in this land."

"No," the other man responded, "He can speak six languages. He's our best communicator and speaks for all of the Seminole."

"Are you Seminole?" Debalo queried him.

"I am."

"You black man. How Seminole?" Debalo queried further.

"My mother..." the man had begun to answer Debalo's questions when a cheer of approval set up over something Pacheco had told his listeners.

"Excuse me," the larger of the two black men stood up and grabbed Debalo's shoulder with a friendly shake, "I want to go see what's going on over there," he said as he stepped away from him and moved toward Pacheco's audience.

Debalo looked to the other man who was looking after the cheerful gathering.

"I do not know how is your name," he spoke to his companion.

"I'm sorry," the man apologized as he turned his attention back to Debalo, "My name is Charlie. My mother is Seminole, a member of the Bird clan and my father is a former slave. He escaped from a home in Alabama and came to Florida. I have lived free all of my life, but now Spain has abandoned the territory and slavery is coming to this territory on the heals of the white soldiers that remove us from our homes and tell us that we have no right to live free in this land."

Debalo was trying to follow along and understand everything that he was being told, but lifted a hand to stop Charlie before he became too confused.

"I hear you and am trying to know your words. Whites come to take you from your homes?" he asked with great concern.

"Yes," Charlie began again, "Florida has not been a slave territory, so for many years, ex-slaves and many Indians have come to Florida to live free from the rule of the white man. Many white men have lived here also, but they live as we have lived.

"Now, those who believe they can own another man as his own property are coming here. I will not become another man's slave and I will not give up my home, so I come here to fight."

Debalo's heart began to sink as he began to understand what Charlie was telling him. He thought of the Arab slavers that surrounded his village in Africa and the way that all of them who did not resist were chained together and led away, leaving those who would resist lying dead or dieing amongst the smoking ruins of what had once been a happy village.

He looked into Charlie's eyes, which were studying his own and shook his head.

"Do not let them come to your village," he told him. "Arabs brought me and my village to the white men. I was slave," and with fear and anger he vowed again, "But Debalo no slave no more!"

"There are many forms of slavery," Micanopy approached and spoke to them.

Turning to face him, Charlie asked what he meant by that as Debalo listenend carefully to understand.

"Then you will fight the white soldiers with us? The militia?" Charlie asked him in earnest.

"I am a hunter," Debalo answered softly and casting his eyes aside, "I no with skills of the warrior."

"You can learn. Killing white men doesn't take skill, it takes will!" Charlie told him with insistence.

Another cheer arose from the gathering near the council fire pit. The crowd had nearly doubled and Debalo could see that Pacheco was now standing upon one of the log benches so that everyone could hear his words.

"You were a slave Debalo," Charlie challenged him, "how can you not have the will to resist?"

"Debalo will resist," he replied.

"Good," Charlie told him then asked him sympathetically, "You must surely have seen the evil that the white slave owners are capable of, haven't you?"

Debalo nodded slowly at first, but thinking of the terrors he had witnessed, he stopped nodding and began to shake his head side to side.

"No," he began, "I have seen horror, but not by white men like by black."

"What do you mean?" Charlie asked him with a look of surprise.

"In Africa, it was Arabs came to take us away led by black Warrusha warriors. Overseers at plantation beat, whip, kill. They give little food, little water, much pain. White men not often were to be at plantation. Overseers lead slaves, not white men, but they allow it," he conceded the white man's guilt for the miseries of his people.

"It is happening all over the northern part of this territory, Debalo. White men want to gather all of the blacks and breeds, like me, with the look of the blacks and turn us over to the slavers. They are gathering all of the Indians and breeds with the Indian features and shipping them to another territory in Oklahoma," Charlie tried to convince him.

"You see that they must be stopped?" he asked Debalo.

"Yes," he nodded and looking off toward Pacheco. Renno came jogging over to the two of them with a wide grin and Charlie and Debalo stood up to see what all the commotion was about.

Renno spoke rapidly to them with words that Debalo did not know and he watched as Charlie's face grew bright. Renno lifted the long rifle he carried in the crook of his left arm and shook it with delight.

"Guerro!" Renno repeated a few times and slapped Debalo on the shoulder. Charlie repeated the word to Renno and added some more that was lost to Debalo's untrained ear and widened his grin as Renno moved off.

"What is happening?" Debalo asked with mounting alarm.

"The Seminole nation is going to war!" Charlie told him as all about them men began shouting and gathering in the center of the compound near the council house until Debalo was swallowed up in the sea of bellicose exaltation.

The evening was turning to nighttime and the crowd dispersed for a while, Pacheco invited Debalo to follow him to one of the smaller thatched shelters where a cooking fire had been burning with a large roast broiling above it and a large copper pot containing a thick stew boiled slowly. There were other men gathered around the fire, some eating and some caring for their weapons and all chatting quite enthusiastically.

Pacheco gratefully accepted an invitation of a meal for Debalo and himself and they both were served large portions of the roast on palmetto leaves and wide wooden bowls of the stew. The roast, Debalo recognized as having belonged to a deer, had been seasoned and cooked to his liking. He thoroughly enjoyed the stew and ate it with relish.

One of the men commented on Debalo's appearance and Pacheco mumbled something to him, which sent the fellow scurrying off into the dark, only to return minutes later with a pair of leather breeches and a spun shirt similar to the one worn by Pacheco himself. He as well produced a deer hide, which was spread out upon the ground near the fire and the clothing items laid upon it. Pacheco nodded his approval while Debalo looked on with much interest.

The other Indian mumbled a few things to Pacheco, who reached into his bag and produced a small sack of blue beads and laid them upon the deer hide. The other man shook his head and Pacheco then produced a twist of tobacco and a small pipe. Again the other man shook his head no. Pacheco appeared to study the clothing a moment further and picked up the sack of beads and replaced them with another twist of tobacco and two shiny round coins. The other man smiled and picked up his items as Pacheco claimed the clothing, which he then presented to Debalo.

Debalo was overwhelmed for a moment and covered his mouth in the polite manner of his people and bowed his head before offering his sincere gratitude. He took the items and carried them out of the light to change, but not before bowing again at the waist.

Pacheco was smiling as he told him, "You are welcome. If you are to travel among us, you should not be expected to do so in rags. Now go change and I will meet you at the council fire later."

Debalo moved away from the light and sought a secluded spot in the corner of the camp to change into the new clothes. It was time to work on his appearance. He removed his belt and knife and laid them gently with the new clothes and removed the tattered shirt and pants. He felt about on his face for the few curly hairs he'd not bothered about for some time and plucked every one he found until his face was smooth again.

He finally decided to cut his hair away with the big knife. He started carefully, working from the front to the back, scraping the keen edge across his scalp to trim the hair at the skin. He sat in the cool grass and continued to feel for and trim away all of the hair that he could detect on his head. He was bleeding from any number of nicks and cuts by the time that he was finished, but he would look more presentable at least, he thought to himself.

After wiping his scalp down with a handful of sweet smelling grass he crushed and rolled between the palms of his hands, he stood and dressed carefully. The leather breeches fit quite snug, but he knew that the leather would stretch and loosen after being worn a while. The shirt was a bit long and billowy, but fit comfortably after being held tight to the waist by the wide leather belt and the big knife sheath.

By the time he finished dressing, it seemed that the entire encampment had arrived at the council house. There were a few hundred Seminole warriors and free black men milling about together, quietly straining to hear the words of the speakers. He left the old clothing where it lay and joined the throng of standers by, trying to locate Charlie, Pacheco, or some other of the men with whom he was familiar.

Words were shouted from the far side of the gathering and the crowd parted across the burning fire pit and the Council of the Seminole Nation arrived and began to fill up the log benches.

The assembled Seminole council was composed of the wisest and most skilled warriors and chiefs from both the combined Indian nations and the leadership of the free Black men. Dressed in their finest ceremonial clothing they took their seats row upon row beneath the long rectangular council house.

The coppery skin of the Indians held little contrast to the black skin of their fellows. In honor of the occasion, many wore decorative leggings covered with colored beads and strips of metallic lace. Each man wore a bright scarf around his neck and some had donned brightly decorated cloaks of blue and scarlet about their shoulders.

Necks ears and wrists were adorned with silver medals and gorgets, chains, or bracelets and many wore earbobs of many designs. Some of the Indians wore turbans of fine cloth with a silver brooch at the front from which extended a plume of feathers, and others wore beaded head bands.

Pacheco stood before the gathered council and was the first speaker of the night. It took him only a half of an hour to describe the news about the soldiers being marched to Fort King to round up the Red Sticks and to welcome the Red Stick warriors to the council and introduce Osceola. He could have spoken much longer, but Debalo sensed that the crowd was in great anticipation to hear from the man Osceola.

Debalo watched intently as Pacheco was seated and a taller man rose from a seat on the bench and removed the blue cloak he was wearing before turning to address the gathering. He had fine features that showed up well in the firelight and from the distance Debalo could tell that the man had fire in his eyes and there was a look of confidence and power about him as he spoke to the council.

"I am Osceola. Hear me!"

TWENTY-ONE

Silence settled over the throng of spectators as every man leaned in close to hear. Debalo was acutely aware of the heat of the men around him and the energy that was coursing through them. He watched the tall Seminole pace back and forth as he waited for the silence to deepen. As he walked before his eager audience he looked into their eyes, one at a time, and held Debalo's eyes too for a moment, and in that moment Debalo felt a stirring in his chest. It was as if the man had looked all the way down into Debalo's own spirit and found his strength for him. As Osceola continued to parade before his followers, Debalo grew proud to be a follower of his as well.

"I come before you tonight," Osceola spoke slowly and evenly, "as your servant. I bring with me the warriors of the Baton Rouge, the Red Sticks and a pledge to stand together with you all against the spread of the white settlers from the states.

"Without our consent, the Fathers of the United States have claimed the land as their own. They claim that Florida is now an open range for settlers to homestead, but they have not asked us if we will allow this. They give away our land as if it is their right to do so and not once has a man among us been paid for that land which has been taken.

"My Indian blood cries out that it is an injustice for the whites to push always toward that which is ours; but there are some among us like Chief Charley Emathla who believes that in order to survive we must become more like his white neighbors. He has given me his council and my ears have heard him, but my heart tells me that he is wrong."

He paused as a murmer of agreement swept through his listeners and he waited for them to quiet again.

"Should we turn aside our hearts to our black neighbors who will not live as slaves to the white man? I will not. A man, regardless of the color of his skin is born to labor. To provide food and clothing for his family a warrior must leave his home, his woman, his children. There are times when he must travel far. When his hunt is successful, it is necessary for him to dress his kill, butcher the meat, preserve it by drying, and then carry it home upon his own shoulders.

"When he is engaged in this activity, which must be repeated time and time again, he will face cold, thirst, hunger, and the danger of accident, of being killed by a wild animal or by an enemy. Often he may fail. And yet he does not ever stop his labor."

"White men would prevent our Black brothers this life of labors to force them to become slaves to their own needs. They would deny them a family, the freedom to hunt and fish and live as they wish. They would deny them even the right to turn the land and plant the crops of a farmer. They deny them these things with chains and whips and hunt them with dogs should they try to escape their bondage and when they are found they are often killed slowly, so that others might fear."

He paused again and paced slowly befor his audience to assure that his words were sinking in.

"The Fathers of the United States have voted to remove the Indian from Florida to make room for the settlers of white skin. All of our Black brothers are to be made as slaves to the white man. To be bought and sold as cattle and the Seminole are to be removed to land the whites do not yet want."

"For years, the Fathers of the United States have sent to us Indian Agents to pass along empty promises and lies. They wish to live in peace and they offer promises, which are empty, so that they can steal even more Seminole land. I am here to tell you that the agent Wiley Thompson is dead. The man sent to us by the white fathers of the United States, who would initiate false treaties, will lie to us no more."

He paused in his speech as a murmur of approval and excitement coursed through the Indians and Blacks alike. A few shouted their approval, but they all quieted quickly as Osceola lifted both hands, palms outward, to quiet them before beginning.

"There is nothing to celebrate in the death of this man. I was glad to take his life and he died well, but there is nothing to celebrate. When the soldier chief in the white man's forts hear of this man's death, there will be many that will want to see me hang. There will be many that will want to see any Indian dead."

"Even now, my brothers, I have word of soldiers marching from Tampa's Fort Brooke. They are to arrive in Fort King to strike against us. I propose that the soldiers never make it to Fort King."

He raised his hands again to calm the crowd, which had erupted in shouts and celebration at the mention of his proposal. Debalo felt the crowd surge to and fro and he was nearly squeezed breathless amongst Osceola's jubilant audience.

"Hear me! Hear me!" Osceola was calling to the gathering beneath the palm-thatched roof. Pacheco and a couple more men of influence stood and helped to calm the congregation.

Debalo looked around him at the fierce pleasure the men were experiencing. They were eager to fight and Debalo felt that same doubt begin to crowd in on him. He had seen too much of death and killing and suddenly he realized that he wanted to be away. He understood their reasons for wanting to fight, but the images flashed in his mind of Bwana lying on the table, the torn body of the cannon gunner lying in the mess of blood and seawater on the floor of the stinking ship, the surprise in the eyes of Roundbelly as he reached for the knife that had plunged deeply and ended his life, and the pitiful remains of the slave he had buried in the stinking mud of the plantation.

Debalo turned to leave, but the revelers held him fast amongst them. So tightly were they crowded around the speakers that he could not escape their midst. Osceola and the others were regaining order and Osceola was shouting for their attention.

"Hear me! You must hear me my brothers!"

Debalo watched the tall man as he once again gained control of the meeting and Pacheco and the others reclaimed their seats. He was miserable with doubt, but he calmed as the powerful young man began to speak.

"It is time for us to rid ourselves of those who would ignore the treaties and take away our land and drive us away from our homes. It is time for us to rid ourselves of those who would tear apart our families and separate us from those whom we love. The Seminole nation must rise together as brothers. It is time for war!" He finished with a shout and both arms raised upwards, eyes flashing with confidence and power. Debalo's fear began to subside, but there was much he needed to contemplate.

As Osceola finished with a shout, the gathering exploded into shouts and whoops of support from the warriors gathered around the council fire. Someone placed more wood on the fire and it blazed brightly behind the Seminole war leader. Gunfire erupted at distant intervals around the compound. Over the din of the excitement Debalo could hear the chiefs calling the crowd back to order. In that moment he realized that the crowd had surged outward and he found room to turn and make his way out of the midst of the revelers.

He walked back to the place where he had left his rags and took a seat at the base of a large pine tree that grew there. He watched the shadows of the men moving about and swaying, silhouetted by the light of the council fire. The rest of the compound was alive with men gathered together and talking animatedly in groups here and there near much smaller fires. The gathering at the council house erupted again in a chorus of shouts and he wished that he had not left, but rather had remained to hear all there was to know.

He sat there beneath the tree and thought over his situation. He knew that he could easily slip off into the night and not be missed, but he felt drawn to these people. They were gathered to fight against the very evil that had torn his world apart and the world of his mother and extended family in Africa. It was a good reason to fight, but he hated the thought of death. It made him tired to think of it. Some doubt still lingered in his mind and that too familiar knot was building in his stomach.

He lay back against the rough bark of the pine and stretched out his legs in the fallen needles and closed his eyes. Sleep was difficult to find him with the noise of the encampment, but that was just as well. In the back of his mind he feared the nightmares and hoped that the dreams would not visit him that night.

Debalo padded softly along the narrow trail, tiny puffs of reddish dust spurting from beneath his wide calloused feet. He carried his spear easily across his right shoulder as he walked, the fire hardened point upwards, glowing gold in the fading light of the late afternoon. Wiping the sheeting sweat from his young forehead, he thought of a pot of soup he expected his mother to have on hand when he returned and licked his dry lips. He thought he could almost taste the sharp flavor on his tongue as he passed the deep, conbretum thicket, its waxy green leaves masking deep caverns of shade.

Terror grabbed his chest with the first report of gunfire up the trail, which was followed by a regular volley of shots. It was too close he knew, too close to the village ahead. He froze for a moment of confusion. No guns were in the village; the shots he was hearing could mean only terrible events were unfolding. He found his legs in a burst of adrenaline panic as he flew down the narrow, grassy trail. Debalo covered the last couple of miles to the village in record time.

The village was bursting with activity as he arrived, running past a group of tall Warusha warriors he easily recognized by their bright red cloth kept tied around their mostly naked bodies and the plumed ostrich feathers that adorned their war bonnets. They made no attempt to stop him, so he continued past until passing through the opening of the boma where he froze at the sight of dead bodies littered about the compound and dozens of Warusha standing about his people gathered in the village center. He then noticed the Arabs with their flowing robes and dark bearded faces bristling with knives, swords, and the long rifles he had heard earlier.

He froze again, unsure of what he was witnessing, when he was struck from behind. He flew forward and landed face first, sprawling in the dust of the village grounds. He rolled over to see that one of the Arabs was standing over him with a wickedly curved sword. He spoke a few words to some of the Warusha whom had come trotting up upon Debalo's appearance inside the boma. Before he could gather his wits about him, Debalo was grabbed up from the ground and dragged to the mass of villagers standing under guard of the enemy warriors. He was dropped at the feet of three older women and they assisted him in rising. He felt a large knot rising on the back of his head where he'd been hit and he placed a hand back there to ease the pain. It felt wet and he pulled his hand away to see that he was bleeding.

A few more guns fired nearby and the villagers wailed and screamed in their fear. The Arabs shouted orders here and there as Warusha warriors began setting fire to their homes and to the protective Boma encircling the living compound of the little village.

As the smoke blew about them and stinging ash settled upon them, the Arab captors began sorting through the villagers. Old and infirm members of the small tribal community were relocated to another area of the burning village and the others were beaten and shoved into line. Iron cuffs were laced around their ankles until they all were tethered together in a long line.

Many resisted, some quite violently, but those who struggled the hardest were merely cut down by a swing of an Arabian sword or by the lance of a Warusha warrior. One or two tried to run away when it came their turn to be placed in the chains, but they didn't get too far before the rifles of the Arabs belched out clouds of smoke and death.

The smoke of the burning village burned his eyes, but the tears Debalo had running down his cheeks was from the horror he was forced to witness. He twice was able to get a look at his mother, shackled about the ankle and holding her face in her hands as her shoulders wracked from sobbing. He cried out a number of times to tell her he was there, but a crashing blow from a club-wielding Arab silenced him.

Real terror had crawled within him and he could not think. He tried to reason with his own mind about what was happening, but he had no answers and his fright paralyzed his mind. He wanted to close his eyes to the blood spilled about the compound and the torn bodies of his friends and neighbors. He wanted to die himself rather than live in the horror of the moment, but was frozen to resist his captors from fear and confusion.

Before the boma had burned halfway around the carnage of what had been a happy village, their captors led them out and back along that same narrow trail Debalo had arrived on only minutes before. He did not know what was to become of the old ones separated from the rest, but for those in the long line of clinking ringing chains, a long walk to the coast with little rest and less food and water awaited. In fact, the only periods of rest were at times when some one of his neighbors should fall of exhaustion or lack of water. At that time, the others were forced to pause in their miserable march, while the Arabs would shout and beat the exhausted villager back to his or her feet, or take them out of the chains and sever the head of the victim with the swipe of the heavy swords they carried.

After the first one or two fell and were so treated, many would hold up and support those too exhausted to go on, the stronger working hard to save the lives of the less able. They were forced to continue the clinking drudgery of the shackled and forced marching on late into the evening and throughout the night.

Debalo walked until the skin around his right ankle was worn and bleeding. He could easily see that the ankles of the people in line ahead of him were faring no better. The sun had set on the marchers and they were rested only until the moon rose enough to light the way. They were placed back upon the trail despite the dangers of the African night, until the morning's light found them arriving at a city near the coast.

There had been several stops during the night and looking back down the line of marchers by the pink light of early morning, Debalo could see the obvious gaps in the line. There was little doubt as to the fate of the missing tribesman. As the morning light broke in the east and turned the sky from pink to a deep blue, the Arabian captors halted the march of the conquered villagers at a watering hole used by the local cattle. It was a shallow, muddy pond with black stinking water, but so great was the thirst among them, that they flung themselves greedily into the slimy mess, sucking and slurping desperately to quench their incredible craving for drink.

As the light of the morning sun brightened to full daylight, Debalo was able to sit in the mud, rubbing his ankles and looking about him for his mother. He soon spotted her sitting in the fetid muck of the pond. She was shackled amidst a group of other women and for the first time Debalo realized that they had been chained together in a segregated manner. He was linked to a group of men and his mother was tied in a separate chain whose shackles contained only women. Her face showed the strain of the past dozen hours and he began to cry again. He wanted to go to her and comfort her, but could not.

He was not the only one among the chained villagers to cry. All about him, sobs and pitiful whimpers of grief filled the air, but the penalty of crying out loud had been taught well to them and each of them cried openly, but with quiet resignation. None of them could know what lay ahead and Debalo was terribly confused. He could not understand the reason for the horrible treatment of his people, but surrendered himself to whatever fate may await him. He was far too fearful of the quick death he'd witnessed his captor's deal out to the few whom had resisted. Like himself, his chained companions succumbed to the will of the Arabian slave masters.

Shots rang out again and a cheer went up. Debalo opened his eyes from his troubled sleep. It took only a moment to recognize where he was and to get his wits about him and he lay back against the rough bark of the pine tree as yet another wave of cheers came from the open sided council house. He lay awake for a while, rubbing his tired eyes and listening to the sounds of the camp and thought back on his dream.

Debalo continued to lie still as he thought back on the day that his village had been taken away into slavery less than a year ago. As he thought of that day, he better understood the need for these men to fight against such happenings. He wished that he could have known that the slavers were coming that day back in Africa. He could have led his family and neighbors into the brush and hid amongst the mswaki, jungles of the Okavango swamps where the slavers would not follow.

He rose stiffly and stretched with a yawn. He did not know if he would ever again be able to sleep without troubled dreams, but thought it would be a rare pleasure indeed if he could. He straightened his clothing and brushed away the clinging pine needles and headed back toward the center of the encampment.

As he approached the council fire, he noted that the number of spectators had dwindled and he easily moved among them until he could see who it was that was speaking. He didn't recognize the old man who was talking slowly and gesturing wide with his hands. Debalo didn't stay to listen to him, for he recognized no one in the crowd and moved away back toward the tree he'd been resting against.

"Debalo!" he turned at the sound of his name and watched as a black form came toward him in the night. His visitor moved back toward the light of the council house and Debalo followed until he could tell that it was Micanopy who had called to him.

"We looked for you earlier, Debalo. Where were you?" he asked.

"I sleep. A tree over there," he pointed. "Why you are looking for Debalo?" he asked him and Micanopy waved him off.

"Pacheco wanted you, but he rests now. Debalo, do you wish to remain with us?" Micanopy asked him and studied his face in the low flickering light.

"I do," Debalo answered him. "I tell Pacheco so. I go with you."

"It's been decide that we're going to intercept the soldiers marching to reinforce Fort King. We do not have a rifle for you," Micanopy paused and asked, "Have you ever fired a rifle?"

Debalo shook his head no. He had been around them before and knew how to operate the things, but he'd never fired one himself.

"It would be best then, if you come with me. Pacheco is returning to Tampa to guide the soldiers to a spot near the river where they will die. I will be taking fifty men with me. Coacoochee will be there with twenty-five of the Red Sticks and Juan Gavallo will lead forty or more of the black warriors.

"There is work to be done during a battle that does not involve fighting. Until we get you a rifle, I'll need you to help with these chores. I hope I can count on you Debalo?"

Debalo recognized that the man was unsure of him, but was asking for his help, so he answered plainly, "I say yes. I go Pacheco, I go you Mic- a-no-py?"

"Good," the Indian smiled at him for the first time. "Pacheco leaves in a few hours, you go rest. It'll be two days before the soldiers will march up the river. There will be a lot to do in those two days. I will go now and find sleep myself. Thank you."

Debalo nodded and smiled as the Seminole war leader stalked off into the shadows from whence he had come. He liked these people. They reminded him of his own people. He would not want these people to endure the humiliation that his own had faced. He thought that he should have spoken to Micanopy about removing their families to the swamps and jungles where the slavers could not follow, but knew it could wait until tomorrow.

He returned once again to the large pine and lay down again beneath it. He adjusted himself in the needles and lay looking up at the dark sky above him. There was little moonlight passing through the high overcast of clouds, which also blocked out the stars. He could not be sure of the time, but knew instinctively that daylight was still a few hours off.

He dozed off a few times, but caught himself before he could drift into any restive sleep where dreams may torment him. Once he got up and found the ragged clothing he'd discarded earlier the previous evening and put it around him as a cover to ward off the mild chill the morning brought with it. He had wanted to slip off closer to one of the smoldering fire pits around the encampment to take advantage of the warmth from the coals, but thought it best to remain where he was for the time being. Until he came to know and be known better, he knew that it would be wise to await an invitation before approaching the camps of these sleeping men.

He had just dozed off again when he was nudged awake by Renno, who was wearing a wide grin on his face as Debalo awakened and looked up to see who it was that had disturbed him. Behind the happy Seminole, the morning sky was lightening as the sun readied itself to begin its ascent into the sky.

"Deeblo sleepy," Renno said in a humorous tone. "Pacheco ready go," he told Debalo as he reached down and offered his hand to help Debalo rise from his bed of pine straw. He stood and stretched out his muscles and exaggeratedly yawned for Renno's benefit.

"Jambo, Renno," Debalo greeted him in Fanagalo. "Vuku busuku!" he complained of the early hour in jest. Renno obviously didn't understand the language, but he responded good naturedly.

"Futi, mquanda buisa?" Debalo asked about food and pantomimed the act of eating.

Seeing this, Renno nodded vigorously and told him something foreign to his own ears and eagerly led the way. He had come to invite Debalo to breakfast.

Renno led him past several cooking fires until coming to one that was being shared by the warriors he'd arrived with, just the day before. Pacheco was not with them and it was explained to him that he already had left on his return to Tampa. Micanopy was lying on a grass matt a few strides away from the fire asleep and the mood around the fire-pit was quiet, but light-hearted.

One of the Seminoles Debalo recognized was smiling at him as he knelt over a pair of green sticks supporting thin strips of meat dripping into the small fire with a pop and sizzle and told him, "You look better today."

Debalo smiled to him and nodded, "I feel some better too," as he rubbed a hand over his newly shaved head and chin.

"I have some deer that will be ready soon and corn cakes in the bag there if you'd like," he told him nodding at a canvas bag to one side of the fire pit which was full of dozens of the round cakes like the ones he'd eaten that night on the trail."

He covered his mouth with both hands, in the polite manner of his people and walked over to the sack to retrieve a pair of the little cakes. Renno dropped cross-legged next to the Seminole cook and reached for a pair of the corn cakes himself.

Debalo nibbled on one of the cakes and tasted the sweet salty flavor of it and took a larger bite. His stomach quickly awakened and he took another big bite.

"I am Frank Billie. We were not introduced before. I have a family living in Coacoochee's village on the Caloosahatchee River. Do you have any family, Debalo?"

He stopped chewing and a pained look came over his face as he thought of his mother. Frank saw right away that he had asked a painful question and apologized.

"I am sorry, Debalo. I should not ask such a thing. You were a slave for a while, I understand. Am I right?"

"Yes, Debalo was slave, but no more," he told him with emotion. "Debalo mother taken as slave and do not know of where is mother."

He winced at the way he struggled for the words. He understood the language much easier each day it seemed, but the man's question caught him off-guard and he was having trouble answering him.

"You don't have to talk about it, Debalo. Have some meat." He offered Debalo one of the sticks and Debalo removed a strip of the meat. The grease burned his fingertips and he dropped it onto one of the cakes as Renno reached for a strip as well. Frank retrieved a pair for himself and they began to eat in silence until Debalo finished eating and then he asked Frank if he could ask him a question.

"When the slavers come to your village, could you not hide?"

"Hide? What do you mean?"

Debalo licked his lips and thought out the words before he spoke, "Run away for a time to where the slavers cannot harm you or your family. When they go, you go home. Is it not better than killing or being killed?"

"You can't hide forever, besides, I'm an Indian. The slavers will not come after my family, the soldiers will. And we cannot hide only to return later because they will not leave. They are going to force us to move away and leave our homes and our fields that we've worked our entire lives to build.

"No, Debalo we must fight."

"And if you die, will you not lose the home and fields anyway?" he asked

"Perhaps, but I will have an honorable death," Frank answered him wiping the juices from the meat on the arm of his tunic.

"Perhaps you are right," Debalo yielded to the man's logic, "there are times that I wish I died in Africa when they came for my village."

"I'm not willing to let it go that far, Debalo," Frank told him before taking a bite of corn cake and between chews told him, " The sachem, Osceola, says that we can run the whites out of the north. If we can beat them now, my home in the south will not be lost. That is why I am here. I will fight them now, rather than sit back and wait for them to come to me. All of us together, we'll end this war quickly. If we wait, others will go their own way and we will not have the army it is going to take to make the white soldiers see that they were wrong to come here."

Debalo reached for another corn cake and looked at the happy Renno who was stuffing a strip of meat into his mouth. He gave Debalo a quick wink as he continued to eat.

TWENTY-TWO

The next few days Debalo spent in the camp of the Seminole along the bluffs of the river were pleasant for him. The entire assemblage of the camp maintained the same high morale they had enjoyed that first night Debalo arrived and they all had learned that Osceola had declared war on the white men. All of the warriors gathered together, Black and Indian alike, and spent many hours cleaning and assembling weapons while visiting amongst themselves in a high humor. In nearly every spare piece of shade, small groups of the Indians sat crosslegged knapping flint arrowheads and building bundles of the arrows. Debalo had admired the short bows that they carried with them although he had no experience with the bow, he was familiar with the weapon and knew that in the hands of a vapable man, that it could be a terribly efficient weapon.

Debalo as well, began to assemble weapons. He made a long circular walk about the camp accompanied by Renno, whom was becoming more and more of constant companion, looking for a hardwood sapling from which to build a lance. He was searching for one about twice as tall as himself that didn't have too many branches and which grew straight so that it would be strong as possible.

As they walked, Debalo began to really enjoy Renno's company. They talked often, neither understanding very much of the other's language, but they still were able to communicate quite well by utilizing the sign language he observed to be in common use throughout the camp. Many of the Indians assembled represented several different languages, but the dialects overlapped enough that with the use of the sign language, communication in the camp was not a difficulty.

The Black men whom Debalo met and spent short visits with for the most part understood English and he was happy to be making new acquaintances. Several of these men spoke quite an assortment of languages, but the most common in use was the Gullah language that had come into wide use throughout Florida. Gullah, actually was a weird admixture of a dozen different languages including a few words and phrases of Debalo's native language.

During his walk through the forests near camp, he and Renno selected a few saplings to cut and shape for lances and while Debalo worked at shaping the wood into weapons, Renno would sit and watch. Often he would get up and inspect Debalo's work, sometimes offering criticism, but mostly he would give a nod and a smile signaling his approval. Sometimes, he would take out a piece of oily cloth from the bag he carried round his shoulder and spend a little time lovingly polishing up the battle scarred rifle he carried or spend time honing his knife to a keen edge.

Frank Billie came and joined the pair seated beneath a large oak tree on the third afternoon after arriving at the camp. Debalo was completing his work of shaping a lance shaft, using the heavy bladed knife and Frank accepted a seat next to Renno. He spoke a word of greeting to both Debalo and Renno and told them that Micanopy had called for their warriors to assemble on the riverbank the following morning. It was expected that Pacheco should arrive along the river, well to the south and east of the camp, and he would be leading the white soldiers from Fort Brooke.

He repeated everything for Renno to understand clearly and then paused to ask Debalo if he was willing to learn how to use a rifle. He instantly agreed. The long rifles were not much of a mystery to him, but he had never handled one himself and was very eager to become familiar with the powerful weapons.

Debalo finished the work he was doing and set the bare staff of the hardwood sapling aside as he gained his feet and joined Frank Billie as they walked through the camp to a large clearing about a quarter mile south of the camp where several dozen of the Indian and Black warriors had assembled with their rifles. Renno followed along and ran off to join a handful of warriors gathered together beneath the shade of a large tree and laughing out loud at some game they were enjoying.

Micanopy was instructing several Black men as they created palm sized blazes on the trunks of many of the pine trees that fringed the clearing. Frank explained that the blazes were targets for the riflemen to take a few shots at in order to check their aim. A little practice was also good, he explained, for the riflemen to increase their confidence before battle.

Debalo took it all in with great interest. He marveled at the number of rifles among the Seminoles and the differences between them. Most of them, when the butt was rested on the ground, would reach the top of the barrel near the breast of a standing man. Frank had left him to speak with a few others of the Black Seminoles and as he rejoined him, he inquired just how familiar Debalo was with the use of a rifle.

"I have seen used and I watch as they are loaded," he told him before adding, "then I was small," and Debalo held his hand palm down at the level of his chin to show the height he had been at the time.

"Well I'm going to start you from scratch," Frank informed him, but before he could begin a small group of the Black Seminoles led by Charlie, one of the men whom he had met on the night he had arrived at the camp with Pacheco's warriors, interrupted the lesson.

"Frank, you need some help?" Charlie called out to him with a grin.

"I always welcome advice from my brother," Frank called back to him with a smile and reached out as the two grasped each other's forearms in greeting.

"Ever use one of these?" Charlie asked and Debalo shook his head no. "Well then, this ought to be interesting," he said with a chuckle.

A rifle fired and Debalo jumped from the unexpected blast and turned toward the direction of the sound to see a man rising from his knee in a cloud of thick blue smoke. Many men standing behind him clapped their hands together and voiced their approval of the man's aim. Another knelt in the same place as the first man's smoke began to dissipate and raising his rifle, he fired a shot toward the distant tree line, which as well earned him the approval of the onlookers.

"Ready to try my rifle, Debalo?" Frank asked the intrigued little hunter.

Debalo answered with a slow nod. He was comfortable being among these people, but he was a little scared of actually firing the gun. In truth, he admitted to himself, that his biggest fear was looking foolish in front of his new friends. He fought back his doubts and reached out to receive the rifle Frank was passing to him. It was heavy and a little awkward because of the length, but Frank positioned his hands on the rifle and showed him how to carry it across his chest with the rifle pointed upwards in the manner he had seen many others carry their own rifles. Next, he taught Debalo to mount the weapon to his shoulder and to sight along the barrel, lining up the small apertures fixed to the top of the barrel in order to direct the bullets path.

Frank reclaimed the rifle from Debalo and instructed Debalo in detail, how to load and operate the weapon. Once the rifle was properly charged, he led Debalo and Charlie's group of onlookers up to the firing line where several others were now firing their weapons at random.

He instructed Debalo to kneel down then directed him to aim at one of the blazes that had been cut into the trunk of one of the trees. He mounted the gun with great caution and with his right hand, reached up and pulled the hammer back the way Frank had instructed. He took a deep breath and tried to hold the sights steady on the target, but they were moving all about. The rifle began to grow heavy and difficult to hold on the target, so when the sights next swung across the center of the blaze, he pulled hard on the trigger and with a swish and a bang, he found himself blinded temporarily by the cloud of smoke that belched from the end of the rifle.

He stood up with a grin and handed the rifle back to Frank and rubbed his shoulder with his left hand where the guns recoil had banged against him when it went off. Frank asked him, "How is your shoulder?"

"I am no hurt," Debalo answered and then asked the most urgent question on his mind, "Did I hit it?"

Before Frank could answer, Charlie stepped up and patted his shoulder and told him, "You weren't even close, but you did well. Frank is a good teacher and I expect you to learn fast. You'll be sure to get a rifle soon, then you will stand by the Seminole nation and kill many soldiers."

Debalo sobered a little upon hearing speak of killing men and responded, "I want rifle. I want not to kill a man," he paused a more shots rang out near by. "When hunting, Debalo has seen the good of a rifle. It is good to know the rifle to hunt."

Frank looked a little confused and asked him, "You have said that you will fight, no?"

Debalo, nodded his head, "Yes, Debalo will fight if there is need."

"I think what he's saying," Charlie interrupted, "is that he wants a rifle to hunt with, not to make war, but he'll make war if he must."

"Yes," Debalo agreed as he nodded again while looking up to Frank.

"Then you must reload the rifle to learn to shoot the rifle," Frank told him, then handed over the metal flask containing gunpowder.

Debalo took the flask and after removing the cone shaped cap from it, he filled the cap to the rim with powder and poured it into the muzzle of the rifle. Replacing the cap on the flask, he handed it back to Frank, who in turn handed him a lead ball about the size of the end of Debalo's thumb and wrapped in cloth, which he pushed into the end of the barrel. Then, as he'd seen done many times, he pulled the ramrod out of the hole in the rifles stock where it was kept beneath the barrel and used it to shove the wrapped ball all the way down the barrel until it was seated firmly upon the powder.

Replacing the ramrod into its position, Debalo lifted the rifle upward until it was cradled across his chest and he pulled back the hammer to expose the little covered pan where more powder was to be placed. Frank handed the flask back to Debalo, who placed a small amount of it into the pan and replaced the cover. Frank reclaimed his powder flask and then showed Debalo how to hook his thumb over the hammer and pull the trigger at the same time, so that he could lower the hammer back down slowly without causing the rifle to discharge.

After the rifle was loaded and uncocked, Frank and Charlie both complimented him on having learned the procedure so quickly. Charlie stepped closer and asked Debalo to kneel beside him. Once Debalo had knelt, Charlie knelt beside him and directed him in aiming the gun. He reached around him and pulled the stock firmly into Debalo's shoulder and corrected his form.

"line up the sights on the mark. Let them float over the target and squeeze the trigger. Don't pull it fast, but slowly squeeze and once the trigger releases, stay on the target. Don't move a muscle until well after the shot has taken place. You must give the bullet time to clear the gun," he directed and Debalo studied the target over the alignment of the rifles sights and squeezed slowly. Knowing what to expect, he didn't shy away from the noise of the powder igniting in the rifles barrel and held steady on the target as the cloud of blue smoke exploded from the barrel and swirled all around him.

Grunts of approval behind him turned into encouraging applause and Charlie slapped him hard on the back. When the smoke cleared enough that he could see the target, he could see that a large white hole had appeared in the bark of the tree, just inches above the blaze he'd been aiming at.

"I hit?" he pointed to the target with a grin.

"You hit," Charlie confirmed.

They stood and walked the few steps back to where Frank and the others were watching and Debalo returned the fine rifle. Before he could speak, however a cheer swept through the shooters and spectators throughout the clearing and they all turned to see Osceola leading a score of his Red Stick warriors into the clearing, each warrior bristling with weapons. Each man carried a long rifle, pouch, and knife like most of the other warriors, but these as well had small axes tucked into their belts, which Frank told him were tomahawks and many carried very short guns with curved handles Frank called pistols.

They walked into the clearing in an orderly fashion and it was clear to Debalo that these men were senior warriors. The sachem of the Seminole nation watched as his warriors each knelt and fired their weapons with a look of satisfaction. Many men gathered around him, but none disturbed him as he supervised the target practice.

Frank and Charlie both fired a shot each and were satisfied with the results. Debalo headed back to the camp as the sun began the evening descent toward the horizon, leaving the others to continue to watch the shooting. He went back to his woodworking beneath the oak and smoothed the long wooden shaft until he was satisfied with the results. The end, he still had to harden over a fire pit, but that was something that could be done later that night after the evening meal. He felt the balance of the new lance and it felt good, but after firing the rifle, it seemed terribly inadequate for battle.

Later that day as the evening shadows filled the sky, many dozens of the men assembled in the camp gathered together beneath the thatched roof of the council house. They filled the seats and those arriving late, sat cross-legged on the floor. One man in a black coat moved amongst them leading them in strange, soft songs that he enjoyed hearing. After each song the man would speak for a while about a child's birth.

Debalo had come close to listen to the singing and tried to understand what it was the black-coated man was telling them. He assured them all that Jesus loved them and wished them all a merry Christmas. When the singing ended the gathering slowly dissipated and Debalo spotted Micanopy and the several warriors of Pacheco's scouts heading over to the fire pit where they gather to eat and followed them.

Renno was already squatting near the cooking fire and had large slices of deer meat suspended from green sticks all around the fire as well as fresh corn cakes baking in an oven he'd built from palmetto leaves and mud. The best treat was a large pot of pumpkin soup seasoned thickly with special herbs and pieces of deer meat. Deep into the night they ate and talked of their homes and families and Debalo sat quietly and listened.

Even Renno, who seemed to always wear a smile, grew solemn and he took a seat beside Debalo and watched the fire as it danced its timeless dance. After a while they fell off to sleep as did Debalo, who dreaded the simple act.

The next day the small band of Pacheco's warriors had gathered near the river as had been directed and Micanopy led them south for several miles. They moved at the warriors pace, strung out in a single file line, moving soundlessly through the forest. As they ran, a few of the warriors positioned in the back of the line took turns bringing up the rear and each man carefully matched his pace to that of the man ahead of him, so that even though they were many men, they continued to move as one.

They pushed deep into the wilderness along the river, where the sweet scent of pines was strong and the fields of palmetto gave way to the darker greens of tall grasses and briar. They stopped near the edge of a large hammock of oak and Micanopy gathered them round as he spoke in a soft voice.

"Ahead is where the trail from Fort Brooke turns to the east and crosses the river. Pacheco is to lead the soldiers along the trail and will traveling in the lead as a scout. His arrival will signal that the soldiers are approaching. We must find a spot to meet them, which will give us the greater advantage," he paused for a moment and looked at four of the men including Frank Billie. "You go forward to the trail and follow it to the river crossing and be alert us of any movement. Do not fire upon any white men that may travel this way. The sound of gunfire may alert the soldiers and ruin our plans."

Frank and the other three moved quickly off toward the trail and Pacheco gave similar orders to four others he expected to travel two miles in the other direction to act as sentries along the wilderness trail and they sped off to their task. Micanopy then led the remaining handful of warrior forward until they reached the trail and careful not to leave any sign of their passing, the warriors fanned out along the trail where it passed beneath a wide canopy of oak and other hardwoods, which blocked out the sun so that the underbrush was sparse. Micanopy then directed the men to remove many of the smaller trees from the area, cut close to the ground and carried a hundred or more yards away from the trail, in order to open the field of fire for the many warriors whom would be joining Micanopy's small force by mid-day.

When the preparations of the battleground were complete, the warriors withdrew from the trail and rested in the shade of the oaks. After a few mouthfuls of dried meat and corn cake, Micanopy stood up and left them there as he made one last tour of the battle field to make sure all preparations that could be made, had been made. In the distance Debalo heard the calling of an owl and he noticed the reaction of the others including Renno and correctly surmised that the owl call had been given to alert them to the presence of the approaching warriors. No one spoke, but they each stood to look for the approaching warriors.

Debalo was the first to spot a flicker of movement far off into the forest and he raised a finger to point it out to the others and soon they all could plainly see the arrival of a large number of Indians, armed with long bows and quivers teaming with arrows and their Black counterparts carrying firearms of many descriptions. Renno flashed a grin at Debalo and whispered something he could not understand, then turned and slinked off toward the trail. He turned to see if Debalo was following and motioned with his hand for Debalo to come along, he intended to find a good spot before they all were taken and wanted Debalo to join him. He had no desire to witness the event, but Renno's good-natured insistence won out and Debalo followed him to a slight rise of the ground about fifty or so paces away from the trail. They knelt behind the trunk of a fallen palm tree and cleared away the leaves and litter of the forest so there might be no sound from any movement that may become necessary. They lay side by side, Renno readying a rest for his rifle and Debalo clutching his lance beside him.

Groups of warriors began to fan out all around them and conceal themselves amongst the trees and foliage of the hammock. A small number were seen climbing high into the tops of several trees overlooking the trail and they flattened themselves out amongst the branches. It didn't take long until all of the warriors were in place and the waiting began. Throughout the evening, Micanopy and a couple of the other leaders moved among the concealed warriors offering encouragement and urging patience.

Hours passed and the sun climbed ever higher and began to fall toward the horizon. Thirst became a nuisance, as he lay still and quiet beside Renno. A trio of men had taken shelter a short distance away and one of them noticed Debalo watching him as he drank from a leather-covered canteen. He held up the canteen and offered Debalo a drink and slid soundlessly closer to pass the canteen to him. He covered his mouth as he nodded thanks and turned on his side so that he might accept the water with both hands in the polite manner of his people. He took a few sips of the cool water and returned it back to the man who then offered it to Renno. Renno as well took a few sips and with a smile and a nod, passed it back to the man.

He smiled to the pair and returned back to his position as an owl hooted down the trail. At the sound of the owl, Micanopy and one of the other warrior leaders acting as sachem made their way through the warriors a last time before the soldiers arrived and the sound of hammers being pulled back snickered all along the trail for a few moments and they waited. Debalo was fighting back the twisting fear that had been building in his stomach. His body was rigid and sweat began to break out along his forehead. He raised a hand to wipe the perspiration from his brow and Renno flashed him a confident smile.

The wind, which had been blowing lightly all day, began to pick up a little and Debalo could smell rain carried on the breeze. He watched a large red ant walking along the rotting trunk he was hiding behind as it went about its business oblivious to the events unfolding around it. He glanced at Renno who nodded his head slowly to their left and Debalo could hear the rhythmic plodding of men marching toward them. As the sound neared, he could hear the rattle and clank of equipment and the sound of voices. Pacheco soon arrived at a trot and passed by along the trail.

Debalo watched him as he stopped past the last of the concealed warriors and knelt as if studying the ground. Soldiers appeared then, coming along the trail in a long blue line. They marched three men across and were following two men on horses. As they approached Pacheco, who was knealing in the trail, the column stopped and an owl hooted again. But this time, before the sound died away, the terrible thunder of a hundred or more rifles firing at once filled the air and a dense curtain of blue smoke hung thickly in the air. Renno's rifle was one of those fired in the opening volley and he rolled quickly to his side to reload the weapon. Screams filled the air as men died along the trail and the howling of the warriors around him sent tremors along the length of his body as terror enveloped him. He breathed the acrid stink of the smoke and recalled the horror of the canon fire while he carried sand in the belly of the pirate ship. Tears filled his eyes and he wanted to run away, but he did not know where to run to, so he huddled behind the log and waited. More shots began to ring out and the firing increased as the riflemen finished reloading and began to pick and select their targets.

Erie whistling and low twangs reported from all sides and the air filled with the flying arrows or the Indian warriors. Shouts and screams were everywhere and soon there was firing by the soldiers on the trail as they rallied themselves to face the attack. A bullet whizzed by clicking branches as it sped away and Debalo looked up over the log as Renno raised his long rifle and sighted on a blue clad figure busily trying to reload his own rifle. There were bodies strewn all over the ground including both of the men whom had been mounted on horseback. Renno's rifle belched flame and smoke and the man stopped loading his rifle and slumped forward across the body of another.

Above the smoke, a hail of arrows whisked here and there, like an angry swarm of bees seeking out tartgets, now cowered and desperately trying to rally themselves to meet the attack. Debalo ducked back below the trunk of the fallen palm and clenched his eyes shut tightly. His heart was pounding in his ears and his chest tightened up to where he thought he might not be able to draw another breath. His hands were clenched tightly around the shaft of the lance and more tears escaped his eyes as Renno fired, reloaded and fired again.

The smoke of the many rifles poured thickly over him and he covered his mouth and nose beneath the neckline of his shirt as he lay there beside Renno. Twice, the palm log shook violently as bullets impacted it near his head and he knew that they had been aimed for Renno, who was even then reloading for another round. An arrow skipped overhead, and clattered to a rest amongst the debris of the forest floor.

Slowly the firing died down and Debalo looked down upon the group of soldiers fighting to bring a small cannon into action against the Indians manning the far side of the clearing.

Renno grabbed Debalo by the shoulder and shook him hard as he yelled his name before leaping over the trunk of the tree with a terrifying shout.

Not wanting to remain alone, Debalo as well jumped up with a shout and followed Renno toward the soldiers on the trail. There were Indians and Black men alike charging down upon the last of the soldiers rushing to load and fire the small cannon and he arrived at the scene of the battle as Renno leaped upon one of the soldiers as he knelt to take aim at another Indian running in from the opposite direction. He sank his knife deep into the man's back, but the soldier leaned way forward and Renno's momentum carried him past his opponent.

Despite the ragged wound in his back, which had just begun to pour forth a flood of crimson the soldier righted himself on one knee and brought the barrel of the long gun down upon Renno, but before he could fire it, Debalo's lance struck home between the man's shoulder blades with all of the force the young bushman could muster. The point of the lance continued through the man's breastbone and pushed out the front of his shirt as he fell over gasping.

Debalo noticed the blood beginning to flow from the mouth of the dying man and watched his eyes roll upward into his head as he died. A few more shots were fired farther down the trail and shouts and war whoops of the victorious Seminole warriors replaced the dying screams of the white soldiers lying about them spread in grotesque poses of death.

Renno was back on his feet and ran over to embrace Debalo, who was far too stunned to return the affection his friend offered. Instead, he walked shakily back from the body of the man whose life he had just taken and fell to his knees beside the wheels of the carriage drawing the cannon the man had died trying to defend. The horse that had minutes before been drawing the small field piece was lying before him, dead in the harness with the body of a soldier fallen across its neck.

The smell of the blood and recently released bowels became too much for Debalo and he bent forward as wave after wave of vomiting overtook him. Renno helped him to his feet and handed him the rifle of the man he'd just killed and spoke a few words that he could not understand and shook his shoulder hard. Debalo turned back toward the bodies of the dead men lying scattered beneath the hardwood canopy. The shouts of victory had died down and the coppery smell of blood filled his nose and Debalo fell to his knees and vomited again.

TWENTY-THREE

The acrid stench of smoke from the muskets, blood, and vomit continued to assault Debalo's senses and his now empty stomach fought hard to purge itself further. He weakly regained his footing and steadied himself by leaning heavily on the long rifle Renno had presented to him. All around the trail beneath the cover of the hardwoods, both Indian and Black alike were engaging in the looting of the corpses and equipment of the soldiers for what booty they could gain. Renno called to him and catching Debalo's attention, he hurled a satchel toward him and shot a wide grin his way.

Debalo caught the bag and looking inside, he found a flask of powder and a dozen or more of the heavy lead bullets with which to load the rifle he was still leaning on. Various other items had been stored there by its previous owner, but their significance was lost on the small bushman. He started to toss a few items out, but thought better of it and left everything as it was. Slinging the satchel across his right shoulder, he picked up the rifle and walked over to the trunk of the palm tree he and Renno had hid behind. Reaching it, he looked once over his shoulder at the swarm of warriors picking and plundering through the remnants of the soldier detachment.

Far off along the trail, he could see Pacheco standing atop of one of the dead horses that had fallen in the opening volley. He was shouting and pointing, but clearly no one was paying much attention to him as he tried to regain control. Debalo sat down upon the trunk of the dead tree and studied the rifle he now owned. The wood was very dark and lightly scarred by use in the wilderness. The metal of the barrel was still a deep blue-black and had no silver showing through. Debalo correctly guessed that the weapon was fairly new and appeared to be in good shape.

He removed the ramrod from the rings, which held it firmly below the barrel and slid it gently down the barrel. It bottomed out with nearly three inches of rod sticking up above the end of the barrel, which told Debalo that the gun was still loaded. Replacing the metal rod back into it's proper place, he turned the gun over and observed that the action still had a charge of powder beneath the pan opening and that the flint was in good condition. There was no need to fire the weapon, so he lowered the hammer in the manner in which he had been instructed and sat watching the activity down on the trail.

The sun began to lower itself toward the horizon, firing spears of crimson and copper through the leaves of the canopy of trees. Renno came to where

Debalo sat quietly grieving and offered him a drink of water from a round flat container, which had been carried by one of the dead white men. He had been too miserable with lamenting to know how terribly thirsty he had grown until those first sweet drops of water passed his lips and he drank deeply.

Renno said something to him, pointing at the new rifle and Debalo offered a tight smile and a nod of his head as he returned the canteen. Renno stood up and motioned for Debalo to follow. They walked past dozens of dead and denuded soldiers and scores of the Seminole warriors sorting out their plunder. Renno quick stepped over to one in particular, who was sitting on the ground beside a pile of heavy wool blankets and speaking a few harsh words, confiscated a pair for Debalo and himself. The seated Indian scowled, but made no attempt to deny him the blankets. Handing one to Debalo, he rolled his lengthwise and draped it across his shoulders and the little bushman did the same.

Frank Billie called to them and they walked over to where he stood with several black men.

"Debalo," Frank began, "Pacheco has to run to Fort King and join Osceola in the attack there. By morning, this territory will be crawling with soldiers looking for revenge. It is his idea that you come with me to the south. Once we leave this place, we will go to Coacoochee's town on the Loxahatchee River and spread the news of this battle and the war, so that others may join us in this fight. What do you say to that?"

Debalo had difficulty finding his voice, but husked out a nodding reply, "Pacheco idea for me go to this place, I go." Then looking to Renno asked, "where will you go?"

Before Renno could respond, Frank answered for him, "Renno will be coming with us. He is at home along the Caloosahatchee."

Debalo was eager to leave the trail and it's bodies far behind. He was ready to travel far in any direction, and if these men were leaving, he did not wish to remain behind. He stood beside Renno and noted that the faces of the other men around him bore no traces of joy or celebration, but instead were tired and grim.

Pacheco came over to them and Debalo read the sorrow in the man's eyes, "Major Dade lies just off of the trail there."

"That is good. His reputation as an 'Indian Fighter' was not quite accurate for a man who died so easily," Frank said and looked off toward the covered body of the officer.

"I do not wish for him to be disturbed. He was a good man all the same," Pacheco told the men gathered there.

"It is my wish that you should go now to Coacoochee's town to the south. I will try to find Osceola as soon as I can and join him, but soon, I must return to Fort Brooke with word of this attack on Dade's men or I will never be allowed to travel among the white men again and we need to know their minds," Pacheco spoke with little emotion.

He turned away and walked farther down the trail in the direction of Micanopy. The barrel chested Indian was carrying a bundle of rifles across his shoulder and was wearing a wide grin.

Frank started off into the wilderness on the south side of the trail, leading his small escort of warriors away from the carnage. Once on the trail, Renno jogged ahead of the rest with Debalo hot on his heals and they set a blistering pace as they traveled through the hardwoods forests. There were seventeen men in all traveling behind them and they moved with ease through the lush foliage of the Florida wilderness. After a few days on this trail, the men began to know Debalo as a man of uncanny skills in the forest. For despite the differences in the foliage, he felt at home in the forest. Once as the group settled into a night camp on the banks of a small lake, Debalo disappeared into the woods and a short while later he returned with a pair of rabbits he'd discovered and clubbed.

When he returned to the beach, he found that Renno had caught a turtle, which was already stewing. The two young men feasted and shared their fortune with some of their companions. Others had elected to fish the lake and likewise were eating well that evening. The strips of dried venison and parched corn had long been eaten and now they traveled on what they could gather along the way.

Another day he froze in mid stride and crouched low to the ground. Renno had been trotting ahead of him and Debalo let out a low whistle, which upon hearing it, Renno slid to the ground quietly at the base of a large tree and waited. The others were quietly coming up on the two and Debalo stood slowly and motioned for them to stop and then slipped off to one side and disappeared. None of the warriors traveling in the group had any idea as to what the reason for stopping and maintaining silence, but their training told them to remain hidden and silent until the signal to resume march was given.

Time crawled slowly by for the assembly of warriors waiting on the edge of a thick pine and palmetto forest and there was no sound in the forest other than the occasional buzzing of a fly, attracted to the perspiration moisture on each man. Renno was out ahead of the rest of the main body of warriors and slowly he righted himself and looked back down the trail to see if he could get a hint as to what had caused Debalo to stop their advance when the roar of a rifle exploded nearby. The little bushman was completely concealed by the palmettos, but the thick cloud of smoke rising fifteen yards to Renno's right marked his position.

As the shot echoed through the pines, the crashing and thrashing of an animal mortally wounded, slowed and ceased in the thicket ahead of Debalo's position. Minutes later, the scrub and palmettos parted and the little Masarwa tribesman rejoined his companions carrying the body of a large buck across his shoulders.

Knowing that the shot could well alert an enemy to their location, Renno started off again to the south and east and ran for another six or seven miles before coming to the banks of a small river coursing through the heart of a high pine studded flat. There, Debalo all but collapsed on the ground beneath the weight of the large buck. Ignoring his own discomfort and fatigue, Debalo set aside his rifle, shirt, and possibles bag and readied to dress out the deer. He moved the animal closer to the waters edge and positioned it onto it's back and using the large knife, he slit the skin open from the groin to the neck and cross cuts along each leg and began to peal the skin down each side.

Once the skin had been cut all the way down to the ground level on each side, he made a small cut in the animals groin and inserted two fingers into the cut to act as a guide for the tip of the sharp knife as he opened the body cavity to reveal the entrails, which he offered up to any who wished to receive them. Several men stepped forward and each walked away with a choice cut. The heart he selected himself and carried to Renno whose ever-present grin widened further as he accepted the choice organ.

When all of the entrails had been picked over, the remnants were slid into the waters of the river and the carcass was then divided up amongst the warriors, again Debalo saving a large piece of the favored meat for himself and Renno. As Debalo washed himself clean of the deer's blood in the waters of the narrow river, his happy companion prepared the cookfire and started cooking the meat for their supper. They ate well that night and it was clear that the opinions of the quiet little man and his capabilities had risen higher yet.

That night as the cooking fires burned low Frank Billie joined them for a visit and brought out his pipe. They sat cross-legged on the ground and remained quiet as Frank filled his pipe from a small pouch he carried in his large bag some of the men referred to as their "possibles" bag. After tamping the tobacco into the bowl, he lighted it with a small coal fished out of the fire pit. He breathed deeply of the aromatic smoke and passed the pipe to Renno, who was seated on his left side. Renno as well drew on the pipe stem and breathed in the smoke before exhaling it upwards in a slow stream.

Debalo received the pipe next and followed the example of his two companions. The smoke burned as he drew it deeply into his lungs and to his dismay, he began to cough. He fought hard to regain his composure and recovered quickly before passing the pipe back to Frank, who drew once again on the pipe and passed it again. The passing continued until the tobacco was spent, then Frank quietly cleaned out the pipes bowl and it was returned to its place in his possibles bag.

Only after the pipe had been put away did he speak, "You move through the forest like an Indian. I have watched you and you take care to be silent as you move. I understand that you were not a warrior back in Africa, but you move like one. How is that?"

"I am a hunter. My father was Bantu and was warrior, but he teach Debalo to hunt. To kill animals, not people," he replied

"The skills are the same though aren't they?"

"Yes. The same, but it is the will that is not the same," he answered him.

"How so?" Frank queried.

"I do not know to tell you," Debalo tried to find a way to explain what he meant. "I kill animal for eat and tool. I am glad to do this for village, for people," then pointing to a piece of meat leftover from the evening's meal of venison, he had provided, "deer dies for us and has purpose. Kill a man, there is no purpose."

"Yet, you have killed a man, Debalo," Frank told him. He watched the almond shaped eyes of the dark little man as they narrowed.

"Yes," he told him, then asked impatiently, "why you are asking me of these things?"

"Because, Debalo. I want to know where you stand," Frank eyed him with intensity, "once we've made all necessary arrangements for the town and all is well with our families, we will take the war to the soldiers. We will kill them all Debalo and you are a man whose skills we can use."

Debalo looked down into the dying fire and they grew silent again. Renno spoke a few words in his own strange dialect and then repeated Franks words, "kill them all." He smiled over at Debalo who didn't return the toothy grin.

"Our homes and families are in danger Debalo. You have lived it already. I don't want my family to live through what you have."

"I want only to go home," Debalo told him miserably, "but if I must remain here, I will live as you live and fight as you fight. I ask this of you," he hesitated trying to find the right words.

"If there is another way, find it. Home, warriors fight against warriors of other villages. Bantu, Masai,

273

Warusha, all fight. They fight before Debalo, they fight before Debalo's father, they fight before that. If there are any left after the slavers come, I know they will still fight. There are many ways of dieing. Do not create another if can be another way."

Frank let it sink in what Debalo was trying to say and solemnly assured him, "I will always try to find another way. But, the soldiers and their leaders are determined to see all of us rounded up and accounted for. I will not stand for it. Tomorrow we will come to the town of the bird clan near the Caloosahatchee River and will warn them of the war so that they may begin the preparations for their defense, if needs be."

"What pre-per-a-tion means?" Debalo asked.

"It means that they will lay in enough meat and material that they will not go hungry in our absence. Extra wood will be brought inside the village so that the women and children do not travel far into the woods when there is danger about. Fields must be harvested and extra grain stored away. We must pass the word to all of the towns that war is declared and let all of the young men know that it is time to take the warriors path."

"We will hunt then?" Debalo asked.

"We will. Can I count on you as a hunter for the towns?" Frank asked him.

"You can," Debalo assured him, relaxing now that the talk had changed from killing. He did not want to talk of it any more, it was bad enough that it visited him still in his dreams, he certainly didn't want to think on it during the day as well.

"Once we cross the Caloosahatchee, we will come to the traders road. We will follow it to the town, from there, we will go to the big water, Okeechobee. There are many small settlements around the lake and soon we will come to Loxahatchee.

"And I will hunt?" Debalo confirmed.

"Yes," Frank answered. "We will need much meat."

The answer satisfied Debalo who returned a smile to the still pleasant Renno and began to relax. Soon Frank left them and as the coals continued to glow red in the fire pit, Debalo stretched out on the ground where he had been sitting and tried to sleep.

He awakened well before the sun and shivered from the cold air of the early morning. He reached out for the wool blanket Renno had procured for him and wrapped it about his shoulders. He stirred in the ashes of the fire pit for a live coal and added a handful of dry grass to it. At first the grass only smoked and Debalo found the smell pleasant. It finally ceased to smoke and a small tongue of flame licked upwards to devour the grass and to that flame Debalo added a handful of small stick and soon had the fire kindled to his satisfaction.

Wet swirls and splashes at the waters edge caught his attention and he remembered the entrails of the buck he had placed there last evening and quickly jumped to the opposite side of the fire, keeping the flame between himself and the small river.

"Ngwenya!" he thought to himself as fear began to swirl in the pit of his stomac like the sound made by the feeding reptile.

He reached over for the rifle he'd kept loaded and flipped up the striker to see that there was priming powder still in the frizzen in case the ngwenya came ashore towards him. He rose slowly to his feet and over the fires glow he could see the red glowing eyes of the alligator peering back at him. The gator, having become aware of Debalo's presence had stopped feeding on what had remained of the buck and lay still in the water returning Debalo's stare.

"Deebalo," Renno spoke quietly to him, then snaked his hand out from beneath his own blanket and wrapped it around his rifle, lying beside him.

Debalo, waved him off, then pointed to the water and told his friend the source of his alarm, "Ngwenya. All-gat-or!" he hissed through clenched teeth.

Renno withdrew his hand from the rifle and pulled it back beneath the blanket and muttered something that Debalo didn't quite hear.

The little bushman, lowered himself slowly into a squatting position and pulled the blanket tighter about his shoulders and tried to relax. He listened to the splashing sounds as the alligator resumed feeding and watched the fire continue to burn as he held closely to his rifle.

The sun did arrive eventually and the warriors began to stir. Each man retired into the privacy of the forest to relieve himself, before breakfast was consumed rapidly and the march southward resumed again.

Crossing the shallow river, Debalo had the highest level of caution as he was intensely alert for signs of the alligator, which had finally left before the sun fully brightened the sky. As he ran at the warriors pace through the tropical wilderness, instinctively finding cleared areas to land his feet so as to move soundlessly, he thought of the similarities he found between this new land and that of the land of his birth.

It was true that he could make himself comfortable in this wilderness. The animals were very different, but could be hunted the same. Now, he carried with him a rifle with the ability to kill at a far greater distance than he'd ever have been capable. He took note of the various game trails and tracks as he traveled. The area was rich with deer and more than once he spotted areas of ground overturned from the rootings of wild hogs, like those he'd seen penned on the Plantation.

There was still very little sign of any large predators and he thought to ask about that when they next stopped for a meal near midday. Predators were a big part of life in Africa and he and his fellow villagers had lived with the constant knowledge that each day might well be their last.

He looked up from the ground, where he studied the terrain for quiet footing, in time to see Renno leap sideways, with arms flailing as he shouted. Debalo froze in his tracks as did the others and they knelt in the palmetto scrub to await the cause of Renno's alarm. Renno appeared soon wearing his usual grin and motioned for them to come up with caution. Debalo approached with confused caution, but was even more puzzled by the low buzzing sound coming from the brush directly in front of Renno.

"Rattler," one of the other men called out to the others and they all relaxed and came forward to walk around the large diamond patterned snake coiled into a pile of scaly muscle. He noted the wide triangular head with the pits above the flickering tongue.

Debalo was very willing to walk in a wide arc around the serpent and resumed the run with Renno, now in the rear of the line of march. He was impressed by the relative calm displayed by the warriors when passing the snake. He well knew the fear that caused such a panic in men at the mere mention of the names Cobra or Mamba and thought these men either brave or foolish to show such a casual familiarity with a poisonous snake.

Stopping for water along the edge of a cypress rimmed pond, Debalo spotted the tracks of a large cat in a muddy spot near the waters edge. He likened them to the tracks of ingwe, the leopard, but saw that they were noticeably narrower and would have been made from an animal weighing near ninety pounds.

Attracting Renno's attention, he pointed to the tracks and Renno nodded and pursed his lips and mumbled a word Debalo didn't understand. Another member of the party, an Indian with a scar running from cheek to cheek across the bridge of his nose, stepped over to see what was attracting their attention and looked over at Debalo and told him, "Puma."

"Eat of men?" Debalo asked.

"It has been done, but they eat well of the deer and smaller animals," he told him, "Puma will be no danger to us, you will see."

"And bear?" Debalo asked the man.

"Bear must be respected. He has great strength and has been known to kill men, but if he is left alone, it is not often that brother bear will give you reason to fear him."

Renno said something to the man, who chuckled and spoke at length to Renno and they both shared a good laugh. Seeing Debalo's confusion, the scar-faced man chuckled again and patted Debalo on his shoulder and walked off to where Frank and the others were preparing to resume their travels. Renno pointed at the track, then took his arm and led him over to the others grinning.

"Deebalo, like puma?" he asked with a chuckle.

Debalo didn't understand what was so amusing, but he was sure that they were mocking him for fearing the large cat. He marveled at how unconcerned these men were to the presence of predators. "They wouldn't survive the night in Africa," he thought to himself as he joined in the run again and resumed the mile-eating pace they would maintain until late evening.

TWENTY-FOUR

The temperatures were dropping noticeably and the midday sky began to grow dark. The group of warriors arrived at the banks of a wide shallow river as the first cold drops of rain began to fall. None of the men complained of the inconvenience, but accepted it with stoic indifference. Renno showed Debalo how to carry his rifle in a manner so that the lock containing the priming powder was beneath the wide leather flap of his possibles bag to keep the lock as dry as possible. He stressed the need to keep the powder dry in order to prevent the weapon from misfiring.

They turned onto a narrow path paralleling the river for a time and late in the day arrived at a narrow place in the channel. The rain was still falling lightly and the wind had turned onto them from the north and carried a stinging chill to it. Debalo quickly understood that this was where they intended to cross to the opposite bank as his companions began to step down the low bank and wade cautiously across. Each man held his possibles bag, rifle, and blanket high above his head and Debalo followed their example.

On the opposite shore, they headed toward a large oak hammock and began to set up camp. Lean-too shelters were quickly erected with their backs to the wind and a hunt for dry wood and kindling began. Soon a large pile had been gathered and fires were started. By this time, however, many of the men including Debalo were shivering terribly from the wet and the cold. Renno, whose company Debalo expected and was grateful for, worked at building a fire in front of the small lean-too he and Debalo would share while Debalo finished putting the final touches on their temporary shelter.

Once the fire was blazing and in no danger from the little rain filtering through the canopy of trees, both men removed their wet clothing and suspended them from the opening of the lean-to facing the fire so that the clothes might dry. Renno stuck a handful of palmetto leaves into the ground, standing upright, on the opposite side of the fire. The leaves served effectively to reflect the heat more towards the pair shivering beneath the saturated blankets.

Debalo began to warm considerably and as his comfort grew, so did his exhaustion. Sleep was still something he dreaded since the dreams continued to haunt him. He knew he must rest some in order to be able to continue pushing himself to travel with these warriors of the Seminole. He continued to lay awake, however, until long after Renno's breathing had slowed and evened, which told him that his companion was asleep. He closed his eyes to the black moonless night, his mind conflicted with the want of sleep and the fear of it. When fires had burned low to smoldering coals, Debalo fought to clear his mind, hoping that tonight the dreams would not come again.

Debalo sealed his eyelids and gradually he faded into sleep. He knelt at the edge of the mukwa, or hardwood forest, with the green curtain of vine hiding the beast from his sight. He sniffed the air and the familiar, urine-tinged animal smell reached his nostrils. The wind was still in his favor, so he remained still, not wanting his presence to become known.

He knew that it was there, and he knew that he was close, but still he could not see it. He wondered how anything as big as a jumbo, or elephant, could be so hard to spot in the brush. He had no intentions of wandering so close to jumbo, attempting instead to skirt the heavy timber for an opportunity at one of the small antelopes he had hoped to find there. Debalo recognized the gurgling sound they made to let others in the vicinity know where they are when he heard it.

It obviously had been resting in the shade of the trees when Debalo arrived on the scene. He hoped to be able to make out which direction the elephant's head was facing, knowledge that could serve him in making his plans to retreat without alarming the giant. Normally jumbos are content to shy away, but when startled at such close quarters, they do often react with aggression, usually stomping whatever poor creature had the misfortune of disturbing them.

His mind raced as he knelt there in the tall grass. He knew that climbing was out of the question. Too many men had found out that jumbo's trunk can still reach them as they scramble up the tallest trees. Outrunning one was certainly not a sound choice. An elephant's shuffling gait looks awkward and slow, but he knew that was not the case. A running elephant could easily overtake a man running on open ground. His best chance was to slip away undetected and try to put as much distance between himself and the jumbo as he could without ever having disturbed its rest.

He moved back a few inches at a time, slowly and quietly retreating to a safer distance. His heart was pounding in his chest and he fought to control his breathing. His first impulse had been to turn and run, but he felt that he had made the correct decision. As fear pumped adrenaline throughout his young body, Debalo felt a tickle of wind against the back of his neck and his pounding heart stood still for a moment as he realized the wind was changing against him.

Debalo froze again and readied himself to run. With a trumpet so loud it hurt the young Masarwa's ears and reverberated through his stomach, the elephant broke free of the cover of the forest's edge and halted for a microsecond before its fist-sized eyes detected the form of the young man sprinting away through the tall grass of the African plains. The huge ragged ears of the giant bull jumbo swished wide and the trunk drew back, coiled against its chest, waiting to strike out to capture the fleeing form. In the next moment, it charged.

Daring a look over his shoulder, Debalo was overwhelmed in terror and amazement at how unbelievably fast the giant gained on him. He saw great clumps of dirt and grass exploding from beneath his smashing feet as it ate up precious yards. Debalo looked ahead of him, desperate for any route of escape; he redoubled his effort with an intense will to live. He traveled fewer that ten more strides before he felt the rough weight of the tip of the trunk crashing into his back...

Debalo awoke with Renno's hand on his shoulder shaking him gently. His breathing was ragged and he swallowed and cleared his throat.

"Deebalo," Renno spoke slowly. "Deebalo."

He removed his hand from Debalo's shoulder, who continued to lie in the complete darkness, still wrapped in his moist wool blanket, wide awake and feeling the cold air as it slowly returned. He listened to the quiet night and soon Renno's breathing told him that his friend had returned to sleep. Debalo felt ashamed at having had to be awakened from the terrible dream, but was very grateful that he was.

He reached over Renno and picked up a small pile of pine splinters and tossed it onto the lightly smoldering bed of coals. The rain had stopped falling and the temperatures dropped lower. As a small flame flickered brightly, he could see his breath reflected in the fire's light.

By the light of the burning pine splinters Debalo was able to crawl over the prostrate form of Renno and retrieve an armful of wood that he fed into the flame.

Once the fire was again throwing its heat beneath the roof of the lean-to, Debalo returned to his blanket and lay awake listening to the crackling of the fire and the light wind swaying the tops of the trees. He tried to remain awake but it was of no use. After a long time his eyes closed again and he slept, although his was not a restful sleep.

They rose with the sun and crouched close to the fire pits, taking advantage of the warmth while they breakfasted on a few strips of dried venison. Debalo wished that there were more of the corn cakes he had grown fond of. He also thought of the gourds filled with egg soup his mother would prepare for him and missed her terribly.

He asked Renno in Fanagalo, since he didn't understand him anyway, "do you know how to make bird egg soup?" His breath hung heavy in the cold morning air.

His friend grinned and nodded before answering something equally unintelligible to Debalo who returned the grin and nodded as well. They hadn't yet begun to work out a common language, but it had not become a problem for them. They still managed to get their point clear to each other when it was necessary.

Debalo chewed the last of his venison and stood upright arranging the blanket around his shoulders. Many of the others were nearly ready to return to the trail and Debalo left Renno to walk over to where Frank was standing with his backside toward a dying fire.

"Rest well, Debalo?" Frank asked him as he walked over.

"I slept," he answered. "We are to be in town today?"

"I expect we will this afternoon. We'll have a meeting with the men of the council and explain all that has taken place. Why?"

"You ask Debalo to hunt. Debalo hunt while you are in town?"

"We won't be there long. We will leave in the morning to spread the word to the other towns on the way to Coacoochee's. I'll want you to hunt for sure when we get there. We'll be wanting a lot of meat dried and set aside. If soldiers come this far south, the smaller villages will come there." Frank pulled his own blanket tighter around his shoulders and blew a long stream of steam from his mouth. "There are a lot of deer around the fields after dark. If you just want to hunt, I will ask the Micco, the leader, of the town to see if meat is needed in any home," he told Debalo.

Debalo shrugged his shoulders and looked back to where Renno was kicking dirt into the fire pit.

"We leave now," Frank told him and Debalo followed the man as he left the clearing. He didn't need to look over his shoulder to know that all of the others were falling into line behind them.

After following a deer trail winding through a field of shoulder high palmettos, they broke through the noisy brush onto a wide and well marked travel route running to and from the still rising sun. Turning onto the path in the direction of the sun, they quickened the pace to a blistering run and Debalo welcomed the exertion. His body ached from the cold and uncomfortable ground, but he could feel his muscles loosening up and his breathing steadied as he found his pace.

Twice they encountered deer on the trail and Debalo delighted as he watched them turn and bound away with their white tails flagging high in the air. There were great areas of turned over ground indicating the presence of wild hogs and Debalo looked forward to hunting them. Although he had yet to encounter one, he suspected that they would be nearly as easy to ambush as the heavily tusked warthogs he had known in his homeland.

They did not stop for water until late in the afternoon and after drinking their fill in a small creek winding its way toward the not to distant river, Debalo watched curiously as the party of warriors stripped and bathed in the creek. He too stripped and following their lead bathed and redressed carefully. Renno tied his long hair into a tight bun and held it in place behind his head with a strip of rawhide and into it he placed three striped feathers.

The others were taking their time arranging their clothes. Some were tying their hair up beneath tightly wrapped turbans of colorful cloth and holding them in place with plumes and metal pins that had been carried in the wide bags they traveled with.

Debalo needed no explanation, for he was familiar with the custom of wanting to make a good impression. He felt along his jaw and found some new growth sprouting and he was careful to remove it before the group continued their march to the town.

He made himself as presentable as was possible and was eager to see the town of the Seminoles. He knew that he should be a little apprehensive, but he had been comfortable in the company of these men and could think of no reason that he would not be welcome. They trotted casually around a bend in the trail and came to a wide, open space planted with corn, beans, and pumpkins in long rows. There were several young, dark skinned girls in the fields pulling grasses away from the stalks of corn. Each stood and waved as the warriors passed by.

Debalo noticed that none of the men gave any attention to the now giggling girls as they passed by on their way into the palm-thatched town. He didn't understand their reluctance to acknowledge the girls, but he offered them a shy smile in return. Many dogs poured out of the gathering of Chikees, the rectangular thatched houses favored by the Seminoles, and swirled around them in a yapping, dusty cloud.

The residents of the town gathered to see the warriors enter the town and assemble in the center compound in front of a large open-sided council house with a wide fire pit. Frank, acting as the leader of the warrior group, addressed a tall man with graying hair and furrowed brow, who stepped into the shade of the council house wearing a bright yellow turban with a perfectly white plume. They spoke for a few minutes before the elder man spoke a few sharp words to the crowd and a dozen or so men of obvious stature came forward and were seated on low benches of hewn logs. Frank and a few others of the traveling warriors were seated opposite them across the fire pit and the older gentleman began speaking.

The crowd gathered around, but Renno grasped Debalo's arm and led him out from the throng and motioned for him to follow him. They walked over to a smaller, open sided structure where a low fire was smoldering in the fire pit. Two women were tending to a large metal pot seated on the edge of the fire.

Aside from the girls in the field, these were the first women he had seen since leaving the island of Baritaria on board the privateer ship. They were slightly built and kept their long black hair flowing freely down their backs. They had long colorful skirts and loose fitting white blouses that Debalo found decidedly attractive. One of them offered Debalo a wooden bowl of stew from the pot and he eagerly accepted the bowl in the polite two-handed manner of his people.

He smiled widely at the young lady, who quickly averted her eyes and turned away. Renno had received a bowl himself and the two ate merrily. They were joined by several other of the warriors with whom they had been traveling, whose appetites were equally keen. They ate silently for a long time until the urgency of their hunger had waned and they joined each other in quiet conversation. Several men of the town joined them and had many questions about the declaration of war and the massacre of Major Dade and his men.

Debalo was surprised to learn that many of these men had heard of the man Dade and expressed mixed feelings about his death and that of the men that died with him. While they were impressed by the fact that a successful ambush had taken place, there was no comfort in it because they all feared retaliation by the soldiers.

One man in particular was concerned about an attack by the white soldiers in retaliation for the slaughter of Dade and his troops. His face was lined with wrinkles and his skin hardened from many years in the sun. His eyes were dark and serious and his expansive forehead underlined by oversized gray eyebrows. A red cloth turban was kept tightly wrapped around his graying hair and held a small white plume that bobbed up and down as he spoke.

"No good can come from declaring war on the soldiers," he told them, shaking his head side to side. "I have seen it. I was a young man then, but I remember. My mother was a maiden of the Biloxi tribe who was taken as a wife by my father who was a runaway from slavery in Georgia. They made their home near British Fort along the Apalachicola River in the north. I grew up there and I will tell you about it." He paused long enough to accept a pipe that had been lighted and was being passed around. He puffed politely and nodded, then passed it to the next man before beginning again.

"British Fort we called it because it had been built by the British when they thought to claim our land, but the Americans drove them away. When they left, my people took over the fort. It was well built with tall walls fifteen feet high and was built thick to stand against an attack." He raised his hands up and out as if to outline the fort's size. "There were eight sides with walkways around the tops so that you could see anyone approaching."

He lowered his arms to his sides. "We called it British Fort because it had been, but the Americans called it Fort Nigger. That is the term they used for all of us with blood from the Blacks. Fort Nigger was a place for any of the slaves to come to from the Georgia territory to be free and for us to live and hunt and fish. Our fields were full and life was not hard, but the Americans did not want us there. They built a fort of their own on the Flint River. They called it Fort Scott and it was not far away. After the soldiers were living in the new fort for a while, they began to ride into our territory, burning some homes and setting fire to our fields."

He turned slowly to the circle of listeners, emphasizing the importance of each part of his story. "There were many of us who were young then and wanted to make war on the Americans and let them know that they were not to do such things. Many old men told us not to do it, but we wouldn't listen. We said it was a matter of honor and we marched off to make war on the white soldiers. We fired some shots from what rifles we had and we launched a lot of arrows over the wall of their fort. A couple of us tried to build a fire against their wall, but they poured a bucket of water on it. We went home and none of us ever knew if we had hit anything with our bullets or arrows or not, but we were happy to have let the American's know we would fight back. We still had our honor."

The pipe, which had been passed around once again came to this old man and once again he accepted it politely, smoked, and passed it on. Debalo also smoked the pipe when it passed around to him and listened with interest to the story the man was telling.

"Their Sachem was the man called Andrew Jackson," the old man continued. "He had been the man responsible for defeating the British and making them leave. He was outraged that we should attack his fort and he ordered his entire army to attack and destroy us.

"We watched from the walls of our fort as the Americans gathered in rows by the hundreds and lined up six of their cannons with the big wheels. They pulled them in place with horses and the men loaded them and aimed them at us. By midday they were in position to attack and they fired one shot from a cannon at us that landed near the house where our foods were kept. After that there were some men sent forward with a message from their General Jackson.

"It said that if we would abandon the fort, our lives would be spared. It said that all blacks were the rightful property of the commonwealth of Georgia and would be taken back to Georgia to be enslaved. The Indians could go free. We were Seminole was what we told him. Some were Indian and some were black, but we were all Seminole and told him to leave."

"They began to fire on the fort after that. The big guns were dropping their exploding shells inside the fort's walls and it was very horrible to see. Everybody pressed against the walls of the fort and the cannon fire went over our heads, but it was destroying many buildings inside of the fort. Then one of their cannon balls hit the house where all of our powder was being stored and it blew up. It was a powerful explosion and many of our people were torn to pieces by the blast. My parents were both killed. There were piles of bodies and pieces of them laying all over the fort. I could not hear for a long time afterwards."

"We that survived ran away and left the fort. The Americans moved in and burnt everything to the ground. The fields were all burnt and destroyed and even the wells that had been dug for water were filled in with the bodies of our dead. That was in 1818 by the soldier's calendar and the man Jackson is now the great father of all of the Americans. He lives in the town of Washington and is again calling for the blacks to be enslaved. We are no better at resisting him now than we were back then. If the soldiers march at our town with cannons, we cannot expect to fight back."

The old man fell quiet and no one commented on what he said right away. Debalo held out his bowl to the pretty girl with the colorful skirt and she filled it again with stew. She kept her eyes lowered as she returned it to him and he thanked her. Renno broke the silence by holding out his rifle and speaking a long string of unfamiliar words. Debalo looked to him and Renno reached over and clasped his shoulder and finished his statement firmly. A couple of the others looked as confused as Debalo himself until the man with the scar running from cheek to cheek translated for him.

"Renno of the Seneca, now a Seminole warrior, wishes to tell you that he was there when the soldiers were defeated and he is confident that they will all die. He says that to wait for them to come here would be wrong. To fight the white soldiers we must go to where they are and kill them there in the same way we killed the soldier by the Withlacoochee."

The old man asked the translating warrior if he agreed and the man looked at Renno and nodded in affirmation with a low grunt.

"And you," the old man asked Debalo, "What are your thoughts? You were there, weren't you?"

"I was," Debalo answered, "but I am not one to ask. I would not have men die if there was another way."

"Do you know of another way?" the man pressed him.

"I do not know. Renno is maybe right, but to see men die and to kill a man..." Debalo trailed off for a moment and sat the bowl of soup down on the floor between his feet. "To kill a man makes Debalo hurt," he said as he ran his hand over his chest, "and is hard to sleep. I want another way, but will not be a slave." He held out his left hand, palm up so that the brand of slavery he carried with him could be seen. "I would not have this happen to your families," and looking toward the pretty girl said, "would not want this done to her," he answered shyly, then picked up his bowl of stew and sipped lightly at the broth.

Conversation continued, but Debalo emptied his bowl and picked up his rifle and stepped out into the late evening sunlight. He was growing tired of the talk and wanted badly to take a walk alone in the forest to think, so he started off toward the fields he had passed earlier when they had arrived at this town. Hearing a trotting step coming up behind him, Debalo turned to see Renno hurrying to catch up with him.

"Debalo," Renno called to him and Debalo was pleased to hear that he finally pronounced his name correctly.

He smiled at his friend and waited for him to come alongside before he started off again. They walked out of the town and through the fields and Debalo studied the tracks of the animals in the loose dirt and took note of the directions from which they came and went. They walked the edges of the field and took turns pointing out the tiniest bit of tracks to one another. After only an hour or so, Debalo was more eager than ever to be allowed to hunt. They were almost back to the town as the shadows lengthened and darkness was about to close in when Debalo spotted movement on the field's edge ahead of them and froze. Renno froze as well and he was instantly alert for whatever it was that had stopped Debalo.

There was no more movement for a long time and the pair remained unmoving as they studied the area for any sign of life. Debalo slowly tilted his head back, lifting his nostrils to the wind, searching for any telltale scent. He signed to Renno that he had seen something ahead of them and received a slow nod of comprehension. Just as he was about to begin to creep forward to investigate, there was more movement amongst a large stand of waist-high cornstalks growing in rows. No doubt about it now, Debalo was staring at a large wild hog and he was thrilled.

The night was quickly coming on and after sneaking up closer yet to the feeding brute, there was no longer enough daylight to see the sights of his rifle. Renno motioned that he would remain where he was and for Debalo to crawl closer yet. He slid to his hands and knees and with great caution he closed the distance to the unsuspecting hog.

He could make out that it was a boar hog and its size was close to twice that of Debalo's lean frame. It was turning over great clods of dirt with its nose and was completely ignorant of the bushman lurking nearby. It was as black as the gathering night and had a ridge of stiff wiry hairs growing from the top of its head and down its spine. The boar carried its weight forward into its massive chest and shoulders.

Debalo could now smell the musky odor of the animal as it continued to feed, its black tail swishing back and forth in a relaxed manner. Debalo lifted the rifle. Although he could not see the sights in the darkness, he knew that he could not miss for being so close. He held his fire for not wanting to alarm the people of the town. With so much talk of war being made, he thought it might be better to not use the rifle and wished he had a good spear at hand.

He reached down and grabbed the cool handle of the big knife at his side. It slid quietly from its sheath and he tested the weight of it and enjoyed the balance of it. He was confident that he could not miss a throw from this close range. Debalo raised himself onto one knee, lifted the knife high and threw the heavy blade forward with all of his strength.

He heard it strike home and the beast exploded out of the corn with a grunt and ran in a wide circle around Debalo headed to the safety of the dark timber. Debalo listened to it running and heard a loud crash and thrashing sounds as the animal fell and stilled in the underbrush a short distance inside the treeline. It was nearly completely dark, but Renno ran up to where Debalo stood and the two clasped forearms and exchanged wide grins.

Searching the ground from where the boar began its flight, they quickly found the blood-covered knife, which Debalo cleaned off on a leaf from a corn stalk. Together they entered the timber to recover the dead boar. Both of them had pretty well marked the position where the animal fell by the sound of its crash and went straight to the area. It took a few minutes to find the boar, which Debalo located by its smell and they drug it out to the field edge. It was a very large animal and the pair struggled beneath the weight of the boar as they carried it from the field and into the village. Debalo delivered it to the open-sided council house where he and Renno had eaten.

Many people had drawn around to see the boar and Debalo asked if there were any families willing to share the meat. A few spoke up and the carcass was carried away from the hut to be butchered by several women. Minutes later the men who had spoken for it returned to Debalo with gifts of tobacco and corn cakes which delighted him greatly. He accepted them humbly with both hands and a slight bow.

TWENTY-FIVE

The night air had grown chilly again and Debalo was happy to remain near the council fire. Children of the Seminole kept the fire roaring throughout the night as the elders sat, ate, and smoked. There was further discussion of the war having been declared on the Americans and each man was eager to have his own opinion heard. Debalo much preferred to remain silent and listen to the speakers after having stated his own position earlier in the evening. He ate a portion of a baked fish and drank from a cup of fermented fruit juice trying to show interest in the thoughts and opinions of the others.

Renno had taken a seat across the fire pit from him and was engaged in quiet conversation with two older men. A young man was standing and addressing the thirty or so gathered beneath the thatched roof of the council house. He was dressed in leather breaches, much like the ones Debalo had on and was wearing a woolen shirt with bright colors wrapping around him in up and down patterns, which Debalo thought was quite attractive. A red sash was tied loosely about the youth's hips and a red wool blanket was thrown across his shoulders for warmth. A hint of hair was beginning to show on the fellows chin and upper lip and his black hair fell loose about his shoulders.

The language was not one that Debalo had learned, but the youth spoke with such desire, that Debalo hung on every word. He didn't need to know the exact words of the youth's speech to clearly understand his meaning. Debalo understood that the young man was ready to fight the American soldiers and was clearly willing to go join Osceola in the north.

It hadn't taken Debalo long to understand that the Indians dearly loved to make long eloquent speeches. He had been listening long into the night, but was quickly growing tired and was pleased when the young man finally ended his. Nobody else rose to speak and the spectators murmured amongst themselves making their own opinions of the young man's reasons for wanting to go to war.

The talk of war was growing tiresome so deeply into the night and Debalo began to nod his head. It appeared to Debalo that the general opinion was in favor of the war and very few were as wary as the elder who had cautioned them against tempting the power of the White Americans. He had spoken of how cannon fire had reduced a fort to rubble and killed many of his people and Debalo well understood the man's caution. He was very familiar with the power of the big gun and could well guess how effective it would be if turned against this small village.

Frank Billie stood and came over to where Debalo was seated upon one of the log benches around the council fire and took a seat beside Debalo, "You look tired. Why don't you get some sleep?"

"I wish to sleep, but not now," Debalo answered him with a shy smile.

"Have you understood all that has been said?" Frank asked him.

"No," Debalo confessed, "but I know enough that the people are wanting to fight."

"That appears to be correct," he agreed. "It has been decided that many of these men will be traveling tomorrow to join our army. You will continue to join us to the villages on the Loxahatchee?"

Debalo answered him with a slow nod.

"We are going to separate here and half of our number is going to travel back downriver to the Gulf of Mexico. There is a fishing village at Punta Matanza, or slaughter Point. That is where Spaniards killed Chief Carlos of the Calusa and killed all of his warriors and made slaves of the women and children long ago. If the Americans attack from the sea, these people living there now will need to leave the town and come inland. History has shown us that such a location cannot be defended against an attack by the sea."

"Leave," Debalo said in a soft voice. "I have said such for all of the villages. How can the Americans attack when there is nobody for them to attack?"

Frank sighed audibly, "It isn't that simple here. Even if they left, they must eventually return and when they did, the soldiers would soon find out and return. To be and Indian or to have black skin makes a man a target for the Americans. They claim to have bought this land," he shook his head, "Nobody though to ask any of us if we wanted them to buy it or not, but they are coming. It is not a situation we can run from."

Debalo didn't respond. He'd heard all of these things before and part of him agreed, but still there was a part of him that was very uneasy. He had agreed to join these men and he knew that he would do what was expected of him.

"When do we travel from here?" Debalo asked after a moment of silence.

"After all have had a meal in the morning," Frank answered. "Why not sleep then. You will want to be rested when we resume our march," he told him with a pat on the shoulder before rising and moving on to another man.

Debalo closed his eyes and pulled his blanket a little tighter around his shoulders. Most of the men he had traveled with to arrive in this town had accepted invitations to sleep in the homes of some of the villagers, but he had not received such an invitation, so he remained near the fire on the log and allowed sleep to take him.

He awakened to the sound of wood being added into the fire pit. It snapped and crackled loudly as a shower of sparks flew upwards from the pit as the flames sought to spread over the new woods. The young boy adding the wood to the fire pit apologized for waking him and slipped away quietly. The others who remained near the fire were all sleeping, some stretched out on the ground and others on the benches. Debalo did not know how long he had slept, but he felt rested. He stood and stretched, feeling the bite of the cold on his back and the warmth of the fire to his front. He turned to allow some of the heat to caress his back and stretched some more. As he faced away from the fire, he could see that a pinkish glow was building in the east as the sun began its approach to the horizon.

He sat back down on the hewn log and stretched his feet toward the fire. He was very glad to have received the wool blanket because it felt good to have it wrapped around him. He closed his eyes again, but it wasn't long before he was again awakened, but this time by the pretty girl who had served him the stew the evening before.

"I am sorry to wake you," she told him softly.

"You did not, I was already awake," he told her with a smile.

She had come to hang a large metal pot of soup above the fire. Once it was in place, she turned to ask him, "What is your name?"

He told her and she giggled.

"Why is that funny to you?" he asked with in amusement.

"You do not look like a devil to me," she told him with a soft smile.

"Devil?" he asked her.

"In Spanish, your name Di-ab-lo, means Devil," she explained.

"No," he told her with a quick laugh, "name is De-ba-lo, no Diablo."

"Oh," she told him and added in a teasing tone, "because you are too skinny to be a devil."

"That is why Debalo," he explained with a smile, "my language, Debalo means stick. Mother told me I looked like a stick," he laughed as he ran his hands over his flat stomach. "I never go to fat."

He continued to smile after she turned back to stir the contents of the large pot with a soft giggle. He liked this young woman. He watched her movements as she worked and was happy that the others still slept. Her hips swayed provocatively beneath the folds of her colorful skirt and the loose fitting white blouse she wore did little to hide the swell of her full bosom and Debalo was struck again by how pretty and desirable she was.

"You stare at me?" she asked him.

Surprised, Debalo quickly lowered his eyes and smiled shyly, "Debalo was watching you work," he told her in a whisper, then looking up into her smiling eyes, he asked more boldly, "how are you called?"

"I am Enowara, a maiden of the Bird Clan of the Seminole, but you may call me Eno," she told him.

"Eno," Debalo repeated, "I am glad to meet you."

She bowed her head toward him in acknowledgement then turned again to the pot hanging, suspended by its handle over the growing fire. She stirred quickly with a wooden spoon and lifting it from the pot, she tasted it.

"Is Debalo hungry?" Eno asked him.

"Yes," he answered her although he really wasn't.

She stepped closer to him and picked up the empty bowl he had set there beside the bench during the night. As she began to straighten up, she looked into the wide yellowish eyes of the little hunter and smiled again before retreating the few steps back to the fire pit.

Debalo was stirred by her closeness and felt a yearning for her building strongly within him. She dipped a few times into the now steaming pot until the little bowl was filled and returned to offer it to him. He accepted it into both of his hands with a bowed head and thanked her for it.

He lifted the bowl to his mouth and sipped of the soup and was pleased to find it very flavorful and thick with meat. He looked up and realized that she was still standing near him.

"Do you like?" Eno asked him sweetly.

"Eno is a very good cook," he answered, looking into her pretty face. "Sit beside me, if you wish," he told her and to his delight she did.

"I asked about you last night," Eno began. "They tell me that you fought with Halpatter and Pacheco against the man Dade. Is it true?"

"It is so," Debalo answered.

"My father and brother are gone and the other men are preparing to go north for the war soon," she told him. "I do not like it."

Debalo sipped again at the warm soup and managed to get a chunk of meat into his mouth. As he chewed, she began again.

"Where is your home Debalo?"

Swallowing he answered in the best way he could, "I have no home," he told her, but was not satisfied with his answer, "I live in Africa my life. I was made to come to this new place to work as a slave. I will be no slave, so I runaway."

"You ran away and came here?" she wanted to understand.

"I ran away and this is where I became."

"I'm glad you came here. Will you stay or will you return to the north to fight?" Eno queried him further.

"I go with Frank Billie to other villages. We leave soon," he told her sadly.

She reached out and slid her fingertips across his bald head and he jumped, startled by her touch.

"I'm sorry," she told him.

He quickly recovered from his start and chuckled lowly, "Why did you do that?"

Rather than answer his question, she asked one of her own, "Why did you remove your hair?"

Before he could reply however, one of the men sleeping nearby awoke with a loud groan as he stretched beneath his blankets. Eno stepped quickly from Debalo's side and stirred the big metal pot. The man stood up stretching and mumbled something to the little bushman as he stepped past him quickly and headed for the trees to relieve himself of his full bladder.

The sun was lightening the sky enough that Debalo could make out the forms of the chikees and houses around the village and knew that the others would be soon awakened, ready to eat. He took another sip of his soup and looked toward Eno with a smile, which she returned.

He looked around him at the other men who had slept near the council fire, but Renno was not among them. The Indian who had hurried to the bushes returned and greeted Debalo with a tired smile. Debalo nodded to him and the man reached for a gourd bowl and stepped over to the young maiden who filled it for him from the large pot she continued to stir.

As the morning light continued to displace the darkness, more of the men began to stir around the fire and awaken to a breakfast served by Eno. The village began to come alive as fires were kindled in the various fire pits and women began emerge from their homes to prepare breakfast for their families. The scene was one very familiar to Debalo and he yearned to be awakened once more in the hut of his mother, preparing for a day hunting with the men of the tribe.

Debalo finished his soup and wrapping the blanket tighter around his body, he stepped onto the cold ground outside of the council house and went to relive himself in the trees. Afterwards, he noticed Renno emerging from a small chikee and much to his surprise, a young woman stepped into the open with him. He watched as Renno turned and gave the woman a hug and a pat on her rump before trotting over to the council house.

Debalo called to him as he got near and they walked to the council fire together. Renno's ever-present smile was wider than ever and Debalo gave him a questioning look, which earned him a slap on the back and a laugh from his companion. Debalo smiled back at him knowingly then looked toward the shapely maiden serving soup to the men as they awakened and he sighed.

Debalo hated to leave the small village behind them, but still he was pleased to be back on the trail running. The chill of the morning had subsided due to the exercise and he breathed deeply of the forest air. The clean smell of oak mixed with the tangy scent of pine greeted his nostrils and he felt fit. Every now and then Renno and he would exchange knowing glances and the two would grin stupidly.

They passed long stretches of oak hammock and pine forest laced thickly with palm trees of all sorts and sizes. They came across many deer as they ran, startling them into flight and it never failed to excite Debalo as they bounded away. Several times through the day the trail passed close to the rivers bank and they could clearly hear the jumping of fish and the many melodies of the various birds flitting here and there about the branches of the many trees.

By nightfall the seven men traveling from the Indian village made camp on a high ridge of land overlooking a turn in the river. There were many low growing palm trees scattered throughout the area and Debalo bedded down on the lee side of a small stand of them and curled into his blanket. Renno lay down nearby and the others settled themselves near the small fire they had kindled and used to warm the evening meal.

Debalo lay there in the dark listening to the tiny splashes of fish feeding in the river and the occasional chatter of raccoons as they fed in the shallow water near the bank. He enjoyed the little black-eyed animals with their swinging, hump-backed gait. He hadn't hunted them yet, but did notice several of their pelts drying on the sides of chikees in the Indian village and assumed that they must be fair to eat.

He tried to fight the urge to sleep for fear of the dreams, which had plagued him, but he knew that at some point he would have to succumb. He thought of Enowara and the short conversation they had shared just that morning. He wanted terribly to return to the village to speak to her again, but he knew he must go first to the town with Frank and Renno and the others. He thought of her though, as he lay drowsy in his blankets beneath the limbs of the palm tree and could almost imagine the touch of her fingers on his bare head.

The next morning, they traveled farther south, which carried them away from the river and ran along narrow trails made by deer and other wildlife. For two more days they maintained a blistering pace, resting only when necessary and for short periods of time. As he ran, Debalo's mind kept wandering back to the lovely Enowara standing near the cook pot and more than once he was so caught up in remembering her that he would miss a step and find himself sprawling down upon the debris littering the forest floor. Each time he fell, one of his companions would grab the back of his shirt and help him back to his feet and quickly check that he was unhurt before they would be off again.

On the fourth morning after leaving Enowara's village the group of warriors were slow to leave their temporary camp. Frank had informed them that they were close to the town on the banks of the Loxahatchee River and they took their time bathing in the cold water and grooming themselves carefully before taking the last miles or two into the town.

Debalo readied himself as neatly as he could and was eager to see what he had been told was a much larger town than the one they had just left. Also intriguing, was that he had been told he was to be arriving in a town of Black Seminoles and Debalo was eager to get there.

"Debalo, happy?" Renno asked him joyfully as they waited for the others to finish readying themselves.

"Debalo, very happy," he answered with a nod and a grin.

"Happy," Renno began and said a few words he couldn't understand, but he heard him clearly when he mentioned the name, "Eno?"

Debalo looked at him in astonishment, wondering how his friend could know what had been occupying his mind.

Renno smiled and put his hand on Debalo's shoulder, then shaking his head in good humor, laughed out his name, "Debalo!"

Debalo grinned at the tall man and nodded an admission as he spoke her name, "Eno."

Frank and another member of the warrior group came walking nearer and overheard the exchange between the two friends.

"Am I to hear that Debalo has found interest in the maiden Enowara?" Frank asked them.

Renno answered first and although Debalo was learning to pick up on a few of the Indian's words, he still didn't need to know the language to know what his friend was telling them. A little embarrassed, Debalo didn't want to discuss his attraction for the Seminole girl, but Frank brightened to the subject.

"She asked about you, Debalo. After you returned with the boar, she asked me," he told him. "So, you've taken a liking for her?"

Debalo nodded shyly while grinning despite himself.

"She's a lovely girl for certain, but you should be aware. Her father hasn't any cattle or anything suitable for a dowry. He is a very poor man and she has no fortune to offer a husband," he told Debalo with pity. "No man would think of taking a wife without a fortune."

"I don't understand," Debalo told him in confusion.

"It's not that complicated, Debalo. She's not a fit bride, but take heart. There are many young women in the village ahead of us. Renno here knows most of them and I bet he can introduce you to some. Come on then," he told them looking off to where the others were assembling, ready to take up the trail, "the others are ready and we need to continue on to the town," Frank told him and they all headed into the woods on the trail leading toward the distant village.

Renno patted Debalo on his shoulder as they started after the others and the pair exchanged silly grins.

TWENTY-SIX

The nights had remained bitterly cold, but the days were growing warmer. As Debalo and the others grew closer to the town of the Black Seminoles, the sun was nearing its highest point in the sky and had warmed the day comfortably. It was a perfectly blue sky that was stretched out above the party of warriors as they made their way along the final miles to the town. The clean smell of the oak and hickory nut trees in the enormous hardwood hammock they traversed sweetly caressed his nostrils as Debalo breathed deeply to fill his lungs while running along the narrow trails.

Debalo noticed the increased sign left by people passing through the forest and knew instinctively that they were growing close. Renno, who had been running ahead of the group, halted on the edge of a wide expanse of waist-high grasses and waited for the others to catch up to him. Debalo stepped clear of the thick cover of the trees and drew back immediately to a secure place behind the trunk of a giant pine tree. He watched with growing alarm as the group of warriors stood carelessly in sight of the cattle, oblivious to the inherent danger of the wild herd. He continued to marvel at the unconcerned way his companions acted upon confronting a herd of watusi, the wild cow as he slowly left the cover of the pine and stepped nearer to where Renno stood grinning and motioning toward the cattle before continuing his advance.

He was ready to dash back into the cover of the treeline, but the other warriors followed Renno out across the grassy field at a trot. He fell into line behind the last warrior and followed the party through the grasslands without taking his eyes off of the cattle. There were nearly fifty cows feeding casually in the clearing and Debalo was greatly relieved to have regained the protection of the hardwoods on the far side. He never made mention of his fears to his comrades and he was sure that they hadn't suspected, but he could easily recall the sight of unfortunate villagers having been trampled by the stupid cows and he did not want to tempt a similar fate.

After a short distance they broke out of the cover of the hardwood forests again and came to another clearing, many times larger than the first and in this clearing was a large herd of short barrel-chested horses, many more cattle and in the distance many houses. Crossing the open land to the town Debalo and the others passed several young boys, undoubtedly assigned to watch the horses to keep them from straying. Each one waved cheerfully and a few called out their greetings.

Just as they had acted when approaching the small town on the Caloosahatchee River, the warriors never broke stride when passing proudly by the children without notice while Debalo remained quick to return the waves and smiles. These young boys were dressed neatly in short pants and white-bloused shirts with long sleeves. Their white teeth and eyes fairly glowed against the background of their coal black faces. Each boy's hair was trimmed very short and each carried a long staff.

Debalo wanted to stop and introduce himself, but rather he passed by on his way into the town. The houses were made of sawed lumber, not unlike the cabins he'd been forced to share with the other slaves back on the plantation. Many of the structures were colored white with blue around the windows. Debalo felt that the colored houses were quite attractive, but had been hoping to find a village of mud and stick huts, like the ones he'd grown up and lived in back in Africa. He didn't count the number of houses, but could plainly see that there were many of them. The tall grass of the clearing became much shorter as they neared the first of the wooden houses. The ground surrounding the houses was packed flat and all traces of grass and weeds were cleared to the bare ground.

Several of the houses were located in a center square in the open field and there were many others located along the far edge of the hardwood treeline taking advantage of the shade and cover of the giant oaks growing there. Apart from the homes he could see, there were many larger structures built for housing food stores and one had been set up such as that of the buffalo man he'd met in Tampa, for trading. In an area past the town, the ground had been cultivated and a great many vegetables had been planted there and the ringing blows of a hammer beat out a staccato rhythm that echoed from some place inside the treeline.

The townspeople did not pour out in greeting as Debalo had experienced in the Seminole village. Several women were working in the sun near a large pile of wood that had been accumulated off to one side of the gathering of houses. Debalo suspected this to be a communal gathering of firewood, much like his own village had practiced. A few lean men sat in the shade of the largest of the buildings and worked together building or repairing a large fishing net. Debalo had never been involved in fishing for his village, a task undertaken by the children and maidens of the tribe.

He noticed that the people of this town did not dress in the manner of his own tribe in Africa, but rather were clothed in similar manner of the Seminole Indians. Several of the men who came forward to greet them wore the silk turbans tightly around their heads and the women wore the same colorful skirts with the addition of a cloth wrapped about their heads and tied in the front. They were greeted with kindness and courteously ushered into a long rectangular building that had been built up off of the ground and stood by itself on the eastern edge of the settlement. Food and drink was brought for the newcomers who were seated upon wooden benches.

Debalo was quite pleased to find that although there was great difficulty with the accents of the members of this community, he could readily understand their mixture of African and English dialects. Their demeanor was quite pleasant and Debalo felt very comfortable as he sat on the hewn bench of the long house eating politely from a bowl filled with dried fruit and vegetables. There was much talking and many questions being asked, but Debalo had not been addressed directly, so he chose to remain silent and enjoy the meal and environment.

A dark liquid was served to him. He politely accepted the green metal cup filled with drink from an older woman.

"Lord chile, e don' got no meat for da bones to hide in do e?" she clucked at him cheerfully.

Debalo grinned at her and nodded his head with a smile.

"E don' tink I got to see no starvin' boy now do e? No chile, finish dat in ya bowl now and you go on an hep ya'self for some mo. Heah me now?" she clucked again and Debalo's grin widened.

"I thank for it," he replied and took another bite of the fruit and swallowed it down with the cool black contents of the mug. The drink was bitter, but held a light nutty favor that he found he enjoyed. He took a deeper swallow and savored the taste.

A tall thin man entered the building and everyone quieted as he came forward. Frank stood and returned the man's warm welcome and the two embraced. Debalo noticed the man's high cheekbones and thin nose and wondered if he might have Indian ancestry as well, despite his dark brown skin. Around the man's neck was a large wooden cross that he recognized as a symbol of worship in the new world and wondered if this man might be a healer like the ones he had known in Africa; a lipwereri.

Frank began telling the story of the events leading up to the massacre of the soldiers near the Withlacoochee and told of all they knew of Osceola's plans following that massacre. There was a deep silence in the room as Frank continued to speak and each of the townspeople nodded here and there as they studied all that was said.

When Frank had finished his story, the tall man turned to another of the gathered men and spoke a few words that prompted the man to jump up and run from the room. In a very short time shouts rang out and a bell began to ring furiously.

Talk resumed in the room and Debalo finished his meal. Renno stood from his place on the bench and walked toward the doorway motioning for Debalo to join him. He followed Renno out into the sunlight and down the three steps of the building to stand in the sun of the late afternoon while men and women appeared from all parts of the village to attend to the calling of the bell. They gathered at the building until the room was filled with bodies. Many more crowded just outside, peering into windows for a hint of the reason for the bell to call them for an assembly.

As they passed by, many of them greeted the two men as they stood just outside of the building that many of them referred to as the "church". Several asked Debalo what news it was that they carried, but a stern look and a shake of the head by Renno quieted him and he returned their salutations, but offered no explanations. Instead he leaned heavily upon the barrel of his rifle, in imitation of Renno and carefully studied the people.

They all seemed very pleasant and none looked as if they were starving, but there was a meakness about them that he had not seen in the Seminole village. There was no eagerness to run off to war and no shouts or celebrations as they received the news that war had been declared. Many milled about outside of the church and talked amongst themselves with serious looks and others showed traces of fear.

Renno grunted once and Debalo looked up to his usually pleasant companion whose face was dark and repugnant. He shook his head slowly, nodded for Debalo to join him and lifting his long rifle into his arms, he started off at a brisk walk. Debalo hesitated to follow, but his curiosity over Renno's mood was too great to overcome and he deftly lifted his own rifle and stepped quickly to catch up with the tall Indian.

Coming alongside of him, Debalo shot him a questioning look that brought a half smile from Renno's tightly clenched lips. He halted his march as quickly as he'd begun and turned toward the church and the calm crowd gathered around it and shook his head.

Looking down on Debalo he shook his head again and with a tone more sad than angry he said, "No," beat his chest with the palm of his right hand and added, "Mad," and pointed off toward the church. Debalo understood clearly then that his friend was troubled by the tepid response by these people to the news of war.

The Indian's face slowly began to soften and he patted his friend on the shoulder and turned again and walked away. Debalo didn't follow him, but stood looking after the tall man as he stalked down a well-worn path toward the shade of the trees in the short distance across the small town. Although he didn't understood Renno's disappointment, he couldn't help but sympathize with his warrior friend. Since coming to Florida he'd learned a lot and had been offered plenty of opportunity to reflect on how slavery had turned his own life upside down.

He looked back to the church and at the people quietly milling about it and began to think of them, as Renno apparently did. "Do they not know slavery?" he asked himself and lowered the rifle to lean on it again as he stood alone in the path in the middle of the town.

Debalo rested against the muzzle of his long gun and lost himself deep in his thoughts until a tug on the sheath of the big knife he carried brought him out of his bewilderment. He turned slightly and came face to face with a pair of wide-eyed, wooly headed youngsters with bright white grins shining on their dark little faces.

"Is e come a ways?" one of them asked.

"I travel many days," Debalo answered with a smile, "what are you called?"

"Ma, she call me most anything come to mind, but named me Joshua after da Bible," one of them introduced himself then turned to his companion, "dis hyar is my brother Daniel, he get named right out da Bible too."

Debalo smiled down on the pair and remembered the dirty seaman he'd known and found humor in the image of the nasty man compared to the happy pair he now addressed. The brothers looked to be about eight summers old and he was happy to meet them.

"Why you totin' dat big knife?" the second brother asked while eyeing the knife.

"It is mine," he answered simply.

"Where you get dat?" asked little Joshua, in wide-eyed admiration as he reached out a slender finger to trace the grooves in the bone handle.

Deablo smiled and lifted the heavy blade free of its sheath for the boys to get a closer look.

"It is a little heavy, but with practice, a man learns to value the extra weight," he told them.

"Dat's awful big! Most terrible lookin'! I bet you kilt a gator wid it ain't ya, or maybe a big ol' bear?" Daniel spoke up.

"I have hunt with it, yes," Debalo admitted, enjoying the children's company.

"You gots ta git awful close to kill somethin' wid a big ol' knife like at?" Daniel questioned him further.

"Not if you can throw it," Debalo answered, "See that basket?" he pointed to a woven basket sitting near a smoldering fire pit.

Both boys followed his finger and nodded. As soon as their attention was on the basket, some ten or twelve paces distant, he let fly with the knife. The boys watched in wonder as the polished steel flashed end over end as it arced through the air, coming to a stop with just the handle sticking out of the side of the basket.

The boys erupted in cheers and raced over to retrieve the big knife for him. Carrying it back together, they carefully handed it back to Debalo and admiringly requested that he repeat the performance. He was all too happy to oblige.

"Where ya'll learn to throw a knife like dat," Joshua asked as he again handed Debalo back his knife.

"I learn in Africa as a boy. Father teach to become hunter, a hunter must know how," he answered, proud of their high regard. "Have began training to hunt?" Debalo asked them.

"Heck naw, Ma ain't goin' let us go do no huntin', she say they's too much can happen to us," Joshua again answered.

"You be here some time yet," Daniel asked.

"I do not know, but I think I will hunt here," he told them.

"Why you go an do sumthin' like dat, wid all them cows wanderin' out there and the river so fill wid de fishes ya cain't catch 'em all?" Joshua piped up.

"I don't know," Debalo admitted and looked out toward where he'd seen the older boys watching the herds.

He began walking slowly back toward the church with the pair of boys in tow, each asking questions as quickly as Debalo could answer them. By the time they reached the church, other young boys had begun to flock near to meet the hunter so skilled with the knife and he was asked to select target after target to throw the knife into.

It wasn't too long and he replaced the knife into its sheath and took a seat in the shade of the church with the group of boys, whose numbers had swelled to about a dozen, each listening intently to Debalo's stories of Africa and the animals he hunted there. He sat there for what seemed like hours as the daylight passed away and as evening shadows began to stretch out across the town in the grassy clearing. The doors of the church swung open at last and the people began to pour out quietly, scattering toward their homes.

The children weren't ready for the stories to end, but Debalo excused himself from the group and stood to go meet Frank and the others as they emerged from the white building. A few of the boys clung to him and Frank smiled when he spotted Debalo and his admirers.

"Been making friends eh?" he asked the grinning little bushman.

"Yes, friends," he answered looking down at the boys of the town.

"We'll be sleeping in here tonight," Frank told him. "They'll bring food soon enough and we'll start out in the morning."

"No hunt for village?" Debalo asked with surprise.

"No," Frank answered him sourly. "They do not wish to prepare for a war that is in the north. They do not want our help here, so we will return to the north alone," he told him with a tiredness creeping into his voice.

"Where's Renno?" Frank asked him looking around.

"He walked toward the trees," he answered and didn't offer any more.

"Well," Frank told him, "He knows this town, so he's probably found some young maiden to entertain him."

Debalo smiled at the suggestion and thought of Enowara back in the village on the Caloosahatchee and the realization that if they left in the morning, he could be with her again in just a few more nights. The children seeing him smile began to smile with him and he grinned even broader. Frank had walked over to a couple of the other Indians and was pointing back into the church. Past Frank's outstretched arm he caught sight of Renno walking slowly toward the church with a young black maiden dressed in white clinging to his arm.

Spotting Debalo, he grinned wide and turning to the pretty young woman he bid her farewell and left her after a quick pat on her behind. He left her at a trot and was beside Debalo in no time wearing his customary grin. Debalo was glad to see that his friend had regained his lighthearted demeanor.

Renno pointed to the children standing around Debalo and chucked him on the shoulder, then winking, he inclined his head towards the door of the church and led Debalo inside. Before ascending the three wooden steps into the white building, he remembered to say goodbye to the waving boys and they waited for him to go inside before racing off toward their homes.

Renno and Debalo walked over towards a corner of the building where they lay down their rifles and possibles and sat on a long bench near the wall. Renno sighed a few times and each time he did Debalo would shake his head in mock disapproval. There was no need to talk about the afternoon, even if they had a better grasp on the other's language. They already knew how the other had passed his own time and the looks and sighs were enough to clarify Renno's romance.

The knowledge of Renno's latest conquest flamed Debalo's desire for Enowara even more and as they reclined on the bench awaiting food to be brought, Debalo grew determined that he would return to her village to see her. There was unquestionably an attraction and he felt there was business left undone. He wanted her to understand that he wanted her and needed to know if she indeed wanted him.

TWENTY-SEVEN

Tiny flames licked hungrily upward and around the black ebony log and a shower of brilliant sparks flew upwards toward the countless twinkling jewels adorning the cloudless night sky. Debalo stepped back from the fire pit and knelt at the feet of the older man who sat removing bits of fat and scraps of flesh from the hide of a freshly killed kudu calf. He watched as the man's leathery fingers drew the edge of the scraper in neat lines across the surface of the skin, leaving nothing but moist white skin.

"Why don't you go to bed, Debalo?" the older man asked a little slurred from the gourd of tshala, beer he'd been sipping from while he worked.

"I am not tired," he answered.

"You had a big day today. Most boys would be ready to go to their beds, but you wish to sit by the fire and watch me work," the man chuckled. "You are an odd boy," he told him as he chuckled and reached again for the gourd.

After a good long drink of the fermenting liquid, the old fellow placed the gourd back on the ground by his feet and stretched his feet out closer to the fire. A hyena laughed his challenge out in the darkness down by the river and was answered from farther off into the blackness by the unmistakable grunt of a lion. The hyena called again and the lion grunted again, the hyena laughed long and comically and the lion roared loud and commanding and there was silence again in the night.

"What do you think Debalo, does fisi wish to tempt simba tonight?"

"No, I think that would be foolish," Debalo answered. "Father?" he asked looking to the older man.

"Yes," Debalo's father responded as he continued to work his scraper across the kudu hide.

"Why are you not tired?" he asked him.

"Ha, I am tired," his father answered with a quick laugh, "but, I have to finish this skin. Even in the dry air the hair will be slipping off by morning if I do no care for it now."

The fire snapped and crackled in the pit as the log caught and burned brightly. Debalo studied the puckered scars that ran diagonally across the wide chest and asked his father about them.

"Were you scared when simba gave you the scars?"

His father looked down at the long welts crossing his body and chuckled, "How many times are you going to ask me that question?"

"I don't know," Debalo answered, awaiting his father's story.

"No, I was not scared," he started and then took a swig from the gourd. "You've heard this a thousand times. I had no time to be scared. One minute I was walking beside my brother and the next minute I was lying in the grass bleeding and my brother was gone."

The lion grunted again in the distance and the old man asked, "Debalo, do you really want to hear more of this or can I tell you again in the morning. I'm almost finished here and I want to go to bed. Why you aren't already in bed, I do not know."

Debalo didn't answer him, but rather turned to look into the darkness toward the river where the lion grunted again, then looked back at the parallel scars crossing his father's body.

"When you are older, Debalo, you will have times when you will be scared. Everyone is afraid, Debalo. Some scare easier than others, but everyone is afraid. How you react to your fear is what makes the difference between men."

"I think I understand," Debalo looked back into the fire as his father returned his attention back to the job he was doing with the kudu hide.

The night was black and as the fire began to die away, Debalo asked his father without looking over to the older man, "May I hunt again with you in the morning?"

His question brought no reply, so he asked again as he turned back toward his father, but his father was no longer there. Confused, he looked around, but there was no sign of him except for the kudu hide and the half empty gourd of tshwala sitting upon the ground.

"Father," he called out to the shadows beyond the fires light, but received no response.

The night air had taken on a noticeable chill and there was no sound, not even the crackling of the fire or the hum of the innumerable insects keeping vigil in the night.

"Father!" He cried out in earnest.

"You scared boy?" a deep voice boomed from the darkness. It echoed through Debalo's head and body and terror seized his heart as recognition of the voice came to him. It was Roundbelly!

"Father!" he cried out again, but heard only a laugh from the darkness. He cried out again and again a deep laugh rang out, but this time closer to the river and moving steadily away.

Debalo sank to the ground and cried. Great sobs racked his body as he released his terror and anguish. After a time, he shouted his grievance to the night and leapt to his feet and he was no longer a boy, but a young man dressed is leather breaches and a Seminole shirt. He turned back to the fire, still shaking and there he beheld Enowara stirring a steaming pot of stew.

"Why are you come to here?" he asked in surprise.

She looked up at him and smiled, but did not answer.

"You should not be here," he told her excitedly, "there is danger!"

She smiled warmly, but remained silent and continued to stir the pot as the echo of laughter rang out in the night.

"Come, we must go!" Debalo cried out to her and quickly stepped around the fire to take her by the arm, but as he drew near, he saw that there were chains around her delicate ankles and they had torn and blistered the skin beneath them.

He looked into the soft eyes and could see they were red and swollen, as if many tears had fallen from them.

"You must come with me," he told her as he reached for her arm, but she shook her head no.

The laughter was returning and Debalo was becoming frenzied to leave, but Eno would not be budged.

"Come now!" he pleaded, but she lowered her eyes again and she opened her left hand to show the terrible rounded scars of a slavers brand.

"No," Debalo shouted and the laughter came nearer.

Staring into the night, Debalo shouted again, screaming defiance against the terrible evil he knew was stalking them as the wicked laughter rose in volume and reverberated throughout him.

"No!" he cried out again!

Debalo jumped to his feet, his blanket falling to the floor around his feet. Moonlight filtered into the room of the church and allowed enough light to see the prostrate forms of his companions stretched out and sleeping around the room. He was greatly upset by the dream and he fought to regain control of his breathing.

"Debalo?" a sleepy voice spoke to him.

He looked down on Renno, who had propped himself up on one elbow and was now studying his little friend in the dim light. Renno reached out and patted his friend on the leg a couple of times and motioned for him to lie back down before he himself settled back beneath his blanket.

Debalo did as he was bid and lowered himself back to the floor and pulled his blanket tightly around him. He listened to the chorus of insects outside the windows of the church and the sound of cattle lowing in the night. There was no danger, but he was terribly uneasy. The words of his father, from so long ago came to him again, "everyone is afraid. How you react to your fears is what makes the differences between men."

As he lay there on the floor of the church house, wrapped in his blanket, he pondered those words he remembered from so long ago and thought of Enowara, kneeling in chains and branded for a slave as he had been. He could not return to the north to fight with Osceola's Red Sticks until he could speak with Enowara again and see to it that she would be safe.

He thought to himself about the possibility of asking her to flee to this village, but quickly dismissed that idea. After seeing the lack of concern in the villagers at the news of war and slavery, he would not expect this village to be safe if the slavers were to come here. A river was said to be nearby, although he hadn't seen it for himself, but he knew that it would easily guide anyone to this place, should they come looking. No, he would have to think on it some more.

As the room's interior began to lighten from the pink light of the new sunrise, Debalo stepped stiffly down the steps of the white building. He was greeted by the sweet smoky smell of the village at morning. He pulled his blanket tight around his shoulders to ward off the bite of the frosty morning air and shuffled quickly around to the back of the building to relieve himself. Afterward he stood in the semi-darkness of the new day and studied the parts of the little town that he could. He did not know what he expected to find in this town of Blacks, but these people, although very pleasant, were not the same as the Blacks of his home in Africa.

There was no disappointment in him, but he thought that they more closely lived like the few whites he'd seen during the short time he'd been in Tampa. The houses were the same, the clothing was nearly the same, albeit patterned somewhat more after the Seminole's, but there was still something very familiar and pleasant to him being in their company. He walked back to the front of the building in time to see a pair of women, one of them the old one from the day before who had insisted he eat more, coming down the bare path toward the steps of the church.

One of the the Indians he'd arrived with came out of the church at a fast hop and grunting something at Debalo, disappeared behind the building as the women drew near. Debalo smiled broadly and bowed to the two as they brought forth a medium sized cook pot filled with steaming soup. The smell was very enticing and the older lady cackled out a god morning to him as she filled a large cup with the thin soup.

"E be so sure to fill yer belly now say. E done got yeself so the bones in e back be nigh to rub a blister on ya belly. E gonna like de soup I done made fo ya, yeah?" the old woman chuckled as she spoke and Debalo accepted the warm cup in the two handed manner of his homeland and bowed again, which pleased the woman.

"Ah, ya gots manners I kin tell. You'll do my bitty, you'll do."

Debalo took a hesitant sip of the broth he'd been offered and his eyes widened in delight as he tasted sweet broth of egg soup, just as his mother used to make for him in Africa.

"You made this?" he asked in great pleasure.

"I did, e like the soup then?" she smiled in pride at he slurped up a mouthful and groaned happily as he swallowed.

"Good, e drink it up and I see you filled."

The two ladies passed him by and stepped up the steps into the church and began to call out to awaken the still slumbering forms stretched out all around the room. Debalo drank lovingly from the cup as the taste and aroma of the soup carried him back to his home near the Okavango and that little mud hut where his mother kept a bed for him. He closed his eyes and saw her sweet toothless smile and missed her so much he hurt inside.

"No venison in the soup?" the Indian had returned from his relief trip and stepped over to see what Debalo had in his cup.

"Egg soup," Debalo answered brightly.

"Ugh, I should be at my home. My wife would have soaked corn with bits of venison cut into it. I haven't eaten her food in a long time," he sighed.

Debalo thought hard to remember the man's name before it came to him, "El-Ichi?" he asked tentatively and the man looked down to met eyes with the little bushman.

"Will you go your home, that we carried the news to these people? Or, do you go back to fight the slavers?"

"I will follow Halpatter and Micanopy as they make war on the white soldiers," he answered with a shrug and turned to go up the steps into the building, but Debalo wasn't satisfied yet in his curiosity.

"Do you not miss your family?" he wanted to know as he took another sip of the flavorful soup.

"No family, only a wife. She has a big mouth, but she is a good cook. There is no hurry," he grunted and ascended the short flight of steps.

The sounds of voices and movement inside the church continued to increase as his fellows awakened and were treated to their breakfast. Debalo drained the cup of the egg soup and hurried up the steps for more, wearing a smile.

The small group of warriors had assembled on the edge of the town, prepared to leave as Frank met once again inside the church with a few of the elders of the town. The sun had been up full for some time and as the warriors of the Seminole waited, they visited openly with a few men of the village while Debalo was surrounded by several wooly headed youths, all of them admiring his knife and his short stories of the hunt.

Renno stood to one side with an expressionless face and kept his arms crossed over his chest with his long rifle resting against his side. Every now and again Debalo would toss a comment his way, but Renno only grunted in reply. Debalo did not know why Renno disliked children so much, but with their still limited understanding of the other's language, he didn't bother to inquire. He felt it would be too wearisome and tiring to figure it out.

Frank emerged from the church with the elders and after taking the hand of each in turn, he trotted over to the warriors and gave the signal to go. Renno jumped into motion and slapped Debalo sharply on the shoulder as he started out to take the lead. Debalo lifted his rifle to his shoulder and saying a quick goodbye to the boys, turned and ran quickly to catch up to his partner.

A chorus of youthful goodbyes rang out behind them as they made their way across the open field away from the town. When Debalo caught up to Renno and fell in beside him, he noticed that Renno was wearing a broad smile and they both began to laugh as they hurried away from the little town. Neither man fully understood the humor that the other found in their laughter, but it lightened their hearts as they took to the steady pace of the warriors run and they ate up the miles as they headed northward, back to the Caloosahatchee.

The grasses were still quite wet from the heavy dew that had settled during the night and soon the legs of his leather breaches were soaked through. The wet leggings began to slap against his legs as they flew back and forth in his run and started making a hollow popping sound at each step.

Renno eased their pace and finally stopped and pointed to the noisy leggings of his little friend and Debalo knew what was troubling him, so he knelt and rolled up first one then the other of his pants legs up to the knee to prevent them from making the wet noise. As he stood again, ready to resume their run, Renno coughed behind a smirk, then roared out in laughter at the same time slapping his little friend on the shoulder. He straightened his face up and pointed to the skinny little legs of Debalo and whistled before speaking one of the few words he knew in English, "bird."

Realization washed over Debalo and he burst into laughter as well, "Bird legs you call them, then let me see you catch them."

Debalo jumped into a lightening sprint and flew off down the trail. He knew the big man would be hard pressed to catch him and he ran for all he was worth. His feet pounded the earth and his lungs filled nearly to bursting as he flew down the well-worn path as it entered a thick hammock of hardwoods and pine trees. He looked behind him once and saw that he had taken such a lead that Renno was no longer in sight behind him and his chest swelled with pride knowing that he'd taught the tall warrior a lesson about laughing at his skinny little legs, for they could easily outrun his long muscular limbs any day. The path took a downward angle and wound around a small stand of cypress before ending at a narrow creek and a small wooden platform laid out along its bank.

Debalo halted his run as he neared the creek bank and his heart sank as he realized why Renno had not been close behind him. He hadn't outdistanced the big man, but instead had taken the wrong path out of the clearing and was now standing before a washing platform where women would come to wash laundry and bathe.

There was no way out of it, Debalo realized. He had to go back up the trail to where the others had turned off and rejoin his comrades knowing full well that he was destined to be the brunt of quite a bit of teasing for getting himself lost. He started back up the trail at a trot and in less than a mile he came within sight of the others who had waited at the fork in the trail for him to realize his error and to rejoin them.

As soon as the little bushman came into sight the others set up such a roar of laughter that more than a few of them had tears running down their cheeks. Debalo trotted past them flushed with his embarrassment and as they pointed out the trail for him and he wordlessly took the turn and resumed his run, much more carefully now. It took awhile before Renno drew alongside of him still chuckling as he ran and holding his side with one hand and gasping his breath as he ran.

Debalo was terribly embarrassed, but after awhile even he found the unusual humor in his mistake and it would take only a look from one of them toward the other to break them up into laughter again as they traveled together through the cool shadows of the forest.

TWENTY-EIGHT

The group of warriors pounded out a blistering pace as they traveled through the tropical forest, stopping only for water and handfuls of parched corn or dried venison. In less than a day and a half after leaving the small Black settlement, the group arrived at the campsite they had used above the banks of the Caloosahatchee River the first night after leaving the Seminole village. The sun had passed overhead already and was well toward the western horizon when they stopped, but there remained a good three hours or so before nightfall.

Frank spoke up to the others about remaining in that campsite for the night and moving on in the morning. All of the Indians appeared to be in agreement, so Debalo didn't press for them to continue on. He was not so tired from the day's run that he couldn't continue on for another few hours, but he withheld his dissention, but openly frowned upon it.

"Debalo," Renno quietly called to him while shaking his head and gesturing toward the setting sun with a grin.

"I have no fooled you, Renno?" Debalo smiled at the big Indian.

Renno nudged him and together they walked over to the far side of the campsite to where they had slept beneath the cover of the short stubby palms. Other than the sign of several birds walking and dusting themselves in the ashes of the fire pit, the camp showed no sign of having been visited since they left it. Lowering their blankets, rifles, and possibles bags onto the ground where they intended to bed down later, Debalo was startled to see Renno begin to strip down.

Sensing his smaller companions confusion, Renno nodded toward the river and made a swimming motion with his hands and Debalo understood that he was going down to the water for a swim and a bath. He considered joining him, but the air was beginning to cool again as the evening wore on and Debalo didn't want to be damp in the night air. Instead, he decided to take a short walk around the campsite and explore the area a little further.

The others were occupying themselves, some gathering firewood and some stripping to join Renno at the waters edge and noone gave notice to Debalo as he slipped out of the camp amongst the palms and pine trees. He already had an idea of what lay toward the setting sun, since having passed through it after leaving the Seminole village, so he followed the rivers course eastward. He hadn't gone far and the land began to drop lower into a rich hardwood bottom filled with ancient thick trunked trees, whose canopy blocked out the sunlight resulting in very open cover beneath and despite the darker shadows afforded by the canopy, Debalo could see a wide open view.

The ground beneath the oaks had been disturbed in every direction by the deer, hogs and other wildlife that came here to feed on the acorns and hickory nuts, which still lay abundantly on the ground. He stood motionless on the edge of the open woods and watched for the presence of any of the creatures that had left such abundant sign. His hunter instinct had stopped him beside the trunk of a thick tree, which provided him cover as he pressed full length against the cool trunk. He blended well against the rough bark of the tree and wasn't seen by the six deer that fed casually into the open woods, scouring the ground for their evening meal. He thought of attempting a stalk, thinking he might get within throwing range of the big knife, but quickly discarded the idea.

Without the aid of the rifle, the sure way to get a chance at these deer would be to circle downwind into the area to which he suspected them to go and hope to place himself in position for one to wander near enough to become a target. However, the light was fading and there was no need for the fresh meat in the camp, so he remained hidden, unmoving against the bark of the ancient tree.

He watched them feed and interact with one another, listening to their grunts and wheezes, learning more about these thin boned animals until the dying light forced him to retrace his steps back to the campsite. On his way back Debalo listened to the sounds of the forest around him and found nothing in them to alarm him of anything. He'd learned from a very young age that your ears are as important as your eyes when it comes to surviving in the deep woods.

Many varieties of birds danced around in the trees and underbrush, some calling out their whistles and warbles to each other and the soft scurrying sounds of small animals rustling through the leaves, seeking out their own meal of whatever they can find reached his ears in a normal chorus of familiar sound. He paused and drew in a breath slowly savoring the sweet musty scent of the forest. A slight whiff of clean water reached his senses as the light breeze stirred in from the north. He stepped a little faster as he made his way back to the camp. The northern breeze brought with it a bite of frost and as the last of the daylight gave way to shadows and the temperature began to drop quickly.

Closing in on the campsite he could hear an occasional splash from the river and sporadic soft laughter from his companions. He had a sense of calm come over him as he walked back toward the temporary camp and he was suddenly surprised. He smiled despite himself and shook his head as he stepped into the clearing where the others were resting near a small fire someone had kindled.

"What is it you're grinning about, Debalo?" Frank asked him.

"I was some surprised at my thoughts," he started to explain with a shy grin.

340

"What is it you're thinking about then?" Frank pressed him and a few of the others raised their heads toward him awaiting his answer.

"That, if Debalo no ever gets home to Africa," he paused for a second to be sure of his words, "I will be happy to live this land," he ended with a nod.

"It's good land if I've ever known it," Frank agreed. "It's that girl that's got you thinking about settling down, isn't it?"

The others chuckled a little at Debalo's obvious embarrassment.

"It could be so," he confessed, dropping his eyes shyly toward the ground as he stepped nearer to the palm where he'd placed his things and took a seat. Reaching into the possibles bag, he pulled out one of the corn cakes he'd been saving and took a few bites.

Renno ambled into the clearing, wiping himself dry with a handful of pine needles. He dressed quickly and stepped over to the fire and placed a couple more logs into the pit, turning himself around, welcoming the warmth of the fire.

One of the warriors began to speak to Renno in his own Indian tongue and he looked quickly toward Debalo while widening his grin.

"Debalo?" he called out and spoke quickly a few of the foreign words ending with one that he understood quite well, "Eno?"

Debalo shrugged his shoulders and reached for his blanket to wrap around his shoulders as one of the others translated Renno's question.

"He asks how you plan to take a wife when the only thing you've sampled is her cooking?"

Debalo's eyes flew open wide in shock at his friend's bold question and the look he gave Renno brought squeals of happy laughter out of the others and he quickly recovered from his embarrassment and joined in the laughter.

Renno came and flopped down hard beside him and Debalo gave him a push on the shoulder, shaking his head. Renno reached out for his own blanket to wrap around him and then returned the playful shove.

"You two seem bent upon returning to downriver," Frank interrupted with a more serious ring to his voice, "we were talking while the two of you were out of camp, that we might as well travel upriver to the villages on the north side of the big lake Okeechobee. From there we'll hurry northward toward Ocala to rejoin Osceola."

"What I have in mind," he continued, "is for the two of you to go back downriver, spend a day or two in town and then continue on to the coast and gather as much information as you can while making your way back to the north. Does that meet your approval?"

"Yes," Debalo spoke up while another Indian spoke the proposal to Renno.

"Renno knows the country and the two of you should be able to move easily along the coast roads, but you'll want to be wary of any white militia. Now that war's declared, you can't trust any of the white men."

"Debalo?" Renno asked quietly with raised eyebrows.

Debalo nodded to his friend and Renno's grin returned as he nodded his approval of Frank's proposal, "Is good," he answered and the two of them were quite pleased with their new orders.

There was much talk and speculation that night of what could be taking place in the north and it was quite obvious to Debalo that the others were growing impatient for news themselves. The decision to leave Renno and himself behind to return to the village for a couple of days made Debalo very happy and eventually, he rolled up in his blanket beneath the overhanging limbs of the palm and thought of Enowara and Florida and a life he could come to enjoy here in this tropical wilderness.

His sleep was not troubled that night above the banks of the river and he awakened during the still black morning. There was no wind and Debalo lay wrapped in his blanket and listened to the soft even snores coming from more than one of the Seminole warriors as they slept fitfully. Soft splashes on the water told him that the fish were feeding well and he thought how nice it would be to climb down to the water and reach around the submerged stumps and tangles of root, in hopes of grabbing a slow fish or two for breakfast, but the cold air removed such ideas to the back of his mind.

He couldn't see much of the night sky through the canopy above him, but the tiny pieces of night he could see were speckled brilliantly with twinkling stars. The moon was nowhere in the night sky and he guessed that daylight was still a few hours away. He tried to allow himself the luxury of returning to sleep, but the more he tried to, the more awakened he became.

Finally, he did rise from the shallow depression he'd smoothed into the ground days earlier and pulling his blanket tightly about him, he stepped over to the fire pit and placed a couple of pieces of pine into the bed of red coals. The wood was very dry and in no time dancing flames overwhelmed the dead boughs and Debalo opened the blanket to the fire to allow its warmth to penetrate his stiff muscles.

He sat back on his heels and reached for one of several strips of dried venison that had been placed on a palm leaf near the fire pit to stay warm and bit off a small piece. He chewed slowly, savoring the smoky flavor and watching the ancient dance of the flames in the campfire. He took another bite of the meat and closed his eyes as he slowly chewed and relished the feel of the heat on his eyelids.

A much larger splash came up from the river and Debalo listened as a large animal struggled to regain the opposite bank. A deer he was certain, but it may well have been a wild pig prowling around in the night. There did not appear to be any shortage of game in these woods and Debalo yearned for the hunt, but first there was another issue to settle. Enowara crept back into his thoughts and he remembered the light touch of her fingertips brushing across his scalp.

He wanted to hunt for her, to provide meat for their home, whether it be a mud and stick hut like the one he'd known in his homeland, a palm thatched chikee as he'd admired in the village of the Seminole, or the flat boarded houses of the Black settlers. He thought of stepping proudly down a beaten path leading to the home they could share with a small deer carried lightly across his shoulders and her waiting for his return to make use of the animal to feed themselves and the image in his mind expanded further to include children. He smiled warmly in the light of the small fire as the image played through his mind before he chuckled at his own silliness.

He chided himself quietly for the foolish things he had been thinking. It still was entirely possible that what had passed between them was nothing to her and that she may have no idea just how much he had been affected. It could be as well that she might have no interest in making a life with an African husband. He shook his head again to clear it and chuckled again at his own notions of love.

"What's so funny?" a sleepy voice whispered from across the fire.

"I was just thinking. I did no want to wake you, Debalo is sorry," he answered quietly, ashamed at awakening one of the other warriors.

"That's okay, I was getting cold," the voice spoke up and as the Seminole came close and squatted just beyond the fire, Debalo could see El-I-chi, the tall broad shouldered warrior with whom he'd seldom spoken.

Debalo reached for another stick and placed it atop of the burning sticks and a brilliant shower of sparks danced up between them for a moment before disappearing in the cold night air.

"That feels good," El-I-chi spoke as he opened the fold of his own blanket to allow the fires warmth to spread around him.

"You will go to the girl now?" El-I-chi asked Debalo in a low tone.

"I think yes," Debalo answered softly.

"If you take her as a wife, will you leave her to fight or will you remain in this land?"

Debalo bristled slightly beneath his blanket before answering, "I am told to Frank, I will return with all that I learn."

"I know that, but there should be no hurry for it," El-I-chi spoke sadly.

"I do not know what you say to me," he asked him to explain.

"If you take a wife, you are obligated to her to see she is cared for, do you understand?"

Debalo nodded in the firelight that he did.

"Remember Debalo, you are a free man now. You've nothing to make you rejoin any fighting that may take place. I saw the way you emptied your stomach at the battle on the Withlacoochee." He told him knowingly, "You don't want to be a part of war do you?"

"Does any man?" Debalo countered.

"Oh yes, there are some," El-I-chi observed.

"And you?" Debalo wanted to know.

"Yes, I do. It is one way for a man to gain honors and reputation."

"There are other ways," Debalo offered.

"Of course, but I don't know those ways. I was trained since I was a child to make war and I look forward to honoring my family with my skill as a warrior."

"I was raised to be a hunter, a provider for my village," Debalo told him meekly.

"An honorable profession," El-I-chi commented thoughtfully, then added, "When we left the village of your woman, Frank sent several of our party down the river to follow the coast north to gather news. They will bring all that there is to know back with them."

"You do not want me to fight?" Debalo asked unbelieving.

"I do, but I want you to see to your woman first. I left my wife with enough money and food to last her well until I return home. It is not right for a warrior's wife to suffer when he is not home. That is what I am saying to you. If this woman will have you, see to it that she is cared for and safe. Then, you should follow the coast north and find us."

"I do know what you are saying to me," Debalo answered, "I hear your words and they are good."

El-I-chi nodded across the firelight and the two men sat quietly for a short time before Debalo noticed that the darkness was giving way to the first light of the morning and he stood to stretch. The others would be awakening soon and he wanted to bathe well. He started to excuse himself to his companion, but the large man's chin was resting against his chest and his eyes were closed as he had nodded off again.

By the time he had made his way down to the waters edge, the light had increased enough so that he could see the far side of the river through the thin wisps of fog rising from the water. He stripped quickly, his skin puckering against the bite of the frigid morning air and he stepped into the water of the river.

He gritted his teeth against the raw sting of the icy water. He quickly waded out into the slow moving water until it reached just above his waist and dove in. He broke the surface gaping for breath as the cold enveloped him and he began rubbing and scrubbing at himself frantically. His efforts warmed him very little and he scrubbed himself with handfuls of sand from the rivers bottom. His frantic efforts at bathing were losing out to the deep chill settling into him and he was shaking noticeably by the time he exited the water and stood and wiped as much of the water from his body as he could.

He scampered quickly back to the fire carrying his clothes and deposited them nearby as he wrapped the woolen blanket around him and stepped close to the flames. El-I-chi reawakened as Debalo stood near the fire, shuffling his feet and drying himself the rest of the way with the blanket.

By the time he had reclothed himself, others were rising from their own blankets and the sun was breaching the eastern horizon sending its warming rays through tiny gaps in the trees like little spears of fire falling from between the leaves. The group of men huddled close to the fire and ate well on the parched corn and dried meat they carried, some skewering strips of the meat on thin strips of palm limb and warming it in the fire before consuming it. There was little talk amongst the group of warriors as they warmed themselves and ate, preparing for another day of hard traveling.

Frank finally signaled that it was time to begin their run and each of them reluctantly stepped away from the fire and gathered their gear, ready to set off at his signal.

There wasn't much to be said that hadn't already been discussed the previous night, so Frank bid Debalo and Renno both safe travels and after clasping the forearm of each man in turn, he turned eastward from the camp and the other warriors fell in behind, each calling out a word or two of good bye and good luck as they departed.

Renno stepped over to the fire and urinated on the coals before kicking dirt over them. He turned back to Debalo who was waiting impatiently to get going, shot him a quick smile and led the way out of the campsite on the banks of the Caloosahatchee River and back toward the town of the Seminoles.

TWENTY-NINE

The shadows were lengthening as the sun began it's slow decent toward the tops of the trees standing against the western horizon as the two men raced along the narrow, winding path following the rivers course. The day had passed quickly and the two companions were making great progress on their journey back to the Seminole town.

Debalo spotted a wide trail crossing a sandbar and coming up from the river at an easy slope and halted his run. The sand bar spread out from the bank forming a short beach along the riverbank and Debalo waited for Renno to join him before they stepped out onto the sand and knelt at the waters edge for a drink. As Renno stooped and cupped the water to his mouth with a hand, Debalo studied the tracks leading up the bank and a familiar knot began to form inside of his belly.Renno stood up wiping his mouth on the sleeve of his shirt and noting the change that had come over his friend, followed Debalo's gaze to the trail. Horses had crossed the river at this shallow place, several of them, although it was difficult to be certain of the number since rains had partially erased the sign.

"Seminole?" Debalo asked the big man while tracing one of the tracks with his finger.

Renno's answer was to shake his head and trace the clear outline left by the print of steel shoes on the horse's tracks. Knowing well that Indians never bothered to shoe their ponies, he could only assume that the horses whose tracks they studied, had been ridden by white men.

Debalo drank quickly and the pair followed the impressions of the horse's tracks up the bank and onto the grassy trail leading toward the Seminole village. The pair moved along at a cautious pace, examining every inch of the trail as well as the road ahead for any indication of whom they might run into. There was no way of knowing when it had been since the last rain in that area, but Debalo guessed that it could not have been more that a couple of days and if these tracks were only two days old, the white men who made these could well be camped along the trail. Even worse, they could be in the village of the Seminoles.

Eventually the sun slipped well below the horizon and the two halted their run. The tracks continued on up the trail, but they knew they were getting close to the village. Debalo guessed another mile or so and they would come to the edge of the clearing where the people had planted their crops of pumpkin and corn. Renno apparently guessed that Debalo's hesitation to continue on to the town was because he wanted to clean up a little and look his best, because he flopped cross legged on the ground and opening his bag, he began to comb out his long black hair and retie it up with the leather thongs and hawk feathers he carried.

Debalo followed his lead and began grooming himself, but he hadn't stopped for that purpose. Instead, not knowing what he was about to discover in the Seminole village, he preferred to wait until it had become fully dark before attempting to slip into the town quietly. He did not know that the men with the horses would be there, but if they were, he wanted to know their intentions before he made it known that Renno and himself had arrived.

Feeling the tight curls springing up from his scalp, Debalo unsheathed the big knife at his side and began to scrape away at the unwanted hair. When he was satisfied with the results, he searched his face and found a few that had sprouted anew on his chin and he quickly removed them as well. The pair spent the better part of two hours bathing and straightening their clothes and by the time they were prepared to enter the town the night had grown black and cold.

Debalo started up the trail, but a low whistle from Renno stopped him. Renno stepped up to his friend and opening the primer lock on his rifle, he dumped out the small charge of powder and refreshed it with a new charge from the small canister he carried. Debalo immediately understood the precaution against a misfire and replaced the charge in the lock of his own rifle before beginning again.

As they made their approach to the edge of the fields, they halted and listened to the sounds of the night and found nothing out of the ordinary to alert them to the possibilities of danger lurking in the town. Renno started to leave the cover of the treeline, but halted and through a series of gestures indicated to Debalo that they should circle downwind of the camp and approach from that direction.

Debalo sniffed the air and started out through the edge of the vegetable field, circling in a direction that would carry him away from the river and downwind of the slight breeze coming down out of the north. Half way to where he expected to make his approach to the village, Renno touched him lightly on the back to stop him. He looked closely, but in the dark it was hard to tell exactly what Renno was trying to alert him to, but then the soft sound of a woman's crying came to his ears.

Renno moved silently through the field with Debalo following closely, heading toward the sound of crying. They halted close to the woman whose back was to them while she rocked back and forth on her knees beside the prostrate form of a child. Debalo was greatly relieved to see that the woman was not Enowara, but rather an older woman of the village. Debalo whispered to her and she jumped with a wail and spun around to see who it was that had surprised her.

He placed his hands palms up to show that he intended her no harm and spoke quietly, "Old Mother, do not afraid. Tell what happens here."

"Who are you?" the woman asked with shallow breath.

"I am Debalo, my friend is Renno, we no harm you."

"You were here before..." the woman began, but her words trailed off.

"Yes," he confirmed as he crept closer toward her and the body on the ground.

Once close enough, he could make out that the child had been a boy, not much older than those he had entertained in the town of the Blacks. Debalo had seen death in many ways and forms and could tell that the child before him had been dead only a matter of hours.

"How did this?" Debalo asked in a whisper.

The woman sobbed back a tear and struggled to answer his question.

"Men came to inform us that we will be taken to Tampa. They tell us that this is no longer our land and we are to go to a reservation where we will be happy. They gathered us all in the center of town. This child ran away and a man on a horse ran after him and cut him this way with a long knife, a sword. He was my grandchild."

"How are you to be out here. Why were you to leave when he was not?" Debalo asked as her story sank in.

"I snuck away in the dark," she answered.

Renno spoke some words to her and the woman nodded as she cried anew. He patted Debalo on the leg and motioned for him to follow him, but Debalo still had questions he needed to ask.

"Old Mother, can you tell me the number of these men?"

"Seven," she told him as she reached out and stroked the childs hair.

"Where are the warriors of this village?" he asked her.

"They are gone to the north. They go to fight the soldiers as they were bid."

"Mother can you tell me, of Enowara? Is she safe?"

"None have been harmed but this one," she answered with a trembling voice and began crying anew.

Renno tugged lightly at his sleeve and Debalo followed. Renno moved closer to the village with urgency and as he approached the first chikee, he crept silently to the open doorway and peaked inside. Debalo drew near and Renno handed him his rifle and before Debalo could guess what was happening, Renno drew the knife from his belt and dove into the blackness of the little thatched house.

There was no sound of a fight and Renno emerged directly from the chikee, reclaimed his rifle and sprinted on silent feet up to the next house. Each chikee they visited was empty and at last they could see that the villagers were huddled into the space beneath the large thatched roof of the council house where a large fire was kept burning.

Debalo smelled the horses before he heard them snort at his approach. Renno had left him to circle around to the other side of the council house to find where the White men were, knowing well that they would be guarding the people. Debalo had begun to circle the area in the opposite direction when he came upon the horses.

He slipped to the ground near a small tree and held very still while listening. He was close to the animals and he expected that there would be at least one man remaining with the horses as a guard. He didn't have to wait long until the sound of urine splashing into a puddle on the ground gave away the position of the man. Debalo felt as if a large tree had fallen on him and pinned him to the ground. He knew what was expected of him, that he should kill this man, but he was paralyzed by fear and revulsion. The man in the shadows cleared his throat and spit, Debalo guessed that he was ten steps or so away from him and was glad that the man was not alert.

The rifle was not the weapon for this, but rather the big knife he carried. He slipped it from its sheath at his waist and wrapped his fingers around the smooth bone of the handles. His fingers felt stiff and wooden and his stomach tied into terrible knots. He wiped his forehead with the back of a hand and was surprised to find that despite the chill of the night, he was sweating terribly.

Debalo slipped from the cover of the tree toward where he had heard the man. He approached his quarry in a low crouch, holding the blade of the big knife forward in his right hand. After traveling several unsteady steps, he began to make out the silhouettes of the horses and then that of the man whose job it was to look after them. Bile flowed up into his mouth and he fought hard to keep from gagging.

He gritted his teeth and resolved himself to what he knew must be done and he crouched lower, tensing the muscles in his thighs for the lunge toward his victim, however just as he was about to strike, a muffled scream sounded from the opposite end of the village and the silhouette of the man Debalo was preparing to kill, disappeared into the darkness. Debalo sank to his knees and listened to the sound of the man's boots pounding the hard packed earth, running toward the direction of the scream. He replaced the knife into its sheath and rose to his feet, trembling and fighting to choke down the vomit that threatened him.

He stepped over to the horses and as quietly as he could, he untied them and started them off out of camp. He moved closer to the council house and could see that there was much confusion among the people. Armed men, white men, darted here and there amongst them shouting and threatening what appeared to be about thirty or forty old men, women, and children huddled together beneath the thatched roof of the council house.

He strained to see Eno, but he was too far away to make out individual faces in the poor light of the fire. Of the white men he could see, by the fires light none of them wore the blue uniforms of the soldiers. They were clothed similarly in dark leggings, boots, and heavy coats to fight off the cold. He counted three in the fires light, but knew the others were beyond it in the dark, searching for the source of the scream.

One of the old men stood up from the hewn bench he had been seated upon near the fire and began to gesture around him at the others who remained seated. Debalo could tell that he was making some sort of a plea when one of the white men stepped over to him and hit him in the stomach with the butt of the rifle he carried. The old man sank to the bench hard, clutching his mid section and as the white man straightened himself and began to shout out a command to the gathered Indians, an explosion and flash of light erupted from the darkness a short ways off from Debalo's left side and the lead ball fired from Renno's rifle caught the man squarely in the chest.

The force of the impact threw the shouting white man backwards off of his feet and into the fire. A brilliant shower of sparks erupted from the fire pit and lifted high upon a mild breeze. One of the men who had been standing nearby ran to the side of the stricken man and attempted to roll him out of the flames. The other leveled his rifle and fired in the direction of Renno's blast and before Debalo thought it out, his own rifle was leveled upon that man and a screen of smoke blocked his vision, so he didn't see the man cartwheel backwards grasping at his throat, blood spurting through his fingers in great geysers.

The Indians seated in rows upon the hewn log benches, all ducked and huddled lower. The children cried out in frightened wails as the old men cursed. The stink of sulphur filled his nose as the uproar of the people filled his head. There were so many people calling at the same time that he couldn't understand anything of what was being said, but he had no time to think on it just then.

Suddenly something shoved him into motion and he ran in the darkness as two shots rang out, aimed in the direction of where he had just fired from. It was Renno that held his shirt and pulled him along and into one of the empty chikees while many shouts were sent up from the darkness outside the light of the council fire.

Once inside the chikee, Renno began reloading his rifle in haste and Debalo began to grow feint. Renno grabbed him by the shoulder and shook him, then indicated that he must reload his weapon. Debalo felt the vomit come up in his throat, but swallowed it down and went through the process of pouring the powder, patch and ball down the rifles barrel, driving the charge home with his ramrod, and then pouring an additional measure of powder into the frizzen pan of the rifles lock.

When Debalo had completed reloading his rifle Renno smacked him smartly on the back and dove out the door and into the black shadows of the night. Debalo fought hard to control his ragged breathing and his throat burned from the vomit he kept choking back and his mouth was dry as sand. He listened from the doorway of the chikee to the shouts of the men as they sought out himself and Renno. He lowered himself to his knees and continued to listen. He wasn't sure what was expected of him and he had no idea what Renno had planned, but he knew that there was more death to be dealt to these white men.

He did a quick count and knew that there were four more of the white men in this tiny village who must be accounted for and he left the shelter of the chikee and returned to the area where the horses had been picketed, should one of the men return to check on them. As he approached the area at a crouch, he slid behind the tree he'd knelt beside before just in time to hear a boot brushing against a rock and Debalo slipped the big knife from its sheath as he listened.

Voices soon came to him, in hushed whispers and told him where the men were.

"Damn injun's stole our horses, too. What'n hell are we s'posed to do without our gawdamn horses?" he could hear one complaining.

"Shutup dammit!" the other told him, "You think them dead boys over thar give a tinkers darn about them horses right now. Be quiet and be ready, the moon'll be up in a hour or so and we'll have a little light to see by and we'll get the hell out of here. Just stay quiet now, I think I hear one of them over there," the other answered and started moving in Debalo's direction.

Debalo fought to control his breathing, knowing that the man was now hunting him down. He heard the slow steps of the boot lightly brushing the ground as it slowly arose and lit again. When the man was no more than a few feet away and the sickly smell of sweat filled his nostrils, Debalo could almost make out his silhouette against the nights sky. With all of the power he possessed, he rose from his crouch behind the tree in a lightning fast lunge and drove the blade of the big knife deeply into the chest of the white man.

As he drove home the blade, he released a scream of rage and fear, which mixed with the scream of agony from the throat of his victim. He pushed hard against the man who struggled to get a hold on his attacker, and the man fell backwards and sank to the ground yelling out obscenities and writhing from the pain. A shot exploded nearby and Debalo felt the wind of the bullet passing close by above his head, he threw the heavy knife at the place where white flash of the rifle had erupted in the darkness and was rewarded by a gurgling choking sound and the thud of a body falling hard to the ground.

There were shots fired from the other side of the village square and Debalo grabbed up his rifle and retreated quickly to the chikee that Renno had led him to before and there he remained. The remainder of the night passed slowly and even after the moon had risen, Debalo dared not venture beyond the shadows of the chikee.

It remained a quiet night and even the Seminoles who had been gathered beneath the council house made no noise as they awaited the light of dawn. In the darkness of the chikee, Debalo wept silently and cursed himself for having taken another life. He thought of Bwana lying torn and helpless on the table in the ships galley and of the slave he'd buried back on the plantation. He thought of Round-belly and the soldier, whose lives he had taken as he had taken the life of three of these white men who had killed a small boy and taken this village as prisoners.

When blackness of the night began to give way to the morning's light, Debalo could hear soft voices in the distance and strained his eyes to pick up any movement in the shadows. Images floated in and out of the yet sunless morning and Debalo found his feet and left the doorway of the chikee. He caught sight of a pair of figures standing over the spot where lay the two white men he had killed with the knife and he cautiously moved toward them. As he neared, he could tell that they were Indian and he calmed himself and called to them.

"Have the white men gone?"

The two images in the dismal light of the early dawn turned with a start and one of them asked in a raspy voice.

"Who are you?"

"I Debalo. Are the white men gone?" he asked again.

"Only two," the old man answered and as Debalo neared he could see that it was the same old man who had told the story of Fort Nigger and how the soldiers had blown it apart.

"Are you well Grandfather?" he asked him.

"I am, but how did you know to come here? We had no warriors to resist these men."

"I did not, until I see tracks of horses make and follow them to here," he answered, then concern rising, "Where is Renno?"

"Your friend is near the council fire, he is hurt," the old man told him then quickly added, "but he will live."

"Thank you," Debalo told him as he reached down for the knife that was lying on the ground beside the still body of the man who had pulled it free in the throes of death. He wiped it clean on the sleeve of the slain man and headed for the council house in the center of the village, leaving the two old men behind him with the pair of new corpses.

THIRTY

Renno lay upon one of the hewn log benches near the fire pit, being attended to by a few older women. Behind them there was a pair of young girls putting a large metal pot over the fire pit. A few of the people remained beneath the shelter of the council house's thatched roof and huddled together speaking of the nights events, waiting for better light before venturing out. As he neared the gathering around Renno, he glanced over to the spot where the two white men had lain and was glad to see that someone already had removed the bodies and sifted fresh sand over the spots to cover the blood.

Debalo could see that his friend was awake and the strain on the big Indian's face showed how painful his wound was. Stepping around the women, Debalo could see that the wound was located on Renno's upper thigh. Renno reached out a hand and grasped Debalo by the arm as the little bushman knelt beside him. Through clenched teeth, he spoke Debalo's name and nodded.

The little hunter remained on his knees not trusting himself to speak for fear his voice would crack and betray just how upset he really was. The women cooed and spoke softly to Renno to keep him calm as they cared for him. His pants had been removed and he had been cleansed of any blood. The wound was covered by thick layers of moist cloth and prevented Debalo from seeing how bad it was.

Looking up to one of the old women, Debalo cleared his throat and rasped out, "How bad he is hurt?"

"He's a strong man," the woman assured him, "he will survive." Then to Renno she added, "It will take more than this little hole to kill you, no doubt."

"How bad?" Debalo asked again, his voice taking on a fuller tone as his impatience grew.

The old woman swatted away the hands of another who had been holding the moist bandage cloth in place and lifted it for Debalo to see the wound for himself. There was a small hole in the right side of Renno's left thigh where the bullet had entered and a slightly large hole on the outside of the thigh near the back. The area around both holes was dark from bruising, but there was no blood flowing from either hole now. Debalo was relieved to see that the bullet had left the thigh.

Somewhat relieved, he looked into his friend's eyes and reached over to grasp his forearm and told him softly, "You will heal."

Renno nodded that he understood and offered his little friend a tight smile despite the pain he was experiencing

Debalo rose to his feet and stepped back from the women as they re-covered the wound and offered the wounded Renno a small bowl of thick broth that was just warming over the fire. One of the women assisted Renno in rising a little and another lifted the bowl to his lips for him to drink. Relief flooded through Debalo with the knowledge that his friend was going to be fine and he lifted his rifle onto his shoulder and headed toward one of the several entrances to the council house.

"De-balo?" an old man hesitantly spoke his name as he approached and Debalo recognized him, but could not remember his name.

"Yes," Debalo confirmed and asked turned to face the man.

"We spoke at the fireside," The older Seminole waited for recognition.

"Debalo," he paused for a moment, trying to remember the words, "remember," he told the man and although he tried to force a smile for a greeting, he could not.

"I was of the same mind as you then, that we as a people should leave this place. What say you to that now?" he wanted to know and Debalo didn't quite know how to answer him.

He did not want to talk to anybody, but couldn't be rude to the fellow either, so he thought carefully before answering. He lowered his eyes and shook his bald head a time or two, before responding, "How can I say?"

The old man didn't press further, but stood waiting for Debalo to explain and find his answer.

"Not all of these men are killed. It will be not time to catch their horses and go. I do think that more will come here. Brought by those who no did die," Debalo said, realizing for the first time that they must indeed leave this place.

"It has been talked of a lot since you came to us with the news of war. With the young men gone to fight, we should not stay here. The elders wish to join our brothers in the south, but there are some of us, who wish to travel to the River Of Grass. No horses can travel there and the white men can not follow."

"Where is place?" Debalo questioned with growing interest.

"It is far to the south, four days travel. It is not easy to go there, but there are hammocks of islands amongst the great grasses and the water. You spoke of such a place before. Will you come to this place with the people. We men are old and our women will have much hardship. Our children are strong, but can not do the work of a man."

Debalo nodded as the man spoke to him.

"Debalo, your friend is hurt and cannot return to the north. We will take him with us until he is well. Do you agree?"

"I think that is the right way of thinking. Yes, if there is such a place where the slaver and soldier can not follow, then that is where we go," he stopped himself a moment and looking into the eyes of the elder man he admitted, "I was to return to Pacheco and Osceola after I come here. I do not know the way without Renno. I must stay here until he is well," he looked about him then as the mornings light filled out the shadows. "How soon can the people leave?"

"It would be best to leave by nightfall, no?" the man asked and Debalo shook his head.

"The next morning will be better. We should be ready to leave by tonight, but another nights rest will be better if the trail is a hard one," Debalo suggested and the elder man nodded his agreement.

"I will tell the others," the old man told him and with an urgent step, he started off to spread the word of the decision to vacate the village.

Debalo turned back to where Renno lie still, surrounded by caregivers and his eyes made contact with those of Enowara for the first time since returning to the village. She was just entering the council house with a load of sticks for the fire. He wanted to smile or indicate his pleasure at seeing her, but too soon she dropped her eyes and carried on her business.

He couldn't help himself but to watch her as she placed the sticks she had gathered into a neat pile near the fire and taking a couple from the pile, she fed them carefully into the fire beneath the large metal pot.

She was still as pretty as he'd remembered, but her face was tired from the sleepless night and her blouse was stained and dirty. He leaned his rifle against a supporting timber of the council house roof and he unwrapped the blanket he'd been carrying folded across his shoulder and wrapped it around himself.

The chill of the morning's air was partly the reason, but also because he realized that the front of his shirt was covered in blood and he did not wish for her to see the evidence of his having killed. He shuddered from the thought of the terrible night's activities and reminded himself that there had been no other way.

He turned away and stepped out from beneath the thatched roof and watched the sun as it's light began to filter through the tops of the trees ringing the eastern edge of the village. He wanted to go to the river and bathe in order to remove the blood from his body, but thought first he should go to Renno once more.

As he turned to reenter the council house he was met in the archway by Enowara. She approached him with lowered eyes and a bowl of the thick broth Renno had been given and offered it to him. He reached for the bowl politely with both hands and the blanket fell from his shoulders and crumpled to the ground.

Having both hands on the steaming bowl of broth, Debalo could not pick it up and Enowara stepped around him, retrieved the blanket from the ground and placed it back about his shoulders, saying as she did, "I had hoped that you would return, Debalo."

Debalo fought to control the flood of emotions he was experiencing and was slow to respond as she lifted her eyes to his.

"I have thought of nothing else," he admitted and tried to smile for her.

"You have thought about returning to this village?" she asked him quietly.

He started to answer, but he was too lost in her eyes and that knot he'd carried in his stomach since reentering this village began to tighten up again. He looked to the bowl of broth, but couldn't bring himself to taste it without offering her an answer.

Finally, he found his voice and told her boldy in a firmer voice than he'd intended, "Debalo has returned to Enowara."

As the words spilled from him, he watched her reaction closely and he was greatly relieved to see the corners of her mouth lift into a shy smile.

"That is as I had hoped," she told him warmly and moved closer to him until they were nearly touching.

Debalo removed his left hand from the bowl of broth and wrapped it gently about her shoulders as she came in to his embrace and placed both of her arms around him. His head swam dizzily as she pressed against him, the warmth of her soft body coursing through him and for a moment he felt as if he would lose his breath.

"There is something you must know Debalo," she told him as she lay her head upon his shoulder, "I am poor. I have no family and no presents for you to take me as your woman, but I want that still."

Debalo pulled away slightly from her embrace and she stepped back looking intently into his almond eyes. He took her by her arm and led her back into the council house and over to a low bench away from anyone else and had her sit. He lowered himself to the hardwood bench beside her and as he did, he gathered the blanket and folded it across both of them and lightly pulled her close to him.

"I have no home," he started, "I have no family, too. What I have is what I am. If you can find good in that, I will live for you and we can find a home. Now, these people of your village are to go to the place the elders know. I am to go there too."

As he spoke, she looked deep into his eyes as her own misted over and a tear started to fall. He placed the bowl onto the bench to his side and with his right hand he reached to catch the tear gently on his fingertip.

"Why do you cry, Eno?" he asked surprised.

"Because I am happy," she replied sweetly and she leaned in closer and laid her head upon his shoulder again.

"In my home of Africa, to make you my woman, I first must prove to the people of the village that I am a man," he told her.

"There is no one amongst us that would not agree that you are a man and a brave man too," she responded.

"Then," he continued, "I build for you a house. Afterwards, I must approach your father and challenge him for the right. If he wishes, he may try to kill me, but if he is happy with me he will send you to me before the sun would set. Is that the way of it here?"

"No," she responded against his neck, "it is much simpler here. I have no one for you to go to, but the elders of our village will decide if we shall be united. After what you have done for us, I do not think they will object."

Her assurance moved him deeply and he lowered his forehead to the top of hers as he lightly brushed her cheek with his right hand. Looking down upon her pretty face, a tranquil sense of hope and a new beginning came over him.

"I, Debalo was come to here as a slave, but I am no slave no more. When I would not longer be a slave, I come far from that place and now I am here."

Enowara looked at him fondly. Her kind eyes signaled she had welcomed him into her life.

"In Africa my people I knew are gone and my village was burned," Debalo said. "If I could find a way to go to Africa, there would be no home for me there. Now, Debalo has found Florida and here is where I will be. This land of the Seminole is a good land. Here with you, I am home."

About the Author

Toby Benoit is a native Floridian with a love of his home state and its history. Raised on a small farm in a rural community, Benoit has gone on to lead a life of diversity and achievement. Professionally he has worked as a data entry coordinator for a hospital auditing firm, a family counselor in the funeral industry, an expert in the archery/bowhunting industry, a geriatric nurse therapist and as an admissions director for a skilled nursing facility.

Benoit began writing in 2002 while dealing with a peripheral vascular disease. He began by writing freelance articles for outdoor sporting magazines and the local newspaper from his home. Soon after realizing the therapeutic value of writing, he penned *Caloosahatchee*, his first novel and co-authored *Shootoff!*, with longtime friend Dr. Robert Norman.

Made in the USA
Columbia, SC
07 June 2021

39274574R00211